THE CASE AGAINST
IMMIGRATION

THE
CASE
AGAINST
IMMIGRATION

The moral, economic, social, and environmental reasons for reducing U.S. immigration back to traditional levels

ROY BECK

W · W · NORTON & COMPANY · New York · London

For information about permission to reproduce selections from this book, write to
Permissions, W. W. Norton & Company, Inc., 500 Fifth Avenue, New York, NY
10110.

The text of this book is composed in Galliard
with the display set in Helvetica Condensed and Tea Chest
Composition and manufacturing by the Haddon Craftsmen, Inc.
Book design by Jacques Chazaud

Library of Congress Cataloging-in-Publication Data

Beck, Roy Howard.
The case against immigration / Roy Beck.
p. cm.
Includes index.
ISBN 0-393-03915-3
1. United States—Emigration and immigration—Economic aspects.
2. United States—Emigration and immigration—Social aspects.
3. Alien labor—United States. 4. Afro-Americans—Employment.
I. Title.
JV6471.B43 1996
330.973—dc20 95-51128

W. W. Norton & Company, Inc., 500 Fifth Avenue, New York, N.Y. 10110
http://web.wwnorton.com
W. W. Norton & Company Ltd., 10 Coptic Street, London WC1A 1PU

1 2 3 4 5 6 7 8 9 0

To Warren the milkman,
Freda the homemaker and secretary,
and an era of respect
for the American worker

Contents

Preface

During annual summer treks leading high school students in building houses for the poor, I gradually came to see what became some of the central themes of this book.

In the part of the country where we work, most of the people who qualify for the houses are black Americans with full-time jobs. A steady income is necessary because housing recipients must make monthly payments to Habitat for Humanity for the cost of materials used in building their small, simple houses. But without the free labor provided by volunteers and the interest-free loans provided by Habitat, these American workers' wages are inadequate to secure a 900-square-foot home that meets modern codes. The Habitat efforts are able to help but a tiny percentage of those in need; many of the masses who continue to live in substandard housing do not even have indoor bathrooms. That Americans who seem to play by the rules and work hard would have to live in such conditions, or rely on our charitable assistance to have decent housing, strikes many of the teenage volunteers as unjust.

Questioning the reason for the inadequate wages is a part of the religious tradition of the youths' sponsoring church. The tradition holds that charity is an insufficient response to need if the cause of the need is an unjust system that could reasonably be corrected. I looked further for causes of the low wages. I found that nearly every job these Americans have is in an industry into which Washington brings thousands of additional foreign workers each year through its immigration policies. There are many factors in the poor housing and job conditions of the area where we work, but the federal government inexplicably makes matters worse by running an immigration program that intensifies the job competition for these low-income Americans. Not surprisingly their already low real wages have been flat or declining during the last two decades of radically increased national immigration.

Additional research revealed that a person could step into local communities and neighborhoods all across America and find similar circumstances, not just for the poor and unemployed but even for middle-class professionals thrown into decline by immigration competition. The evidence leads to a disconcerting conclusion: The federal government's current immigration program primarily benefits a small minority of wealthy and powerful Americans at the expense of significant segments of the middle class and the poor. Attempts to protect the current level of immigration by wrapping it in the language of tradition or humanitarianism generally distort both history and the practical realities of our own era while diverting attention from immigration's role as a tool against the interests of the broad public.

This book primarily addresses that theme. It is not about future immigrants' personal attributes, their intelligence, character, race, and nationality; the focus instead is on the effects of quadrupling the annual number of immigrants over traditional levels. The book is not about illegal immigration, despite the importance of reducing it; the focus is on *legal* immigration, because it produces more than three-quarters of the numbers and is the simplest to change legislatively.

The battle to greatly reduce illegal immigration will be a long and complex one. One of the major tools in cutting *illegal* migration, however, is to reduce *legal* immigration. The relatives and fellow villagers from the home country who come as legal immigrants are essential for many illegal aliens in providing shelter from detection and in helping them to enter the labor market. It is also those legal immigrants who send back letters and gifts that entice more people to leave their Third World villages and urban neighborhoods to enter the United States, often illegally. The number of illegal aliens has proliferated over the last three decades as the United States has allowed larger and larger numbers of people to enter legally. A drastic reduction in legal immigration over time will significantly reduce the opportunities for both illegal U.S. entry and for illegally overstaying temporary tourist, student, and work visas.

While the number of immigrants—not their attributes—is the main factor of immigration that causes many U.S. problems, it is the only factor of real significance in terms of environmental concerns. I originally turned my journalistic attention to the immigration issue and moved into full-time study, research, and writing about it in 1991 because of my interest in America's environmental resources. Beginning as a newspaper reporter in the 1960s, I had written on the emergence of the modern environmental era and the giant strides toward restoring environmental health during the 1970s. But by the 1980s, progress had substantially stalled. For every several steps forward in overall environmental quality because of reductions in each American's negative impact, the addition of millions more residents drove environmental results several steps backward. I discovered that immigration, a topic to which I'd given little thought, had become a central environmental issue that I could no longer avoid.

Unfortunately, to write about problems of immigration is to risk seeming to attack immigrants themselves. Even worse is the risk of inadvertently encouraging somebody else to show hostility toward the foreign-born.

I encounter too many immigrants and children of immigrants in daily affairs where I live in northern Virginia to take those risks lightly. From five continents, members of immigrant families pass through my home, especially in the persons of friends of my two teenage sons. They are among the physical therapy patients of my wife; they are participants in youth activities which I lead; they are friends at my church, which has received national recognition for creating local service to new immigrants; they are neighbors; they are business clerks and owners where I trade; they make up nearly half of my sons' high school.

Thus, as is the case for millions of other Americans, I have a very personal stake in not wanting to provoke hostility or discrimination toward the foreign-born who already are living among us.

To be sure, this proximity to so many foreign-born persons includes some less than positive experiences, along with the delightful, which preclude me from a superficial, romanticized view of immigration. The influx into my own community clearly has been too fast and in too large a volume, a key factor in the emergence of dozens of law-violating youth gangs, in the overcrowding of schools, in the rise in the cost of governmental services, and in the difficulty of achieving further environmental progress in the region.

Nonetheless, the local problems of immigration are not the result of bad-acting individuals (except for a small minority) among the new-comers. Rather, most of the problems stem from bad recent public policies that raised the volume of national immigration above social, economic, educational, cultural, and environmental thresholds. Public opinion polls repeatedly have shown that most Americans understand this—that while they oppose continued high flows of immigration, they retain generally positive attitudes about immigrants as individuals. Most Americans seemingly want a pragmatic policy that steers between blind immigration romanticism on the one side and the politics of hatred (nativism) and irrational fear of immigrants (xenophobia) on the other.

For those readers who become convinced that the volume of immigration must be restricted, I strongly urge scrupulous avoidance of nativism. The word "nativism," despite its common misuse by many in public life and in the news media, does not describe opposition to immigration. What it does describe is actions by native-born Americans that are hostile and discriminatory toward the immigrants who already live in the United States. As Joseph Barton, historian at North-western University, has clarified: An American with no malice toward the foreign-born in this country could push for stopping all immigration forever and not be guilty of nativism. In fact, as we shall see in Chapter 3, limiting immigration could very well be classified a kindly act toward recent immigrants since they often are the chief economic losers from further immigration.

Immigration is such an emotionally charged issue that it is difficult to tackle it publicly without subjecting oneself to speculation about motives. There are plenty of ugly motives to be found among people on all sides. At the extremes, there are racists whose prime aim of restricting immigration is to keep out foreigners because they are not white, and there are racists who support high immigration because it provides them with a way to keep from having to hire native-born black Americans.

I cannot prevent speculation about my own motives. I can only hope that the evidence and analyses marshaled for this book will be weighed on their own merits.

The book documents problems that are real, substantial, and pervasive. Those who would argue that immigration should not be drastically reduced have an obligation to the millions of American victims of such problems to outline their own solutions and suggest practical methods to effect them immediately.

THE CASE AGAINST
IMMIGRATION

1

A Nation of
(Too Many) Immigrants?

Since 1970, more than 30 million foreign citizens and their descendants have been added to the local communities and labor pools of the United States.[1] It is the numerical equivalent of having relocated within our borders the entire present population of all Central American countries.

Demographic change on such a massive scale—primarily caused by the increased admission of *legal* immigrants—inevitably has created winners and losers among Americans. Based on opinion polls, it appears that most Americans consider themselves net losers and believe that the United States has become "a nation of too many immigrants."

What level of immigration is best for America, and of real help to the world? Although we often hear that the United States is a nation of immigrants, we seldom ask just what that means. It can be difficult to ask tough questions about immigration when we see nostalgic images of Ellis Island, recall our own families' coming to America, or encounter a new immigrant who is striving admirably to achieve the American dream.

But tough questions about immigration can no longer be avoided as we enter a fourth decade of unprecedentedly high immigration and struggle with its impact on job markets, on the quality of life and social fabric of our communities, and on the state of the environment.

Efforts to discuss these questions alarm some business interests and others who support high immigration. They often express shock that Americans could consider violating what they claim to be the country's tradition of openness by cutting immigration. But they misunderstand U.S. history. It is the high level of immigration during the last three decades that has violated our immigration tradition. The anti-immigration tenor of the times is not nearly so much because Americans have changed as that immigration has changed.

Over the long span of history from the founding of the nation in 1776 until 1965, immigration varied widely but averaged around 230,000 a year. This was a phenomenal flow into a single country, unmatched in world history. It should be noted that during large parts of that period, the United States—with vast expanses of virtually open land—was much better able than today to handle 230,000 newcomers annually. Suddenly in the 1970s and 1980s, at the very time that the majority of Americans were coming to the conclusion that the U.S. population had grown large enough, immigration soared above American tradition, averaging more than 500,000 a year. And it has been running around 1 million a year during the 1990s.

Until recently, policymakers and politicians of every stripe had ignored what public opinion polls found to be the public's growing dissatisfaction with the abnormally high level of immigration. Majority public opinion can be shallow, fleeting, and wrong, but an honest look at major trends during the recent mass immigration shows that ordinary Americans' concerns can hardly be dismissed as narrow and unenlightened:

- Whole industries in the 1970s and 1980s reorganized to exploit compliant foreign labor, with the result that conditions have deteriorated for all workers in those industries.
- Long trends of rising U.S. wages have been reversed.
- Poverty has increased.
- The middle-class way of life has come under siege; income disparities have widened disturbingly.
- Aggressive civil rights programs to benefit the descendants of slavery have been watered down, co-opted, and undermined because of the unanticipated volume of new immigration. A nearly half-century march of economic progress for black Americans has been halted and turned back.

- The culture—and even language—of many local communities has been transformed against the wishes of their native inhabitants. Instead of spawning healthy diversity, immigration has turned many cities into caldrons of increased ethnic tension and divisiveness.
- A stabilizing U.S. population with low birth rates (like other advanced nations) has become the most rapidly congesting industrialized nation in the world (resembling trends in Third World countries). Vast tracts of remaining farmland, natural habitat, and ecosystems have been destroyed to accommodate the growing population. Environmental progress has been set back by the addition of tens of millions of new polluters.
- Numerous organized crime syndicates headquartered in the new immigrants' home countries have gained solid beachheads of operations. Law enforcement agencies have been confounded just as they thought they were near victory over the crime organizations that other ethnic groups had brought with them during the Great Wave.

It is common when discussing those negative trends to focus on individual immigrants' skills, education, and morals, their country of origin, culture, and race. If one side points out that some immigrants are prone to crime and destructive behavior, others note that most immigrants arrive with high motives, good character, and laudable behavior. Some observers fear that the volume of non-European immigration threatens to swamp America's cultural heritage; others welcome an ever more multicultural society. Nonetheless, the chief difficulties that America faces because of current immigration are not triggered by *who* the immigrants are but by *how many* they are.

The task before the nation in setting a fair level of immigration is not about race or some vision of a homogeneous white America; it is about protecting and enhancing the United States' unique experiment in democracy for all Americans, including recent immigrants, regardless of their particular ethnicity. It is time to confront the true costs and benefits of immigration numbers, which have skyrocketed beyond our society's ability to handle them successfully.

* * *

The cumulative effect of years of high immigration has taken a while for Americans to comprehend. But in the 1990s, many Americans have awakened to a rather startling realization: The unrelenting surge of immigration above traditional levels is transforming communities throughout the United States into something their residents often don't like or quite recognize as their own.

The unprecedented flow of immigration has dramatically reshaped the social and ecological landscape up and down America's coasts, and it has spilled over into the hinterlands, carving new economic and cultural channels in the Ozarks Hills, Wisconsin's little northwoods cities, Atlanta's outlying towns, the Rocky Mountains, and the Kansas-Nebraska-Iowa plains. Millions of new immigrants now pulse through the economic arteries of most urban areas, from New York City to Dodge City, and of an increasing number of non-urban regions, from North Carolina fishing villages to North Arkansas mountain hamlets.

None of this has been inevitable. Legal immigration into this country has quadrupled over the traditional American level for only one reason: Congress and the president made it happen.

Legal immigration could be stopped with a simple majority vote of Congress and a stroke of the president's pen—as early as next month, if they desired. Or it could be increased just as quickly. The volume of legal immigration is entirely at the discretion of Washington.

Nobody ever intended for such an onslaught when the immigration laws were changed in 1965; the huge increase in numbers was an accident. But for nearly three decades during various efforts to control *illegal* immigration, Congress stood by as the much larger *legal* immigration soared ever upward and as citizen opposition rose correspondingly.

Finally in 1993 and 1994, a few lawmakers of both parties—but outside their parties' leadership—proposed major cutbacks (of two-thirds to three-fourths) in annual legal immigration. They shocked everybody, including themselves, by drawing almost 100 supporters from among the 535 members of Congress.

Then, in 1995, more modest reductions (of about one-third) were proposed independently by two key Republican subcommittee chairmen, Senator Alan Simpson of Wyoming and Representative Lamar Smith of Texas, and by a bi-partisan federal commission led by former Democratic congresswoman Barbara Jordan. President Bill Clinton endorsed the concept. The emerging centrist consensus, however, quickly drew strong opposition from several top Republican congressional leaders (especially free-market libertarians) and from the Democrats' liberal wing, all of whom wished to protect current high immigration levels or increase them.

The United States entered 1996 with Congress assessing the effects of the unprecedented foreign influx of the last thirty years and trying to determine how drastically annual immigration should be cut.

Despite the loud outcry from immigration advocates that something draconian was being considered, a one-third reduction would leave legal admissions still near the level of the 1880–1924 Great Wave. Even after a one-third cut in 1996, the number of immigrants would be triple the average who entered during America's golden immigration era between 1925 and 1965. In that time of far lower immigration, immigrants enjoyed more popularity and a higher and quicker success rate than at any other time in American history.

Given the three decades of inertia that had made any rollback seem impossible, the leaders who proposed cutting legal immigration by around one-third have to be lauded. But they have approached the issue by starting with the current unprecedented immigration peak, determining that it is harmful to the country, and then asking what can be cut. If instead they were designing immigration policy based on what is best for the American people, they would start at zero and ask what level of immigration actually is needed by the nation. The final number in that exercise would be far lower—and far closer to what the American people most desire.

The country's grateful reaction to a cut of merely one-third might be similar to that of residents of a Mississippi River town after a flood has crested in the upstairs bedroom and then receded to the living room downstairs: "Conditions are improved, but we're still flooded."

This self-inflicted flooding of the past three decades has undercut ambitious efforts during the same period to create a society of more fairness and opportunity for all Americans. Strong evidence amasses that the levels of immigration after 1965 have eroded the country's ability to achieve some of its most cherished goals. Many politicians and pundits have said it is hyperbolic to suggest that the single phenomenon of renewed mass immigration could so negatively affect the country. But major demographic upheavals, like the Baby Boom after World War II, touch every aspect of a nation's life and reverberate for decades. Certainly, the more than 30 million people added by immigration policy during the last three decades qualify as a major demographic phenomenon.

There have been many impediments to reaching some of our nation's highest goals. Immigration has not been the only cause—and not usually the major cause—of various societal problems. But research from numerous sources converges to show that the new massive volume of immigration has played an important "spoiler" role in efforts

Immigration and U.S. Population Growth

The chart on the facing page shows the total growth in U.S. population, from 1970 to 1995, as calculated by the U.S. Bureau of the Census.

The lightly shaded section at the bottom of the chart represents the portion of total population growth contributed by 1970 Americans and their descendants. Tulane University demographer Leon Bouvier calculates, and U.S. Census Bureau projections agree, that this portion of the population will grow slightly for a few more decades as the last of the women baby boomers pass through their childbearing years, but it is on track to level off around the year 2030.

The more darkly shaded section of the chart shows that post-1970 immigration more than doubled U.S. population growth between 1970 and 1995. Of all the new schools and classrooms that the United States has been forced to build since 1970 to accommodate larger student populations, more than half have been for immigrants. More than half of all other additional public infrastructure needed since 1970 has been due to immigration. More than half the additional people placing pressure on U.S. environmental resources have been new immigrants and their descendants. Because of high immigration and high fertility among immigrants, the country has had to meet far more additional infrastructure demands in the last twenty-five years than it otherwise would have faced over an eighty-year period.

To see what high immigration will do to U.S. population in the near future, see facing page.

By 1995, U.S. Population Growth Had More Than Doubled Because of Immigration Since 1970

Total Population
in Millions

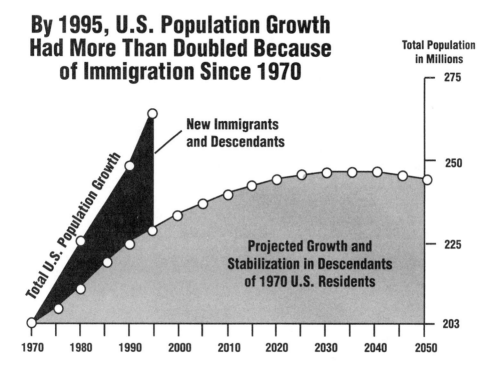

New Immigrants
and Descendants

Total U.S. Population Growth

Projected Growth and
Stabilization in Descendants
of 1970 U.S. Residents

275

250

225

203

1970 1980 1990 2000 2010 2020 2030 2040 2050

Immigration and U.S. Population Growth

In the chart on the facing page, the projected growth in total U.S. population is as calculated by the U.S. Bureau of the Census in 1993. The projection is based on a continuation of fertility, mortality, and immigration similar to current trends. The fertility of today's immigrants and their descendants is not decreasing as that of immigrants in past waves did, but is continuing at a high level—approximately 50 percent higher than 1970 Americans and their descendants.

To a population of 203 million in 1970, another 189 million residents will be added to the United States by the year 2050. Most of that phenomenal increase in population congestion—and 90 percent of the increase after 1995—will be the result of post-1970 immigration. To find similar population growth in foreign countries, we must look to the Third World.

The harsh impact that immigrant-driven population growth from 1970 to 1995 has had on efforts to address national problems—in education, infrastructure, environment, community tensions, crime, and excess labor competition—will pale beside that of post-1995 immigration, if it continues at the present level.

To see what will happen to U.S. population if the immigration reduction bills before Congress in early 1996 become law, see facing page.

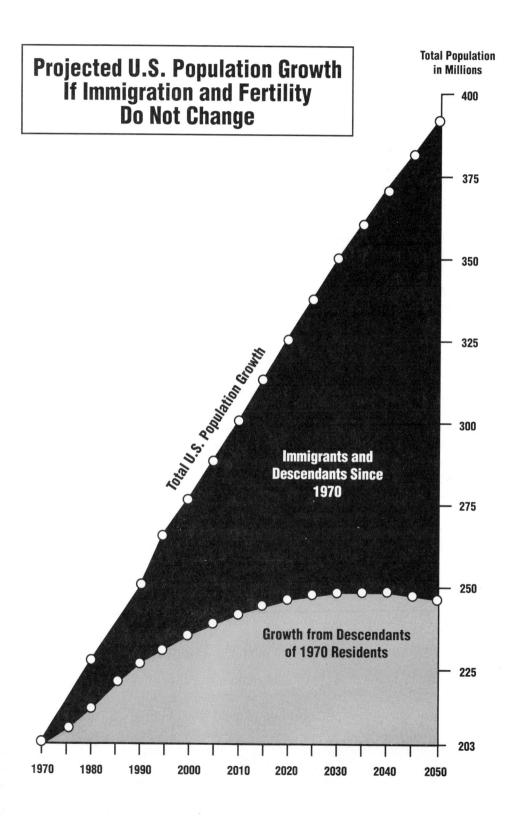

Immigration and U.S. Population Growth

The chart on the facing page shows that even a cut in current immigration of around one-half would still more than triple population growth by the year 2050. Every aspect of American society would face wrenching adjustments to accommodate 145 million additional people over the 1970 population of 203 million.

Beginning in 1995, proposals to cut legal immigration by one-third to one-half arose from key committees in the House and Senate and from a bipartisan congressional-presidential commission chaired by the late Barbara Jordan. This chart is a U.S. Census Bureau projection of what would likely occur if the *largest* of the cuts being considered by Congress in early 1996 was enacted.

The Census Bureau projection assumes net immigration of 350,000 people a year (net, that is, after subtracting from the total number of immigrants in a given year the number of Americans who emigrate to another country). Most proposals in Congress would lead to a far higher net number. But one proposal in the Senate would after several years lower legal immigration to a gross level of 450,000 people per year. If new laws were able to cut the number of illegal immigrants settling here each year from an estimated 300,000 to 100,000 people—and if around 200,000 Americans continue to emigrate to other countries annually—that 450,000 gross-legal-immigration proposal would leave the country with a net immigration of around 350,000 people a year.

Cuts much greater than that will be necessary to preserve the American ideal of a country with both wide-open spaces and widespread opportunity.

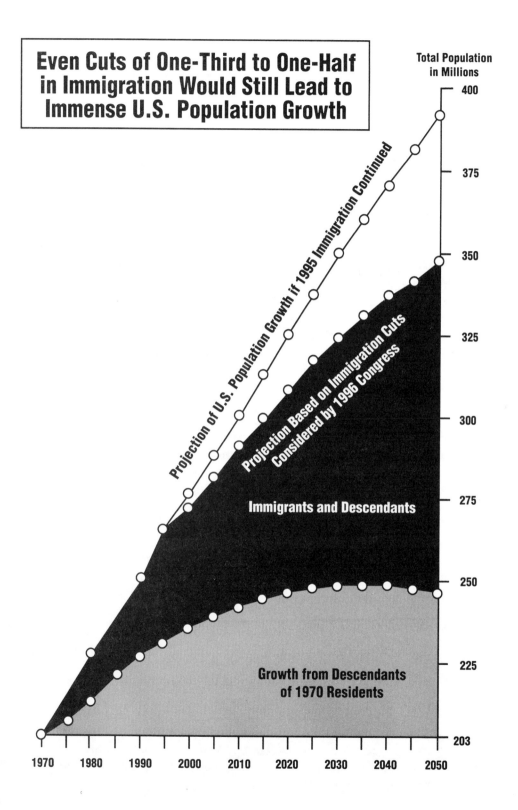

Even Cuts of One-Third to One-Half in Immigration Would Still Lead to Immense U.S. Population Growth

Total Population in Millions

400

375

350

325

300

275

250

225

203

Projection of U.S. Population Growth if 1995 Immigration Continued

Projection Based on Immigration Cuts Considered by 1996 Congress

Immigrants and Descendants

Growth from Descendants of 1970 Residents

1970 1980 1990 2000 2010 2020 2030 2040 2050

to reach at least four of America's goals: (1) a middle-class society; (2) equal opportunity for the descendants of slavery; (3) harmonious and safe communities; and (4) a protected and restored natural environment.

A MIDDLE-CLASS SOCIETY

Today, Americans live in a society of widening economic disparity, with an increasing gulf between poor and rich, and fewer and fewer people in the middle class. This is a reversal of our egalitarian dreams of a society in which all who were willing could find a job, and in which even those who performed the lower-skilled tasks needed by society would earn an income that could support a family in modest dignity.

The Council of Economic Advisors told the president in 1993 that "immigration has increased the relative supply of less educated labor and appears to have contributed to the increasing inequality of income. . . ."[2] That was consistent with a United Nations report on the effect of immigration on the industrialized nations. It concluded that immigration reinforces existing gaps between rich and poor.[3]

Nonetheless, immigration definitely brings some benefits to a nation. In fact, most Americans may have benefitted as consumers because the immigrants have kept the price of labor lower, which may have led to lower prices than otherwise would have occurred. But consumers also tend to be laborers drawing those depressed wages. According to the UN report, it is only for the upper crust that the financial benefits of immigration tend to outweigh the losses. And that serves to increase income disparity.

Who wins and who loses? A glance through the roster of immigration winners quickly finds business owners who have followed a low-wage labor strategy. Land developers, real estate agents, home mortgage officials, and others who tend to profit from population growth are winners. Owners of high-tech industries have lowered their costs by importing skilled immigrants who will work at lower wages than college-educated Americans. People who can afford nannies, gardeners, and housekeepers have benefitted from lower costs. Americans who prize cultural diversity are among the non-financial winners. Others have won by having the security, prestige, or pay of their jobs enhanced by the high immigrant flow. That would include immigration lawyers, refugee resettlement agency personnel, officials of immigrant-advocacy groups, and educators and other social services employees who work with immigrants.

Unfortunately, the roster of immigration losers is much larger and includes some of America's most vulnerable citizens: poor children, lower-skilled workers, residents of declining urban communities, large numbers of African Americans, the unskilled immigrants who already are here and face the most severe competition from new immigrants, and even some of America's brightest young people, who lose opportunities to pursue science-based careers because of some corporations' and universities' preferences for foreign scientists and engineers.

Also among the losers from immigration are all Americans who prefer to live in a more middle class and less economically polarized society. Under low-immigration conditions from 1925 to 1965, the United States enjoyed increasing egalitarianism. But by the middle of the 1980s, it had a larger gap between the rich and poor than could be found in any other major industrialized nation, according to the U.S. Census Bureau. Nearly every community receiving substantial numbers of immigrants has experienced increased disparities among its population and diminished cohesiveness. Even many Americans who would gain financially from high immigration into their community have come to oppose it because of the changes it would bring; they don't want to create a community of rising disparities, even if they would make more money. Consider the recent examples of Clay County, Alabama, and Clay County, Iowa.

In Alabama, the county chamber of commerce helped organize business, civic, and educational leaders in 1995 to discourage an Arkansas corporation from using immigrant labor to expand its existing poultry-processing operations in rural Clay County. Asked if it wasn't a little strange to have a chamber of commerce opposing local economic and population growth, executive director Carolyn Dunagan said: "I don't know about other places, but here when it comes to a choice between quality of life and growth, quality of life is the most important." The Clay County leaders acted out of two primary concerns: (1) The importation of immigrants likely would hurt the county's black workers, harming their already modest economic position; and (2) the impoverished, Deep South county was having enough trouble trying to create a cohesive culture out of its black and white residents, without adding foreign cultures and languages into the mix and contributing to a population growth unlikely to pay its own way.

Mayor Irving Thompson of Ashland, the county seat, told me that many townspeople believed the corporation was preparing to recruit immigrant workers in response to recent protests by local black employees over working conditions. "The fear," high school history teacher Mark Tucker said, "is that the next time black workers walk out over a labor problem, they'll be replaced by Third World workers." It is not a frivolous fear; replacing black employees—more than any other Americans—with foreign workers has become somewhat commonplace around the country under Washington's expanded immigration programs.

In Clay County, Iowa, the economic enticements were greater. An outside corporation sought a zoning change to allow it to start up operations in an abandoned plant in Spencer, the county seat. An enraged citizenry crowded into the high school fieldhouse in an emotional demonstration before the city council, winning unanimous approval to block the corporation.

Why would they kiss good-bye 350 new industrial jobs for the city of 11,000? In a word: immigration. The proposed operation was in an industry with a long track record of drawing foreign workers. Local advocates for the new jobs accused opponents of being racist. Opponents, though, noted that the community had freely embraced refugees over the years, and that their concern about an influx of foreign workers was that the experience of other cities showed an unacceptable change in a previously egalitarian way of life.

The most telling reason Spencer citizens gave for blocking the new jobs was: "We don't want to become another Storm Lake."

Until the 1980s, Storm Lake—less than an hour's drive to the south—had been like a twin to Spencer: neighboring agricultural county seat, same size, similar history and economy, a shared bucolic, safe, midwestern lifestyle with excellent schools, and the same epic prairie sky of uninhibited expressiveness. But a corporation similar to the one just blocked in Spencer moved into Storm Lake and immediately began attracting foreign workers. The steady flow soon turned Storm Lake into one of the scores of new immigration hubs created by federal immigration mandates since 1965.

The unrequested changes to life in Storm Lake followed patterns similar to those in many new-immigration cities. Overnight, Storm Lake schools were dealing with the cultural ramifications of a student body that now is one-fifth immigrant (predominantly Laotian and Mexican) and with the challenges of teaching in different languages. New facilities have been needed to handle the growing population of high-fertility foreign families with their low incomes and low tax payments. Some Storm Lake residents have lost their jobs to immigrants; more have seen their wages depressed because of the loosening of the labor market and the immigrants' lower expectations. The immigrants have tended to occupy housing units in higher densities than natives and have settled in enclaves, changing the character of neighborhoods and causing some elementary schools to be disproportionately filled with newcomers. For the first time, parts of town became undesirable in the real estate market based on which schools had high populations of students who didn't speak English. A community which previously had little reason to think in terms of haves and have-nots became a starkly stratified society.

Especially unsettling—but to be expected in a community of wide disparities, transience, and separate cultures—has been the deterioration in Storm Lake residents' sense of safety. The crime rate soared above that of the rest of Iowa. It is four times higher than crime in Spencer, its former twin.

To a visitor from a coastal city, where the national trend toward economic stratification has been visible longer, Storm Lake still can seem like a delightful place to live. But to those who knew the city before, the changes have been difficult to accept. "It breaks my heart to see what has become of my hometown," said Mary Galik, a Storm Lake native who moved to Spencer.

Given a choice, there was nothing about the creation of sharp disparities in the Storm Lake population that Spencer's citizens wanted to risk duplicating. Even main street merchants did not oppose efforts to block the new industry. As business owners, they favored the new plant because it would have increased their retail sales, explained Bob Rose, program manager of the merchants' economic growth organization. But as parents and grandparents, the merchants did not look favorably on economic development that might endanger what they saw as Spencer's special midwestern small-town culture and quality of life.

Nationally during the last two decades of high immigration, the richest 20 percent of Americans have enjoyed some economic improvement and the richest 1 percent have reaped strong increases of income. But the average wage for most American groups has declined.

No scholar suggests that increased immigration is the chief culprit in America's overall decline in wages. The economist Paul Krugman, of Stanford University, says the obvious central cause of the disappointing economic conditions for the American majority since 1973 is the drastic drop in the rate of growth in output (productivity) per worker. But the experts are uncertain about precisely why productivity growth has dropped so low and stayed there.[4] Clearly, though, Congress picked a terribly inappropriate period of U.S. history to be increasing the number of U.S. workers through immigration.

At the same time immigration was snowballing in the 1970s, the labor market was being flooded with baby boomers who were reaching employment age and with a big increase in married women seeking jobs. Based on recent research by several economists, it would appear that the big increases in the labor supply probably contributed to the drop in productivity growth, and definitely worked against efforts to improve it after it did drop.

Research by the economist Paul Romer explains that the problem with a large increase in the number of workers is that it tends to result in a lower amount of capital investment per worker. It is the capital investment per worker, along with technology, that is the most important ingredient in increasing per capita output, according to Romer's study, published in the authoritative National Bureau of Economic Research journal. Thus, immigration during the last two decades, by greatly increasing the labor supply, would seem to be undermining capital investment per worker, the very process that could send wages upward again.

Romer's research flies in the face of today's immigration advocates, who insist that the federal government must continue to run a high-immigration program in order to boost the economy. Adding workers usually *does* increase the nation's overall economic output, but not by enough to improve the circumstances of the average worker. "In fact, what the data suggest is that labor productivity responds quite negatively to increases in the labor force," Romer maintains. Looking across American history, Romer found that when the growth in number of workers went up (through high immigration and fertility), there was a decline in the growth of per capita output—just as has occurred during this latest time of high immigration and depressed wages.[5]

Studies by Harvard's Jeffrey G. Williamson have found that during those same periods of high immigration, the United States became less of a middle-class society and experienced its highest degree of economic disparity—just as is happening during the current period of high immigration.[6]

It isn't difficult to see how an abundant supply of new foreign workers could retard wage increases. U.S. Secretary of Labor Robert B. Reich fretted in 1994 that constant supplies of foreign labor have enticed many employers to continue relying on low-paid, low-skilled jobs, instead of making technological improvements and then training workers for more productive, higher-paying jobs.[7]

A U.S. Bureau of Labor Statistics study concluded that immigration was responsible for roughly half the decline in real wages for native-born high school dropouts in the fifty largest metropolitan areas during the 1980s. The study found that immigration accounted for 20 to 25 percent of the increase in the wage gap between low-skill and high-skill workers.[8]And economists Timothy J. Hatton and Jeffrey G. Williamson declared in 1994 that all standard mainstream economic models predict migration will tend to lower wages where immigrants settle.[9]

Because the United States has had a surplus of workers, even the profits of the small recent growth in per capita productivity have not been passed on to the workers. Krugman has noted that when the number of workers surges, "the way that a freely functioning labor market ensures that almost everyone who wants a job gets one is by allowing wage rates to fall, if necessary, to match demand to supply." Most of the profits from recent increased productivity have gone to Americans in the top 1 percent of income.[10] According to the research of immigrant economist George Borjas, high immigration during the 1980s helped facilitate a massive redistribution of wealth—more than $100 billion a year—from American workers to the upper class.[11]

The trend in this country during the previous decades of low immigration had long been toward higher wages, less poverty, and a larger middle class. Beginning with the shortage of workers during World War II, more and more Americans found that the toil of their labor earned them middle-class status. The number of Americans in poverty declined for decades. That happy circumstance came to a halt in 1973. Except for minor variations, the number of impoverished Americans has been increasing ever since.

The United States now routinely violates what Washington policy analyst Norman Ornstein has concluded is an implicit, national bi-partisan compact. In words similar to Bill Clinton's during his first presidential campaign, Ornstein says the compact holds that "if people play by the rules, working hard and doing their jobs, they will not have to live in poverty."[12] But his contention has become increasingly difficult to uphold as inflation-adjusted wages have declined for Americans without college degrees and even many with degrees.

What to do about the millions of Americans mired in poverty or struggling just above it? "The best way to help these young unskilled workers is through supply-side interventions," maintains labor professor Robert M. Hutchens of Cornell University. Initiatives that limit immigration of workers "can promote an environment where academic underachievers have at least some opportunity for upward mobility," he adds.[13]

No studies suggest that halting immigration would immediately put middle-class wages into the pockets of a large percentage of today's poor. But America's poor and its working class are not among the net winners of an immigration policy that brings in people who can compete directly with them in the job market. If the nation desires a return to a more middle-class economy, it is difficult to understand why its government would allow more than a nominal flow of immigrants at this time.

EQUAL OPPORTUNITY FOR
THE DESCENDANTS OF SLAVERY

The uncompleted agenda of economic and political equality of opportunity for the descendants of American slavery ranks as perhaps our most troubling and pervasive national agony. No social problem seems untouched by the acrimony of racial recriminations that rises out of the failure to end the massively disproportionate presence of blacks in poverty. Despite a thriving, large population of well-educated, well-paid, highly productive black Americans, one-third of the total black population seems intractably stuck in poverty—and the number has been increasing throughout most of this era of rising immigration.

High immigration has eliminated the best economic friend black Americans had: a tight labor market. Little known to most Americans, the 1924 to 1965 period of low immigration contained the economic golden era not only for immigrants but for black Americans. According to papers in the *Journal of Economic Literature*, tight-labor conditions during that time helped all Americans to make impressive gains. Real incomes of white males, for example, expanded two-and-one-half-fold between 1940 and 1980. But for black men, they quadrupled, rapidly closing the gap between races. The greatest increases for black workers occurred before 1965, the year both the Voting Rights Act and the Immigration Act were passed.[14]

Those who blame racism for the worsening wages for lower-skilled blacks today might consider that institutional and social racism were thriving in the 1940–65 period. But racism—and the absence of civil rights laws and affirmative action—could not halt phenomenal economic progress for black Americans during the tight-labor conditions of that era.

If the black economic trends in the 1940s, 1950s, and 1960s had continued, America would be a far different society today. But progress for the average black wage earner stalled in 1973. The rapid ballooning of the labor supply has conspired to strike most Americans, but black Americans have been hit the hardest. During renewed mass immigration, the wage gap between black and white workers has widened since 1973.[15]

Immigration and loose labor markets hurt black workers more than others in part because American employers always have tended to put African Americans toward the back of the hiring line, Harvard's Ronald F. Ferguson suggested in the American Academy of Arts and Sciences' exhaustive study on the state of black Americans. When the hiring line is short—and especially if it is shorter than the number of jobs to fill—the anti-black prejudice of employers is less harmful. By lengthening the hiring line with so many immigrants over the last three decades, Washington has made the end of the line a lot farther from the front.[16]

Recent investigative reports by the *Wall Street Journal* and Newhouse Newspapers have shown the preference of employers for immigrant workers over African Americans. And businesses owned by immigrants appear to be especially heavy practitioners of anti-black job discrimination, they found.

The federal government's immigration program allows into this country every year: several hundred thousand foreign persons on special work visas; nearly a million legal immigrants; and another few hundred thousand illegal aliens. They settle disproportionately in the neighborhoods of lower-income blacks, with whom they tend to compete for jobs, education, social services, and housing.

The increase in poverty is due to many changes in society. Certainly, there is merit to the arguments of analysts who point to a long list of contributing behavioral traits that have risen in prominence, such as illegitimacy, divorce, single parenting, and involvement in drug use and trade. But the labor economist Vernon Briggs, Jr., of Cornell University suggests an immigration connection to even those factors in his immensely useful history, *Mass Immigration and the National Interest*. "Immigration policy was not purposely intended to harm black Americans, but it has done just that," he says. He finds the increase in labor supply caused by immigration to be a significant factor in the inability of young, non-college-educated black males to obtain jobs that pay enough to support a family and make marriage an option. And that is one of the causes of the incredible increase in black illegitimacy, he maintains. "The longer it [immigration] is allowed to function as a political policy, the worse are the economic prospects for blacks."[17]

According to a 1993 Urban Institute report, 53 percent of black men between the ages of twenty-five and thirty-four did not earn enough to support a family of four above the poverty level. "We hear people talking about black families falling apart," said Roger Wilkins of George Mason University. "But we don't hear anybody talking about putting black men to work, giving black families the economic where-withal to stay together and raise their children."[18]

Some political leaders have been fearful of talking about immigration, saying that highlighting the negative effects of immigration on black Americans risks pitting one group of disadvantaged Americans (poor blacks) against another (poor immigrants). In fact, though, the harm of continued immigration to poor Latino, Asian, and Caribbean immigrants in this country is very similar to what it does to black Americans. The immigrants and other disadvantaged groups among us would benefit from any immigration changes designed to help the descendants of U.S. slavery.

Federal officials wring their hands over the failure of government programs to more appreciably help the black underclass. While Congress argues over which programs actually work, one would think that it would not intentionally take action that would weaken the chances of the members of the underclass resuming their march into the middle class. Yet the federal government continues its program of importing foreign labor into poor black communities.

Considering the political climate and current federal budget realities, it is unlikely that Congress soon will increase the spending aimed at helping poor black Americans. But with a revised immigration policy, Congress could at least take the stance of first doing no harm to the black poor; drastically cutting immigration would cost the government next to nothing, and would take considerable pressure off poor black communities and the programs designed to serve them.

HARMONIOUS AND SAFE COMMUNITIES

Immigration has not been a useful companion to the major efforts of the last three decades to reduce the grievous ethnic tensions in our cities. Ann Scott Tyson of the *Christian Science Monitor* noted in 1994 that many social scientists had anticipated that immigration would encourage greater cultural and racial mixing; instead, they discovered that the "influx of immigrants is provoking sharper racial divisions." Dr. William Frey, demographer of the University of Michigan's Population Center, bleakly observed: "Rather than leading toward a new national diversity, the new migration dynamics are contributing to a demographic Balkanization across broad regions and areas of the country."[19]

Describing California, which is the number-one destination of immigrants, *Time* magazine in 1991 painted an equally dismal portrait of our efforts toward a healthy diversity: "The state is dividing and subdividing now along a thousand new fault lines of language and identity. . . . Los Angeles, for example, is one of the most segregated cities in the world—a horizontal patchwork of ethnic and racial enclaves, all almost self-sufficient, inward turning and immiscible."[20]

This relentless wave of high immigration is transporting ethnic conflict to communities and regions where nothing of the sort even existed in the 1960s. A sweeping Ford Foundation study found that the most prevalent relations among natives and newcomers in communities with moderate to high immigration is competition, tension, and opposition. Every ethnic group in America resents heavy flows of immigrants into their communities, regardless of the ethnicity of the immigrants.[21]

A RAND Corporation study of urban school systems with high numbers of immigrants concluded that the newcomers exacerbate already serious problems in those schools. Education failure is the norm for immigrants and natives alike. Fewer than one of two kids going into these high schools comes out employable. The "size of the wave and the chaos of the situation are too great" for schools to be able to keep poor natives in class.[22]

And then there is crime—the factor that may top all others in driving capital and the middle class from the cities and in creating inhumane conditions for those residents trapped behind. Crime historian Ted Robert Gurr of the University of Maryland explains that this third great crime wave in America's history is similar to the other two in that it is linked to three factors: increased economic deprivation; the aftermath of war (this time, Vietnam); and a big jump in immigration, all of which "interfere with the civilizing process. . . ." It is not that the immigrants themselves are especially oriented toward crime and anarchy, but the arrival in such large numbers of people of different cultures contributes a transience and lack of community cohesiveness that is healthy for neither the newcomers nor the citizens.[23]

Cities—ranging in size from millions to a few thousand—struggle with an immigration influx that few ever requested. And the federal government never asked the local officials if they desired or could handle the flow. Each successive Congress and president simply adopted or maintained policies that forced massive immigration upon thousands of neighborhoods across the land.

Residents have not approved. A Times-Mirror Center poll in November 1994 indicated that 82 percent of Americans think the United States should restrict immigration. Opposition to immigration is not ideological. A CBS/New York Times poll two months earlier found only 6 percentage points difference among those identifying themselves as Democrats, Republicans, or independents; all overwhelmingly objected to current immigration levels. Other polls show that no matter how the populace is sliced into demographic groups—by income, ethnicity, education, region, gender, age, religion, or size of community—a majority of them dislike current immigration levels. It isn't that Americans don't like immigrants. Polls show that most citizens retain generally positive attitudes about immigrants as individuals. But the number of those individuals arriving each year has overwhelmed individual communities. There are numerical thresholds for how many additional and culturally different residents any community can or wants to handle—economically, socially, educationally, and environmentally. But most Americans have had little choice. They have had to stand by passively as Washington sent wave after wave of radically increased immigration crashing over their communities.

Most Americans apparently would like to accomplish what the citizens of Spencer, Iowa, and Ashland, Alabama, thus far have done: Stand up to Washington and barricade themselves against the national tide of immigration. But such efforts are bound to fail if the federal government continues Great Wave–level immigration. Whatever difficulty the nation is having accommodating the post-1970 immigrants and their descendants, the fact that cannot be escaped is that current immigration and fertility rates are projected to increase those numbers by 500 percent during the next fifty years.

A cautious person might question adding another 100,000 immigrants a year—let alone a half million—to the social pathologies and crumbling infrastructures of the cities. Drastically reducing legal immigration and giving the cities a breather for at least a while might be the cheapest and most helpful gift Congress could give the cities to allow them to succeed at revitalization efforts for their inhabitants, including the millions of recent immigrants who now live there.

A PROTECTED AND RESTORED NATURAL ENVIRONMENT

For three decades, Americans have demanded that their government protect and restore the country's natural environment so that it could continue to meet human needs for health, food, recreation, psychic or spiritual nourishment, and commerce.

A nation's concern for the natural resources entrusted to it within its borders is, at its heart, concern for the descendants of the present inhabitants. It is anticipating the pain that our great-grandchildren might have if we destroy their chance of ever experiencing or using parts of our present natural endowment. Conflicts often described as pitting the needs of people against the needs of the environment frequently really are conflicts of the needs of *today's* people versus the needs of our descendants.

At enormous costs, as taxpayer and consumer, the average American since 1970 has slashed his or her destructive impact on the country's environmental resources. The results in aggregate are impressive: rivers no longer catch fire or run in brilliant colors (as I witnessed when I first began covering the environment for newspapers during the 1960s); the air in our cities is far cleaner and even healthy much of the time; the bald eagle has been rescued from oblivion.

But we have fallen far short of our goals. Forty percent of America's lakes and streams remain unfishable and unswimmable. The giant factories of biodiversity—the Chesapeake Bay and the Everglades—teeter in precarious ecological health. Thirty-five states are withdrawing groundwater faster than it is being replenished. In 1988, fifteen years after passage of the Endangered Species Act, five hundred plant and animal species still were listed; by 1993, the number had increased to more than seven hundred.

The most important change in America that has so counteracted all the positive efforts to restore and preserve the environment is this: an additional 65 million U.S. residents. If we were still the 203 million Americans of 1970 whose government committed itself to saving the U.S. environment, most of our environmental goals would have been met or be within reach by now. But there now are more than 265 million of us!

Immigration has been a substantial cause of the negative environmental news that must be mixed among all the good. This is not because immigrants are environmentally bad people, but because they are people. Like the Americans they join, immigrants flush toilets, drive cars, use public transportation, require land to feed, clothe, and house them, and to provide the materials (and space) for their commerce, recreation, and waste disposal. As additional people, they require more streets, parking lots, and all sorts of other asphalting of farmland and animal habitat. More than 1 million acres are blacktopped each year.

Not only do immigrants do all those additional things to the U.S. environmental resources, but they add to the world's overall environmental problems by emitting far more hydrocarbons into the air than they did in their home countries.

Having already destroyed some 50 percent of its wetlands—the prime incubators of biodiversity—the United States is filling in another 300,000 acres a year to accommodate its expanding population. With 90 percent of northwestern old-growth forests gone, there is intense pressure to log much of the rest.

U.S. immigration policy, combined with the much higher fertility of immigrants, has been the number-one cause of population growth since 1970. Using recent U.S. Census Bureau data and projections, demographer Leon Bouvier of Tulane University ran a computer study which found that immigrants and their descendants since 1970 have comprised more than half of U.S. population growth. They will be responsible for 90 percent of the population expansion between now and 2050, if current fertility and immigration rates remain constant.

Thus, to whatever extent environmental problems can be blamed on U.S. population growth, the preponderance of that blame rests on U.S. immigration policy. Changing the composition of the immigration stream—whether by skill, country of origin, education, etc.—will not diminish the threat. Only a reduction in numbers will deal with the environmental problem.

The fight against air pollution may be America's greatest environmental success story. Despite Herculean cleanup efforts, however, about 40 percent of Americans live in metropolitan areas that still fail to meet some of the Environmental Protection Agency's health standards. How different would this statistic be if there were 65 million fewer Americans driving cars and using electricity? And it only gets worse. Each year, the U.S. population grows by another 3 million people, most of them immigrants and the descendants of recent immigrants.

As expensive as it has been to clean up the air thus far, that was the easy and cheap task compared with what lies ahead. Every additional 1 percent of decrease in air pollution nowbecomes much more expensive than before, in terms of both money and restrictions on personal freedom. Because 65 million more people are contributing to the air pollution, the emissions per person must be cut another 30 percent just to make the air as clean as it would have been if our population had remained at 1970's 203 million.

That will take care of this year. But what about next year, and the decades afterwards? The U.S. Census Bureau currently considers the most likely population scenario to be one of fertility continuing close to the present rate and of immigration running slightly below recent levels. Under those assumptions, it projects an increase to nearly 400 million Americans by 2050: that is another 130 million Americans, almost all of them resulting from post-1970 immigration policies.

Such figures pose a chilling threat to biodiversity, farmland, recreational spaces, and air and water quality in the United States. To avoid further encroachment on those resources, federal and state governments must enforce deep cuts in material standards of living and in individual freedoms (such as choices of transportation and where to live) to accommodate another 130 million people. Nothing in the current political climate suggests that such cuts will occur. The more likely direction now appears to be toward cuts in environmental standards and enforcement.

According to the conservation biologist Thomas Lovejoy, the United States doesn't have a lot of environmental leeway. An adviser to the U.S. government who has been decorated by the Brazilian government for his decades of work with the rainforests, Lovejoy says the United States is "demonstrably losing biological diversity. . . . On top of the general threat of pollution and other stresses, we have some areas which are really sort of close to 'last-minute' situations. . . . Population growth is probably the single most important factor in the ability to protect biological diversity and manage the environment."[24]

The United States has pledged itself in international arenas to move toward an environmentally sustainable way of life. That would mean that the total environmental impact of all Americans would not diminish the ability of future Americans or citizens in other countries to enjoy at least the level of lifestyle of today's inhabitants. But if sustainable living can be defined as enjoying the fruit without harming the tree that produces it, then there is ample evidence that 265 million Americans are hacking fairly vigorously at the trunk today.

It is immigration-driven population growth perhaps as much as any other factor that gives many Americans the feeling that they are running in place when it comes to efforts to protect the environment. Environmental efforts too often merely slow the rate of destruction.

The geopolitical analyst George Kennan wrote in his *Around the Cragged Hill* that there is an "optimal balance, depending on the manner of man's life, between the density of human population and the tolerances of nature. This balance, in the case of the United States, would seem to me to have been surpassed . . . the question is not whether there are limits to this country's ability to absorb immigration; the question is only where those limits lie, and how they should be determined and enforced. . . ."[25]

Kennan suggested that the optimal population was passed sometime in the 1970s. Most Americans apparently would tend to agree. In 1992, Americans by a ratio of 7 to 1 told Roper pollsters that the United States was suffering from too many people. In fact, by their own behavior, Americans have been opting for a stabilized population since 1972 by having less than the average 2.1 children per woman that eventually leads to a level population size.

For three decades, Congress has run a government-induced population-growth program through immigration that has negated the low-fertility decisions of America's citizens. Among the winners have been those who profit from converting natural ecosystems and agricultural land into urban development. But the losers have been all who sought to protect America's environmental resources from the assault of an endlessly increasing human population. And the day of environmentally sustainable living in the United States has been pushed much farther into the future.

If Congress had run a replacement-level immigration program (matching in-migration to out-migration) to go along with Americans' replacement-level fertility after 1972, U.S. population never would have reached 250 million, peaking below that mark during the 2030s, according to Bouvier.

Instead, we're already above 265 million and headed to near 400 million by 2050. Virtually every aspect of U.S. environmental protection and quality—and of the quality of life for America's human inhabitants—is changed because of that.

2

Learning
from the Great Wave

In 1910, the fears of many Yankee settlers of Wausau, Wisconsin, came true. For years, they had worried that they would be overwhelmed by the German, Polish, and other immigrants pouring into town as part of what we now call the Great Wave of immigration. By 1910, the demographic takeover had occurred: immigrants and their children were in the majority. They changed the local culture, totally reversed the ruling political ideology, and by 1918 had taken over nearly every elected office in the county. Communities all across America similarly were caught in the social, economic, and political undertow of the Great Wave. Native-born Americans often felt like foreigners in their own hometowns, amidst a babel of foreign tongues and customs. For years, citizens clamored unsuccessfully for relief from Washington. Anti-immigrant hostilities and explosions of ethnic turmoil marred the society.

That is a different sort of history from the rose-colored views preached from many of the nation's political, media, and religious pulpits today: Americans are urged to turn from their opposition to today's levels of admissions and instead to "honor our nation's immigration tradition," as if that phrase describes a past in which Americans eagerly welcomed masses of immigrants. There are constant reminders that "we are an immigrant nation," that "we're all descended from immigrants," and that "immigration made our nation great." The *Chicago Sun-Times* reflected this view of history when it editorialized in 1994 that national policy must be consistent with "the country's historic openness toward immigration."[1]

For all of today's dewy-eyed remembrances of "tradition" and "openness," however, mass immigration always has provoked widespread, deep-rooted objections from much of the public. The historian John Higham of Johns Hopkins University detailed Americans' traditional anti-immigration sentiments in his seminal book, *Strangers in the Land* (1956), which is quoted often by immigration advocates who seek to show that restrictionists generally have been motivated by bigotry and irrational distrust of foreigners. But in the preface to his second edition and in subsequent writing, Higham emphasized that Americans also had some very legitimate reasons to campaign for immigration cuts.[2]

One would never guess from most editorial writers and politicians today that there ever were legitimate complaints against immigration. They still speak of the Great Wave of 1880 to 1924 as a kind of golden era of immigration. Observing the congressional debate over immigration in the mid-1980s, University of California history professor Otis Graham wrote in *The Public Historian* that it was filled with remarks about what "history taught" but without anybody ever consulting a historian: "History was said to reveal a simple story, that mass immigration produced unalloyed benefits: economic growth and creative, law-abiding people like your grandparents and mine." While there was truth in those statements, they left out very important understandings about the costs that accompanied those benefits, he said.[3]

Romanticized and sanitized by sentimental movies, novels, high school textbooks, stump speeches, and Fourth of July newspaper editorials, the Great Wave has been allowed to teach false lessons that have led present-day Americans to distorted positions on both sides of the immigration debate.

The Immigration Restrictionists' Distortion:

Opponents of immigration often blast today's newcomers for being inferior to European immigrants of other eras because they hang on to their language and culture, because they are clannish and live in ethnic enclaves, because they fail to raise themselves to middle-class standards of living, and because they sap public services. In every community I have visited, the most common complaint about immigrants is that they don't live up to the standards of the European-Americans' immigrant ancestors, who "at least learned English" and didn't burden society.

The Immigration Advocates' Distortion:

Supporters of high immigration point to the Great Wave as the reason the United States has nothing to fear from the present wave. Everything worked out fine back then, they reason, so why shouldn't the present wave work out fine, too? Many take that reasoning a step farther and suggest that the only reason the United States ever was able to succeed was because of mass immigration. America simply would no longer be America without it. An editorial in *The Washington Times* captured this sentiment in 1995 with its dismissal of calls to limit the volume of immigration: "The openness of the United States to immigrants—and their openness to the American experience—is an integral part of the lively and dynamic spirit of the country. Quashing that would cause fundamental damage to our society—in ways that no influx of immigrants, of whatever class or education or color, could."[4]

Both arguments are fundamentally flawed. Layer upon layer of family tales and national myths have obscured the fact that most of our ancestors who came during the Great Wave placed an enormous burden on the country. Large numbers didn't learn the language and culture quickly; they were clannish and lived in ethnic enclaves; they remained poor, and their arrival was in numbers that were devastating to many communities. For many of the immigrants themselves, life was a struggle for even a tenuous hold on the American dream. The "running sores" of immigration at the turn of the century were sweatshops, paupers, substance abuse, and fetid slums, according to immigration historian David Bennett of Syracuse University.[5]

If today's immigrants are burdening our society, it is not essentially because they come from countries other than Europe, as many restrictionists claim. And it is not because of some supposed deficiency in intelligence or character in comparison with native-born Americans' immigrant ancestors. If there are problems, it is fundamentally because immigrants today are having much the same aggregate effect on society that immigrants always have had when they arrived in large numbers.

Likewise, to dismiss today's concerns by saying that everything eventually turned out all right after the Great Wave is to trivialize the pain of all who had to live during the time of high immigration. And it ignores the fact that "things turned out all right" only after Washington finally lowered immigration levels in 1924 and kept them down for forty years. To recover tolerance and civic harmony, John Higham said, the United States depended on "a period of relief from heavy immigration, during which an inclusive national enterprise could bring old and new Americans together."[6]

To understand the Great Wave and the current immigration wave, it is helpful to place them in the context of our entire immigration history. Compare the immigration flows during the five major eras below with the average annual admissions of 507,000 between 1965 and 1989, and the more than 1 million entries a year during the 1990s.

1607–1775—COLONIAL ERA: APPROXIMATELY 3,500 IMMIGRANTS (ANNUAL AVERAGE)

These are the immigrants whose numbers were so high and whose arrivals were so unrelenting that they forced the indigenous inhabitants off the eastern seaboard, rolled back the wilderness, and created a new nation. In many of the years, the majority of newcomers were involuntary "immigrants" from Africa.

The first part of the Colonial era was the only time we truly were a "nation of immigrants." But long before the colonies declared themselves a nation in 1776, the majority of their inhabitants were native-born. The country of the United States has always been a "nation of Americans," in which only a small fraction of the population were immigrants or the children of immigrants. As a so-called immigrant nation, the United States is not much different from all other nations which at one time were infused with immigrations from other lands; all but a handful, though, eventually declared themselves mature societies no longer desiring the transplantation of new populations. The United States, Canada, Australia, and New Zealand simply got a later start at nation building and at starting to shut off the outside flow.

The Colonial era represents our immigration tradition in its rawest form. If we honored tradition by matching the immigrant flows to the one era when we truly were an immigrant nation, we would take 3,500 immigrants every *year*. Right now, we take almost 3,500 a *day*.

During the last eight months of 1995, the United States welcomed more immigrants than came during the entire 169-year Colonial era.

1776–1819—THE NEW NATION: APPROXIMATELY 6,500 IMMIGRANTS (ANNUAL AVERAGE)

The legal slave trade came to an end in 1808, but the number of people annually arriving from other continents to join the newly independent nation doubled from the Colonial era.

1820–79—CONTINENTAL EXPANSION: 162,000 IMMIGRANTS (ANNUAL AVERAGE)

The United States bought, fought, and wrought vast territories into a nation from sea to shining sea during this era. With an open frontier to settle and new tribes of Indians to be driven from their lands, America welcomed an explosion of immigrants who took advantage of the invention of steamships that provided relatively safe and quick travel. Businesses imported foreign laborers and the government enticed foreign land settlers. But even then, the annual immigrant flows were less than one-eighth of the volume of total migration in the 1990s.

1880–1924—THE GREAT WAVE: 584,000 IMMIGRANTS (ANNUAL AVERAGE)

Just as the frontier was being declared closed by the U.S. Census Bureau, industrialization created a new market for labor. Employers sent labor contractors and flotillas of ships to Europe to bring back workers. This incredible increase in immigration was extremely unpopular with the American people, who several times, beginning in 1897, persuaded Congress to pass laws to dampen the wave. But three presidents were swayed by industrialists seeking cheap labor, and by the ever-growing immigrant voting bloc, to veto the congressional immigration restrictions and keep the wave going.

The Great Wave could just as aptly be called the "Great Aberration" because it departed so radically from the rest of America's immigration history in terms of its size and long unresponsiveness to the public will.

1925–65—THE RISE OF THE MIDDLE CLASS: 178,000 IMMIGRANTS (ANNUAL AVERAGE)

By 1924, the nation overwhelmingly believed it needed time to digest the Great Wave. Immigration flows were reduced, although only back to more traditional levels. Today's pundits often refer to the 1924 Immigration Act as having "shut the door" on immigration. Nothing of the sort happened. Rather, the law merely returned the country to the annual average flows of immigration from 1820 to 1879 that had dazzled the world with their high volume when the United States was settling an open continent. Nonetheless, the cutbacks were deep enough to allow labor markets to tighten. Sweatshops virtually disappeared, black Americans finally got the chance to enter the industrial economy in major numbers, and most Americans eventually achieved a middle-class economic status during this era. A booming wartime and postwar economy played a significant role in this, but so did the gradual tightening of the labor market as the country caught its breath and assimilated the millions of immigrants who had arrived in the Great Wave.

*   *   *

During each of these eras, immigration numbers went through surges and lulls every few years, oscillating above and below the era's average level. When Congress approved the 1965 Hart-Celler Amendments to the Immigration and Nationality Act, the nation already had been in a ten-year surge and ordinarily would have been ready for a lull. But the congressional action changed that. The tradition of surges and lulls ended.

Since 1965, there have been no lulls, only a precipitous climb upward in numbers, as immigrants flooded the country in nearly the same numbers as during the spasm of the Great Wave. The average rate of immigration from 1966 through 1989 was 507,000 a year.

That flow might be called the "Family Chain–Migration Wave." Current discussion of immigration is filled with references to the country's long tradition of family reunification. In fact, though, relatives of U.S. residents had never been given top preference in immigration law until the 1965 act. If the legislation had extended the preference only to spouses and minor children, there would have been little effect on the numbers. But it also gave preference to adult sons and daughters, parents of adult immigrants, brothers and sisters. If one member of a family could gain a foothold, he or she could begin a chain of migration within an extended family, constantly jumping into new families through in-laws and establishing new chains there.

Then, in 1990, after years of protests from citizens that the immigration numbers were too high, Congress raised them even more in what might be called the "Irish-Booster Wave." Congress approved the huge boost incongruously just before the nation sank into an economic recession. The originators of the action were Irish-American members of Congress who felt that the law's emphasis on relatives of recent immigrants discriminated against people in Ireland, most of whom had only distant relatives in the United States because of the lull in immigration between 1924 and 1965. In contriving legislation that would greatly increase Irish admissions and that could gain approval, the sponsors had to accept all manner of provisions that helped other special interest groups and ballooned the total immigration numbers by 30 to 40 percent.

The bill, which received almost no public attention, was approved with very little congressional debate but began attracting major criticism once the public became aware of it within the next two years. Total immigration has averaged more than 1 million a year since 1990.

When Senator Alan Simpson, Representative Lamar Smith, and the bi-partisan federal commission chaired by Barbara Jordan first proposed cuts in immigration in 1995, they essentially were trying to negate the increases of the 1990 act, while leaving the number near the 1980s level which had surpassed that of the Great Wave.

Advocates of population growth and high immigration—such as the Cato Institute and the Urban Institute—look at the annual flows of the eras just listed and make a remarkable observation: Today's level of immigration really is not very high at all, they say. They can make such a statement because they contend that the actual numbers of immigrants each year don'tmatter. The measure that means something, they say, is immigration's proportion of the total U.S. population. Annual immigration in the 1990s is a smaller proportion of population than it was during the Great Wave. Thus, they conclude, it should not be difficult to handle the present level, and ergo the present level should continue.

The proportion-of-population argument is central in the pro-immigration lobby's justification for keeping the level far above what the public desires.

But the proportion-of-population measure fails to have practical significance for several reasons, including a failure to account for the fact that conditions change. Just because something worked in the past doesn't mean it will do so today. The "proportion" argument also suggests that the more congested a nation becomes, the more immigrants it can handle. This surely is foolishness. It would mean, for example, that overpopulated China should now be taking millions of immigrants each year. It would mean that California should continue to receive far more immigrants than any other state because it is the most crowded with the most people already. It would mean that California should receive even more immigrants in the 1990s than in the 1980s because it now has a larger population, when precisely the opposite is true.

The assertion that the United States can continue to take more immigrants every year as long as the proportion-to-population stays the same also contradicts what Americans can see with their own eyes in communities across the country. It ignores the problems that immigrants and citizens alike face in today's high-immigration situation. One could imagine accepting more and more people if the country were smoothly and productively incorporating immigrants into a thriving, stable, environmentally benign, peaceful system. But that's not the reality.

Above all, the proportion-of-population argument is grievously misleading because it contains the assumption that the Great Wave was, on balance, beneficial to the Americans living in the United States at the time.

There is much to learn from the Great Wave. Stripping away the mythology and encountering the reality of that enormously significant era perhaps would be as helpful as any other exercise in improving the discussion of current immigration issues.

ANOTHER VIEW OF THE GREAT WAVE

We have heard much about the warm personal stories of ancestors who came to America a century ago, but the hard realities and conflict brought by immigration must be restored to the picture if we are to learn anything helpful from the Great Wave experience. First, we must recognize that the Great Wave drew opposition from the beginning; there never was a period of broad public approval.

In 1880, the volume of annual immigration more than doubled over what it had been during each of the previous four years. And it was more than double the annual average of the previous sixty years. The Great Wave had begun. There was no fanfare or official declaration. Only later did Americans realize that something unprecedented was happening. There had been a surge like this in 1872–73 and back in 1854. But this surge was different. The 457,000 level of immigration in 1880 was not a peak but something of a floor for much of the next 44 years.

Many Americans agitated against the increased immigration almost immediately. Their anger was understandable. Manufacturers, such as the shoemaker Calvin T. Sampson of North Adams, Massachusetts, were importing foreign workers to fight the growing pressure from U.S. workers for an eight-hour workday and for other improvements in working conditions. Sounding remarkably like the pro-immigration forces of the 1990s, the industrialists of that time justified their actions on the basis of protecting an unfettered free-market system. They condemned labor organizing and strikes for better working conditions as violations of the "eternal laws of political economy," according to the historian Eric Foner.[7]

Although American workers resented immigrants from both Europe and Asia, they gained their first success in 1882 with the Chinese Exclusion Act. The legislation and anti-immigrant hostilities leading to it included ugly racial overtones. But the special animus against the Chinese immigrants also was driven by the egregious use of them for several years as strikebreakers. In California, the imported Chinese workers had come to make up a quarter of the wage force even before the Great Wave began.

The pressure to cut immigration did not stop with the action against the Chinese. By 1885, Congress was persuaded to move against some of the immigration from Europe. The Alien Contract Law halted the practice of companies contracting to transport immigrants who then were legally bound to work in indentured servitude for at least a year and often for several years.

Those measures knocked the numbers down some. But the volume remained high. John Higham says there was widespread public demand for more curbs on immigration in 1886, the year of the dedication of the Statue of Liberty. Many otherwise well-informed people today have misconstrued that event, suggesting that the statue was placed in New York City's harbor as a sign of welcome to the new wave of immigrants. In fact, the statue and its symbolism had absolutely nothing to do with immigration, as the museum inside the statue makes abundantly clear. It was only coincidence that the statue was placed at a time and place where millions of immigrants were entering the United States. Given the deep opposition to the increased immigration numbers at the time, it is doubtful that the people of New York would have contributed the money to build the pedestal if they had thought the statue, which officially was entitled *Liberty Enlightening the World,* had been intended as *America Inviting the World.*

While the rapid industrialization of the northern economy created openings for many new wage earners, the country did not require hundreds of thousands of foreign workers to meet that need. Large numbers of rural Americans, especially white and black workers in the war-ravaged South, could have taken many of those new northern jobs. But most were shut out of the opportunity by the Great Wave immigrants from Europe. The economist Joshua L. Rosenbloom of the University of Kansas found that immigrants were able to use ethnic networking as a means to fill job openings with workers from their own nationality groups. Like many employers in the 1990s, once northern companies learned that they could easily fill their jobs through immigrant networking, they made few efforts to attract new supplies of American workers. "Only when European immigration was cut off during the First World War were concerted efforts undertaken to develop the machinery necessary to attract low-wage southern workers," Rosenbloom concluded.[8]

The most tragic result of the manufacturers' preference for immigrant labor was a half-century postponement of opportunity for most of the freed slaves to seek higher-paying jobs outside of the South. That left a large percentage of them dependent for jobs from the very class of southerners that previously had enslaved them. The Great Wave began just as the federal government had abandoned Reconstruction and had withdrawn federal troops from the South. With the immigration-filled northern industries having no need of their services and the federal government no longer willing to protect their rights, many black workers were trapped in the South where most of their political and economic gains since the Civil War were stripped away.

Meanwhile, native-born white Americans in the North and West were feeling their own effects of the greatly expanded pool of labor. One reason the industrialists were so eager to enlarge the labor supply was to try to flatten American wage rates, which were far higher than wages in Europe. Because of an abundance of underutilized natural resources (especially open land) and a relatively small population, the New World in 1870 paid wages that were 136 percent higher than in the heavily populated Old World. But by 1913, American workers had lost almost half that pay advantage, after decades of massive additions of foreign workers. Immigrant labor depressed wages for native labor by competing directly on almost equal terms, according to the economists Timothy J. Hatton and Jeffrey G. Williamson, in their book *Migration and the International Labor Market 1850–1939*. They state that the immigrants "marginalized" most native women and black workers, keeping them out of the mainstream of industrial jobs.[9]

Adding to Americans' concerns about the labor competition from immigrants was the psychological shock of being informed in 1890 by the U.S. Census Bureau that so many people had settled in the West that the frontier, under the Census definition, no longer existed. Williamson has written that, around that time, the absorptive capacity of the American labor market declined; thereafter, immigration dragged down wages even more than it had during the early part of the Great Wave.

At that point, it didn't matter what proportion of the population immigration had once been; conditions had changed. The country had reached a level of maturity that no longer needed or could handle immigration at the old proportions or numbers. Frederick Jackson Turner, the most famous of the country's chroniclers of the closing of the frontier, found immigration much more threatening than during a time of open land. He wrote in the *Chicago Record-Herald* for 25 September 1901:

> The immigrant of the preceding period was assimilated with comparative ease, and it can hardly be doubted that valuable contributions to American character have come from this infusion of non-English stock into the American people. But the free lands that made the process of absorption easy have gone. The immigration is becoming increasingly more difficult of assimilation. Its competition with American labor under existing conditions may give increased power to the producer, but the effects upon American well-being are dangerous in the extreme.[10]

A heightened sense of urgency drove Americans to insist on decisive action in Washington. On 9 February 1897, the U.S. House of Representatives began a dramatic series of legislative events: (1) The House voted 217 to 36 to approve an immigrant literacy test. That test would have significantly curtailed the immigration of the next decades. (2) A week later, the Senate voted 34 to 31 to send the immigration restriction bill to President Grover Cleveland. (3) Cleveland vetoed it on March 2. (4) The next day, the House overrode the veto by 195 to 37. (5) The Senate—having earlier approved it by such a narrow margin—did not bother to attempt a two-thirds override of the veto. Thus the Great Wave narrowly escaped being shut off after only seventeen years and before it grew to its greatest strength.

Restrictionism had failed for the moment. There were no public opinion polls to record the actual attitudes of the American people. But the majority of their representatives in Congress worked for the next twenty-seven years to reduce legal immigration levels. That suggests a large segment of Americans who wanted to substantially change the spectacle on Ellis Island where hundreds of thousands of immigrants a year lined up to be processed into the U.S. labor force.

The restrictionist issue carried over to the next presidential election. William McKinley, running on a platform that supported restriction, was victorious; this time there would be no presidential veto protecting the foreign influx. But while the Senate voted 45–28 in 1898 to stop the Great Wave, a reconstituted House narrowly defeated the restriction, 104 to 101. If two members had switched from "no" to "yes," the Great Wave would have lost much of its volume. And the peak decade for Ellis Island never would have occurred.

One branch or the other of Congress was in nearly constant motion during the next two decades, trying to stop the Great Wave. The majority of the members of the U.S. House of Representatives voted to restrain immigration in 1897, 1902, 1906, 1912, 1913, 1915, 1916, 1917, 1921, and 1924. The Senate did the same in 1897, 1898, 1912, 1915, 1916, 1917, 1921, and 1924. But for years, the supporters of high immigration always were able to persuade a president to veto restrictionist legislation and managed to win just enough votes in one of the houses of Congress to prevent a two-thirds vote to override a veto. Industrialists lobbied hard to protect their supply of cheap labor. And leaders of growing blocs of newly naturalized immigrant citizens were influential in making sure immigration continued to add more people to their ethnic power bases.

The country paid high costs for the delay in enacting restrictions. John Higham—who continues to believe that immigration generally has strengthened the American character—has warned defenders of the current wave of immigration that they risk repeating the disastrous mistakes of those who early this century insisted on keeping the Great Wave going. "The inescapable need for some rational control over the volume of immigration in an increasingly crowded world was plain to see, then as now," he wrote. But the business interests, the immigrant leaders, and the traditionalists who feared any increase in the powers of government blocked all reform and allowed problems to fester and grow. As another 14 million immigrants entered between 1897 and 1917, the social fabric frayed, as exemplified by the upheaval in Wausau, Wisconsin. Frustrations among Americans overflowed. America endured a nationwide spread of intense anti-Semitism, anti-immigrant hysteria, and the heyday of the new Ku Klux Klan as a "nationwide, all-purpose vigilante movement," according to Higham.[11]

It was that extreme reaction to the extreme volume of immigration that has tended to cause immigration restrictionists today to be suspect as right-wing racists. But Otis Graham of the University of California, Santa Barbara, has noted that "Restrictionism attracted some of the best minds in America, including many liberal clergymen, spokesmen for organized labor and the black community, and socialists."[12]

Part of the concern of the liberal restrictionists was the abominable conditions for many immigrants. A congressional study found that new arrivals were three times more likely than natives to be on welfare in 1909; immigrants comprised more than half the people on welfare nationwide. Chicago was especially hard-hit; four out of every five welfare recipients at that time were immigrants and their children. Foreign-born residents constituted a third of the patients in public hospitals and insane asylums in the country. The situation was worse in New York City, where the president of the board of health said that almost half the expenditures were for the immigrant poor.

A national commission studied the impact of immigration for five years and concluded in 1911 that it was contributing to low wages and poor working conditions. It was not until 1917, however, that immigration restrictions finally were enacted into law as the House (287–106) and the Senate (62–19) overrode President Wilson's second veto.

In the public's view, the 1917 action did not block enough immigrants. Another act in 1921 set a numerical ceiling for the first time. And then in 1924, Congress decisively gave the American people the respite they so long had sought. The "Great Aberration" was over, after forty-four years.

* * *

To criticize the Great Wave—or any period of immigration—is not to criticize the individuals who were part of it. Often through no fault of their own, the immigrants were used by certain Americans to undercut the wages and power of other groups of Americans.

Because immigration was drastically reduced after 1924, the problems caused by having too many immigrants gradually subsided; we now can look back positively and affirm the sizable fraction of the current population who descended from that wave. None of that, however, should blind us to the reality of the damage the Great Wave level of migration did to this country at the time—or the further damage that likely would have occurred had the era not ended. Nor should the reality of consequences necessarily take away any of our admiration for the courage, hard work, and perseverance of the majority of immigrants who endured despite harsh conditions. "Obviously, immigration has given this country wonderful people," says Jim Placyk, a self-described New York leftist activist. "I'm glad my grandparents came from Ireland. I'm glad about all kinds of specific descendants of immigrants. But let's not pretend that nobody got hurt because the immigrants came."

With the flow of immigration cut back so substantially after 1924, urban turmoil began to subside throughout the country, including in Wausau, Wisconsin, the very setting of which is symbolic of that part of immigration history. Wausau scenically nestles on rolling land shaped over the ages by the confluence of the Wisconsin River from the north, the Eau Claire River from the east, and the Rib River from the west. The power of these rivers is evident from the famous Wisconsin dells and smaller Eau Claire dells carved out of land both upstream and downstream. Settlers during the 1800s decided they liked the lay of the land and didn't want any more flooding. They constructed dams to regulate the flow of the rivers, restraining them from significantly changing the terrain further while channeling their power for the benefit of the community.

The 1924 immigration law functioned in much the same way as gates on a well-placed dam: Over the next forty years, immigration policies regulated the flow of foreign migration streams to keep them low enough to be beneficial to native and immigrant alike. Immigration no longer was allowed to transform the social landscape of local communities against their wills.

American municipalities were given a long "cooling-off" period to create tranquility out of their caldrons of human divisions and enmities. In Wausau, the quarreling Germans, Poles, and Yankees began to explore ways of creating a common local culture with common goals.

By the time Chinese refugee Billy Moy pulled into Wausau's train station in 1952, the city's different ethnic groups had mixed into something close to a common culture. Moy was a teenager fleeing

Chinese Communist authorities. He arrived in America during an era that was especially welcoming to the modest number of immigrants coming at the time. Moy remembers that as a refugee he was a novelty in Wausau: "I didn't know a word of English when I arrived. People were very nice, especially the teachers. Kids never harassed me. Never a bad word." He was able to learn English quickly and move into the local job market. Because migration numbers were low, nobody had reason to fear a loss of local control from people like Billy Moy.

And so it was in most of the United States. Partly because of the low immigration from 1925 to 1965, Americans developed a whole new attitude toward immigrants, becoming substantially positive about them for perhaps the first time since the country's birth. A poll in 1965, for example, found Americans had an overwhelmingly positive attitude on immigrants and immigration, with only about one-third desiring that the immigration level be lowered.

Many Americans today have been surprised to find themselves changing from supporters to opponents of immigration. They had been so welcoming and admiring of immigrants in the decades before 1965 that they mistakenly assumed that was how Americans usually had reacted. Americans may have been blinded by the unusual profile of immigrants who had arrived in the reduced numbers between 1924 and 1965. Those immigrants had much better education than the average American and made contributions highly valued by natives. Some were geniuses who fled Nazism, World War II, and communism. They assimilated quickly and enjoyed great economic and career success. George Borjas, an economist at the University of California-San Diego, suggests that Americans came to attribute the qualities of 1924–65 immigrants to the immigrants who had arrived much earlier, during the Great Wave. That led to a false memory of a kind of golden Ellis Island era of mass immigration.

In fact, though, progress for the Great Wave immigrants was extremely slow. One reason was that there simply were so many of them. Borjas matched 1910 Census data with recent data to discover how long it took the descendants of Great Wave immigrants to reach educational and economic parity with the descendants of American natives of the time. He discovered that they haven't yet done so. His calculations showed that it is taking around one hundred years, four generations.

Progress was far more swift for those who arrived in smaller numbers in the 1924–65 era. Billy Moy, after years of hard work, perseverance, and saving, bought the abandoned train station that sat on an island in the middle of the Wisconsin River across from downtown Wausau. He opened his restaurant, Billy Moy's One World Inn, in the island depot in 1965. It was the same year Congress inadvertently unhinged the immigration floodgates.

By the 1990s when I talked with Moy, Wausau again was reeling from swollen streams of immigration like those that overwhelmed it during the Great Wave. The accelerated immigration—this time from Southeast Asia—had once again dramatically changed Wausau, creating deep resentments among the citizenry and sharply diminishing the ability of foreign migrants to move into the city's mainstream. As we talked in his restaurant, Moy showed printed cards with sketches he had made of the low-water Wisconsin River while the nearby dam was being repaired some years ago. "Good food in a town of good people," one card read on the back. Moy spoke in puzzlement about local ethnic tensions that now are common and the fact that recent refugees tell of hostile treatment at the hands of the native-born.

Any visitor to Wausau can observe stark lines of social, economic, and cultural differences between the native-born and the large—and largely poor—new Southeast Asian population. But a careful observer, says local history professor Jim Lorence, can look at who wields local power and at memberships in churches and other organizations and still see some faint signs of a continuing divide between the descendants of the Yankee settlers and of the Great Wave immigrants. Such signs remain even though it has been more than seventy years since the Great Wave ended. Americans contemplating the assimilation of the current thirty-year wave of immigrants might want to consider what America would be like today if Congress had not adjusted the gates on the immigration dam in 1924 and had not given the nation's diverse peoples forty years to adjust to each other without the constant large infusions of newer groups.

3

How Many Refugees?

Support for today's high-immigration policies often is wrapped in the language of refugees and compassion. If the United States is to be a "good" country, according to some Americans, it must annually accept hundreds of thousands of foreign citizens. To do less, they say, is to renege on humanitarian obligations and to abandon the country's necessary role as a refuge for people fleeing persecution.

But of the 1 million immigrants who have been arriving each year during the 1990s, people requiring refuge from persecution comprise only a small fraction. Just a little more than 100,000 of the slots have been designated for refugees each year. And even that number gives an inflated image of actual refugee admissions.

Most of the people who enter the country in those 100,000-plus refugee slots are not recognized by the United Nations as refugees; Congress and the president merely call them "refugees" so they can use those slots, according to the State Department.

The U.S. refugee program obviously does not follow the internationally recognized definition of a refugee as a person who has *fled* a home country after facing an *individualized* threat of persecution based on race, religion, nationality, membership in a particular social group, or political opinion. Incredibly, most people who have been arriving here as "refugees" had never fled their country; most were still living in their home country—under no individualized threat of persecution—when they got their notification that Washington had invited them to come as refugees: 67 percent in 1990, 73 percent in 1991, and 80 percent in 1992.

The United States even allows "refugees" to get their visas now but stay in their home countries until a more convenient year to move.

The reason for the official subterfuge is that Congress uses the refugee program as a way to help preferred nationalities—usually with a vocal American constituency—to get around other immigration quotas. For example, long after the fall of the Communist government of the former Soviet Union, Congress, through its Lautenberg Amendment, has required the State Department to bring in many Russians as refugees. A Scripps-Howard investigation by Michael Hedges in 1995 examined internal government documents about the approximately 300,000 Jews, Christian Pentecostals, and other Russian religious minorities who had been allowed into the United States as Lautenberg refugees since 1989. Hedges reported that U.S. memos indicated that by 1993 less than 1 percent of the tens of thousands of Russian "refugees" each year actually met refugee criteria, an incredibly loose operation that allowed significant numbers of hardened criminals to expand crime syndicates in the United States.

The bi-partisan federal commission chaired by Barbara Jordan recommended in 1995 that the number of annual refugee slots be cut from more than 100,000 to 50,000. That stirred a huge outcry from religious groups and other organizations that are paid by the federal government to handle refugee settlement. But 50,000 still is far above the number of refugees to the United States who actually have been internationally designated for resettlement.

* * *

Despite a total worldwide refugee population that often exceeds 20 million, the United Nations High Commissioner for Refugees does not advocate large-scale refugee resettlement because its drawbacks far outweigh its benefits. International humanitarian officials know that even if the rich countries were generous to the point of totally disrupting their own societies, they never could take more than a small fraction of the refugees. So, humanitarian efforts are concentrated where they can help the most people—in the camps near their home country, and in clearing barriers to the refugees going back home.

Each country's limited funds for assisting refugees are much better spent on the camps and repatriation than on settling a lucky few in a place like the United States. Roger Winter, director of the non-profit U.S. Committee for Refugees, has estimated that a day's worth of the funding needed to settle a single refugee in the United States would cover the needs of five hundred refugees abroad.[1] Humanitarian concerns about helping the most people with available money would seem to dictate that the United States take as few refugees as possible and instead spend the money abroad to help far more people. Refugee analyst Don Barnett wrote in *Newsday* that the total costs of resettling refugees in the United States during 1994—including direct resettlement costs, and public assistance at the local, state, and federal level—approximated the entire U.S. foreign-aid budget of $13.5 billion for all purposes.

Refugee settlement in the United States is one of those "nice" things to do that can end up harming more people than it helps. Hearing that a few of their fellow countrymen have been settled in a rich country can entice far more people to flee their countries than otherwise would, thus swelling refugee numbers. The initial openness of the West to Vietnamese refugees in the 1970s is widely suspected of having given false hopes to masses of people still in Vietnam who had little chance of meeting true refugee criteria but who took to boats and risked their lives for the slim possibility of being allowed into a rich country.

In order not to trigger unnecessary—and often dangerous—refugee migrations, the United Nations asks the advanced countries to be cautious with refugee resettlement.

The power of even the remotest possibility of settlement in the United States could be seen in Southeast Asia again in 1995. Two decades after the end of the war and the subsequent Communist takeover that sent hundreds of thousands of Vietnamese fleeing in boats, the United Nations began trying to shut down refugee camps in nearby countries. Conditions again were safe for living back home, according to the international diplomatic community, including the U.S. State Department. The would-be refugees had been screened and judged able to travel home safely. "We feel sure that it is now time for these people to go home," said Werner Blatter, a UN official. "It's time to wrap this up."[2]

But columns, editorials, and news stories in U.S. newspapers carried arguments that the camp people be offered another round of interviews to give them one more chance to come to America. A few members of Congress introduced legislation to try to halt the repatriation.

Ruth Marshall, a spokeswoman for the UN High Commissioner

for Refugees, responded, calling for a larger view: When refugees who have entered another country uninvited refuse to go home although they don't face personalized threats of persecution, they have become illegal aliens. "There is no moral or legal principle that requires the international community to continue to assist a large population of illegal immigrants," she maintained. U.S. journalists interviewing returnees inside Vietnam found that they commonly expressed regret that they had not gone home sooner. "I left because I dreamed of a better life," one man said. "I found that nowhere is better than your home."[3] But the chance to go to America had a much stronger hold over those still in refugee camps, where the Vietnamese resisted orderly relocation and even turned to violence and rioting.

Because of such volatility in Third World communities, the United Nations asks industrialized nations to concentrate their settlement efforts on the relatively few refugees with special needs. These are the people who face imminent persecution, death, or critical health concerns. In 1995, the United Nations requested all countries to resettle a combined total of only 31,900 refugees. Yet U.S. policy required bringing in 112,000 people under the heading of "refugees."

The U.S. refugee resettlement program has had very little connection to true international humanitarian efforts. In 1994, for example, only 18,543 of the 112,573 people entering the United States under the refugee heading actually were recognized by the international relief community as special needs refugees requiring resettlement in a third country. U.S. refugee admissions easily could be cut to 30,000, or even 20,000 a year; at that level, the United States still would meet its international obligations to those who actually require permanent refuge and who are refugees in fact and not just in name.

The possibility always exists that America from time to time may need to provide temporary first-asylum protection for larger numbers of refugees fleeing neighboring countries. But temporary asylum protection should not on humanitarian grounds increase the number of people permanently settling in the United States. Since the purpose of refuge is to save lives and protect from persecution, temporary refugees should go home as soon as the dangerous conditions subside there. Bad economic conditions or a climate of discrimination in the home country should not be allowed as justification for temporary refugees to stay in the United States indefinitely. If those two conditions were criteria for permanent residency here, hundreds of millions of people around the world—who live in dismal economies and under a government that does not respect their full human rights—would qualify to come. The U.S. population today contains large numbers of supposedly temporary refugees from a couple dozen countries who never went home. Salvadorans and Nicaraguans, for example, are allowed to remain here, even though it has been years since the wars in their countries ended and since democratic government was established. Their refusal to go home and the federal government's unwillingness to insist that they do so has led most people to believe that there is no such thing as temporary refuge. That opinion undoubtedly has contributed to the increasing reluctance of the United States to provide temporary refuge to other nationalities in recent years.

* * *

Although true refugees make up less than 3 percent of all U.S. immigration, the proponents of high population growth and high immigration often speak of the entire program as a form of international humanitarianism. They say that although few immigrants actually are fleeing for their lives, most are fleeing desperate economic circumstances. Immigration then becomes an important way for the United States to show compassion to the Third World.

Immigration, though, is not an effective humanitarian tool. While having an anti-humanitarian effect on many vulnerable people within U.S. borders, taking in a half million or more immigrants a year does virtually nothing positive for the economically distressed people in other countries. Consider that the International Labour Organisation estimates that some 800 million people are unemployed or underemployed. And the UN Development Programme estimates that 900 million people are malnourished. U.S. immigration cannot make a dent in those numbers.

If indeed our immigration policy is driven by humanitarian concerns, Mexico appears to set the standard. From 1981 through 1990, 23 percent of all U.S. admissions were from Mexico. A humanitarian case can be made for rescuing people from Mexico, where per capita income is only about 15 percent of the level in the United States. But more than 4,500 million people live in countries with annual individual incomes *below* that of the average Mexican.

Consider also that during a year in which the United States takes a half-million immigrants from Third World countries, for example, the excess of births over deaths in those countries adds another 80 million or so to the impoverished population. By way of illustration, we could say that the year begins with 4,500 million people living in misery in the Third World, and after U.S. immigration, ends with 4,499.5 million, plus the additional 80 million. Neither the United States, nor the industrialized nations as a whole, can possibly take enough immigrants to serve as a population safety valve for the Third World. Clearly, for anything significant to happen for the sake of Third World residents, it must happen where they now live.

From the standpoint of the people of the Third World—almost none of whom will ever get a chance to immigrate—the international humanitarianism of immigration is at best a mixed blessing. Let's take a closer look at four areas of impact:

- *Loss of U.S. capacity to help.* Geopolitical analyst George Kennan believes that the United States remains one of the great sources of hope for the Third World. But the hope is not that Third World people can move to the United States, because "even the maximum numbers we could conceivably take would be only a drop from the bucket of the planet's overpopulation." Rather, it is important that the Third World have a United States to help them "by its relatively high standard of civilization, by its quality as example, by its ability to shed insight on the problems of the others and to help them find their answers to their own problems."

  Kennan worries that current immigration may be creating conditions within this country "no better than those of the places the masses of immigrants have left" . . . "As that happens, Kennan says, the United States becomes more and more inward-looking, with less and less ability and willingness to help others. Recent political trends concerning foreign aid seem to bear him out.[4]

  Then there is immigration's effect on the food-producing capacity of America's land. That capacity is of major humanitarian importance to more than one hundred grain-importing nations. Lester Brown of the World Resources Institute suggests that U.S. farm production may already surpass a level that is sustainable. "By definition, farmers can overplow and overpump only in the short run. For some, the short run is drawing to a close. . . . The United States already has converted 11 percent of its cropland to grassland or woodland because it was too erodible to sustain continuous cropping. The USDA reports that water tables are falling by 6 inches to 4 feet per year beneath one-fourth of U.S. irrigated cropland, indicating that eventual pumping cutbacks are inevitable."[5]

  As immigration drives the U.S. population sharply upward, there are more and more Americans who are forcing the conversion of prime agricultural land to urban use. An average of 1.5 million acres of arable land per year are being destroyed through urban development and erosion from overuse. When agricultural land disappears under a parking lot, it is gone forever. "Asphalt is the land's last crop," in the memorable phrase of Rupert Cutler.[6]

Immigration puts the food-producing capacity under a three-pronged attack. It is responsible for a rapidly growing U.S. population, which (1) converts farmland to urban use, taking it out of agricultural production; (2) competes with agriculture for water; and (3) eats more of what otherwise would have been an exportable food surplus to the world's hungry nations.

· *Bad population example.* No humanitarian gesture from the United States is likely to reduce the future numbers of people in poverty by a larger amount than participation in massive, international efforts to halt the Third World population growth that annually is adding another 80 million to the ranks of the impoverished.

Leaders of most countries recognize the need to slow that growth or to stabilize their populations. But most must contend with counterforces which suggest that a growing population is a source of power. The United States is the chief model for those counterforces, who can point out that the world's most powerful nation not only refuses to stabilize its own population but has government policies that force a U.S. population growth of nearly 3 million a year (primarily recent immigrants and their descendants), higher than all but a half-dozen countries. With that kind of record, the United States lacks credibility in its efforts to preach environmental and population responsibility in the world arena.

· *Remittances.* Here is a factor with obvious benefits for the people left behind by immigrants. U.S. communities discover a whole new phenomenon at their local post office soon after immigrants begin to move in: long lines of foreign workers on payday, waiting to send money orders back to family members in their home countries.

In 1992, immigrants to the developed nations sent back some $66 billion in remittances to their relatives in Third World nations. Only the sale of oil brings more money into the underdeveloped countries, the United Nations says. Remittances of $600 million a year to El Salvador exceed the value of coffee sales there.

But remittances aren't always enough to compensate for immigration losses to the home communities, according to a study by the United Nations Population Fund. The money usually is spent on consumer goods rather than being pooled for long-term economic development. To some extent, remittances improve the diet and health of the families receiving them. But "fewer than one in five wives has received any remittances from husbands who migrate. And when remittances are received, they seldom account for as much as half of the family income."[7]

A study by the *Hispanic Journal of Behavioral Sciences* found that Mexican communities that had sent large numbers of people to the United States were "now in a downward spiral" despite the remittances. "Yes, they have raised their lives a bit economically, but it is a pity," said a priest in one town. The remittances are a poor substitute in towns devoid of younger men, where tense and saddened women cope with the responsibilities of running a household alone.[8]

And it must not be forgotten that the only reason most immigrants are able to send home remittances based on low-wage earnings in the United States is that they sacrifice their personal lives to work most waking hours at menial labor, as a group of scholars concluded in a study for the *Aspen Institute Quarterly*. The immigrants can send money home because they "submit to overcrowded, deteriorating housing. They trim food budgets and adopt lower standards for mental and physical health, putting up with sickness and putting off medical attention."[9]

· **Brain drain and change drain.** Despite the difficulty that the majority of immigrants are having in succeeding in the United States, very few of the 1 million people who come each year are among the world's most needy and least able. "You can't say this is the most just system," comments Katharine Betts, an Australian sociologist. "What you have now is young, strong able men crossing the borders and the weakest, poorest left behind to endure." Immigration deprives Third World countries of needed skills, says Nafis Sadik, head of the United Nations Population Fund. Africa has lost one-third of its highly educated manpower in recent decades. In Sierra Leone, for example, hardly anybody with an education is left to help a country with only a 15 percent literacy rate. And the brain drain can be debilitating to some countries that are desperate for leadership. Jamaica, Trinidad, and Tobago, with a total of only 3.8 million residents, have lost 38,000 of their professionals to the United States.[10]

A sizable portion of Haiti's population has been admitted to the United States over the last decade—more than 200,000 out of a population of 6 million. Over 12,000 of Haiti's professionals are among them. The effect has worsened conditions for those left behind. Haiti's public and private schools three decades ago were the envy of the Caribbean. Now so many teachers and other educated Haitians have left that a whole generation of schoolchildren is growing up without much education at all, raising the question whether Haiti will have a citizenry capable of supporting a true democracy.[11]

Many Americans who have worked in Third World countries are torn about whether the United States should pressure skilled people to remain to help their own people. While those countries desperately need the assistance of their most educated citizens, those citizens often cannot seem to do much to help because of political and cultural barriers.

In addition, some Third World countries simply can't make much use of one of their citizens who has obtained an advanced physics degree, for example. Immigration advocates argue that the only way for such persons to bloom to their potential is to bring them into one of the advanced industrial nations. On the other hand, if the brightest of the Third World didn't think they had a chance of immigrating, they might not major in physics in the first place. Instead, they would seek education appropriate for their own country's needs, perhaps specializing in civil engineering, agriculture, business and public administration, and public health.

If the political and cultural systems of a Third World country are keeping its residents in misery, who can we expect to change those systems? Immigrants—especially political refugees—often are the people who have the most inclination, energy, or education to bring about change for their fellow countrymen. U.S. immigration then is not just a brain drain but a "change drain," siphoning off the very people who might have been able to help change oppressive systems or contribute to community progress. "You now see skilled people from Mexico coming to take unskilled jobs here [in the United States]," says migration specialist Carol Zabin. "It's a waste for everyone."[12]

The option of immigration also can encourage ruthless dictators and the military to use it as a convenient way to get rid of people they would rather not have around. For that reason, the United Nations was hesitant about endorsing the large-scale immigration of Bosnians to rich nations because it might seem to be endorsing ethnic cleansing. Cuba has been especially adept at using emigration to solve its own domestic problems, says Dan Stein, executive director of the Federation for American Immigration Reform. "As we look at other countries that have overthrown communist or authoritarian governments in recent years, we find that in each case the revolution was sparked from within. With a domestic opposition in place, the forces of democracy were able to pick off, one by one, the rotting regimes of Eastern Europe and Latin America. But instead of an organized opposition in Havana (Cuba), Castro's opposition is comfortably ensconced 90 miles away in Miami. From there they are free to howl about what Fidel has done to their island, and little else."[13]

With few dissidents staying around to model activism for others, Cuba's young people don't imagine that they could change the country from the inside. That has led to cynicism. "Unlike the older people, the young people see no possibility of change," Gerardo Sanchez, a director of the Cuban Commission of Human Rights in Havana, told reporter Nancy Nusser. Typical among the Cubans risking their lives on rubber rafts to reach Florida in 1995 were young adults, many of them "smart, educated people who, if they stayed, might revitalize the economy or drive a political opposition movement," Nusser wrote. But U.S. immigration policies have drained the agents of change out of Cuba.[14]

It is commonly forgotten today that the original symbolism of the Statue of Liberty undergirds the philosophy of helping people in their homelands, rather than trying to help just a few by allowing them to immigrate. Through the years, that symbolism has been largely supplanted by exactly the opposite message which is contained in a poem by Emma Lazarus. It calls for "your tired, your poor, your huddled masses yearning to breathe free" to solve their problems by coming to the United States.

Contrary to claims by numerous politicians and editorial writers, the poem is not carved in the base of the statue that sits in the harbor of New York City. Nor is the poem part of the official "message" of that monument. Rather, it appears on a small plaque that was allowed to be hung privately by friends of Lazarus, an obscure poet, seventeen years after the statue was erected and sixteen years after her death. Virtually nobody knew of the poem at the time it was written or when it was placed on the plaque without any public notice. It is one of thousands of museum pieces in the pedestal. But once it was noticed by the news media in later years and given wide distribution, the poem came to be as well known as the statue.

Anybody visiting the museum under the Statue of Liberty today will encounter the official symbolism of the monument: A French historian conceived of the statue as a way to commemorate the alliance of France with the American colonies during the American Revolution. When it was dedicated in 1886, the French sculptor and all the American officials hailed its representation of democratic freedom and the rule of law. Historians say the statue looked out toward the rest of the world, inviting all countries to emulate the American republican system of government. Nobody ever suggested associating the statue with a promise of new life in the United States for the downtrodden of the earth. Rather, the symbolized solution was to break tyranny in their own home countries. The statue was raised not as an invitation for immigrants to cut and run for the best deal they could get individually, but for them to stay and fight for their own peoples.[15]

Implicit in all that symbolism is that the United States maintain a system of justice for its own citizens that is worthy of emulation. In weighing the humanitarian value of U.S. immigration, one has to consider the effects on America's most vulnerable groups—the descendants of the victims of U.S. slavery and of the land's indigenous peoples who have not overcome the results of centuries of discrimination and persecution; the physically handicapped; poor children; low-skilled workers; and residents of impoverished urban and rural communities, to name several.

Unfortunately, large movements of outsiders into a society tend to undermine support for programs that redistribute resources to the needy, as sociologist Katharine Betts told an Australian government board at a 1995 conference. "Biology may help program us to care for our near kin, but complex social arrangements are required if we are to set up institutions which enable us to care for fellow members of our community, people who are personally unknown to us. The modern nation state is such a set of institutions and it and they depend on borders. . . . A continuing inflow of new members erodes support for social policies, and politics take an ugly turn in which welfare is seen as something paid for by 'us' for 'them.' "[16]

Among the Americans who must be included in any humanitarian considerations in setting immigration levels are those recent immigrants who are now a part of "us." Policymakers, though, rarely weigh the effects of future immigration on recent immigrants.

Increasingly, our nation's program of high immigration appears to be anti-immigrant. Advocates for potential immigrants show little concern for how the continuing unprecedented immigration they seek might lower the quality of life for the immigrants they had worked so hard to bring in during previous years.

There is no question that most new immigrants immediately improve their income upon arrival, given the abysmal conditions in their home country. Even failure in this country can be a financial improvement; welfare in Wausau, Wisconsin, for example, pays twice as much in *one month* as a job in Southeast Asia pays in an *entire year*. Some new immigrants—especially the approximately one-quarter who arrive with advanced education—do exceptionally well upon arrival in this country.

Immigration, however, is not an unmitigated blessing for the newcomers, many of whom seem stuck in the basement of the American dream. Take a look at what has happened to immigrants in affluent Wisconsin: More than 48 percent of Asian children and 32 percent of Latino children live in poverty.[17]

Numerous journalistic reports have chronicled the lives of thousands of immigrants whose income is so low (and debts often so high) they must cram into tiny, windowless cubicles that they share with other immigrants who work and sleep different hours. A study by the United Nations focused on how life changed for women moving from Third World countries to the United States and other industrialized countries. It concluded that most educated women migrants move into the same low-status, low-wage production and service jobs as unskilled women. Although they often end up making more money than back home, the advantages of migration are not clear-cut as the women contend with rape, abduction, sexual harassment, physical violence, and demands for sexual favors, the United Nations reported.

Some people leave unrest in their countries only to live in U.S. urban precincts where the chance of violent death is even higher. When a man who had fled violence in the Sudan was beaten to death while working in the U.S. capital as a pizza deliveryman, a friend noted that the slain man's father had asked him to forget about America and come back to the Sudan where there aren't as many crazy people.[18] By a 7 to 5 margin, immigrants told pollsters that they believe their homelands were safer than the United States has turned out to be.[19]

U.S. immigration policy entices foreign parents to make decisions that split up their families and cause great emotional harm to their children. A RAND study noted that new immigrant families suffer "deep affective losses" from breaking ties with family and other networks necessary for their psychological well-being. Parents often abandon their children in the home country for years while they gain a foothold in America. In other instances, the children are sent ahead of the parents. The principal of one Los Angeles school described a Hispanic population in which 80 percent of the students had been separated from their parents, at one time or another, for about five to eight years. RAND concluded that many recent immigrant children "suffer from severe emotional stress." Many students are separated from parents or have recently moved in with parents they barely can remember. "Even intact families are frequently disrupted by parents' emotional distress and their need to work multiple jobs," the RAND study said.[20]

Recent immigrants in such dire straits do not need the federal government to add to their burdens. Yet that seems to be what it is doing by running a program of such high immigration.

Most economists and other observers of immigration agree that the people who face the stiffest job competition from each year's new immigrants are the immigrants who came the previous few years. A U.S. General Accounting Office study, for example, found a pattern in the pole tomato and tortilla industries in which employers constantly replaced immigrant workers with newer immigrants, or used the presence of each year's new immigrants to undercut the wages of those who had come in previous years.[21]

Gracie Franco, a Mexican-American in San Jose, California, complains that new immigrants take jobs that more established Mexican-Americans otherwise could get: "They come here and in no time at all they have a job because they are willing to work for below minimum wage. Meanwhile, I'm trying to demand fair wages and I can't find anything." The job competition is so great that new Mexican immigrants complained to the *San Jose Mercury News* that the most severe discrimination they face is from other Mexican-Americans.

A group of immigrants and other American minorities formed the Diversity Coalition for an Immigration Moratorium in 1995, claiming that immigration levels disproportionately hurt the minorities represented in its membership. Its members point out that their position against immigration reflects what various polls have found are the majority views held by ethnic minorities.[22] Opinions among Latinos are especially striking. The Latino National Political Survey by Rodolfo de la Garza of the University of Texas discovered that 75 percent of Mexican-American citizens, for example, said there are too many immigrants. That compared to 74 percent of non-Hispanic white American citizens who said so. Probably reflecting the fact that the most recent immigrants face the toughest job competition from additional immigrants, Mexican-Americans who are not yet citizens are even more opposed to further high immigration—84 percent of them.[23] Any survey of Hispanics or Asian-Americans is largely a survey of recent immigrants. Census Bureau tabulations on America's students, for example, find that 68 percent of Hispanics and 72 percent of Asian-Americans are immigrants or the children of immigrants.

Although the leadership of most national ethnic organizations does not agree with the pro-restriction sentiments of the ethnic grass roots, many of those leaders have been acknowledging problems from immigration. "Migration, legal and undocumented, does have an impact on our economy . . . [particularly in] competition within the Latino community," explains Antonia Hernandez, president of the Mexican American Legal Defense and Educational Fund. "There is an issue of wage depression, as in the garment industry, which is predominantly immigrant, of keeping wages down because of the flow of traffic of people."[24]

Po Wong of the Chinese Newcomer Service Center in San Francisco maintains that the continuing flow of newcomers is too overwhelming for his community. And Lora Jo Foo of the Asian Law Caucus says that previous immigrants are seeing "their wages and working conditions eroded" by new immigrants. The greatest adverse impact of new immigrants on wages and employment will be on "minorities and established immigrants," says Paul On, of the University of California-Los Angeles. Sociologist Hsiang-Shui Chen has conducted several studies in the New York Chinese-American community and found that new Chinese entrepreneurial immigrants reduce profits for established Chinese businesses, and the immigrant laborers reduce job opportunities for native and earlier-immigrant Chinese. The *Boston Globe* similarly found resentment among earlier Chinese immigrants to the infusion of new Chinese immigrants who bid down the wages available to them in Boston's Chinatown.[25]

But with the largest number of immigrants coming from Latin America, the greatest impact of our immigration policy appears to be on Latinos. A study by University of Texas professors Jorge Chapa and Richard R. Valencia for the *Hispanic Journal of Behavioral Sciences* concluded that the more the Latino population is swollen by immigrants, "the more they get behind." Latinos are 126 percent more likely than all other Americans to live below the poverty level.

Chapa and Valencia identify lack of educational attainment as a key cause of Hispanic economic stagnation and deterioration. And a major reason for educational problems, they say, is the increasing segregation of this predominantly immigrant population. Why are they becoming more segregated in their schools? Because of "the groundswell of immigration patterns, the high birthrate of Latinos, and the foot-dragging of desegregation efforts."[26]

Although immigrants voluntarily cluster in their housing patterns, they tend to view the resulting educational clustering as negative. In Wausau, Wisconsin, for example, the Southeast Asians pushed for cross-district busing out of the belief that too many of their children in one place created a harmful educational effect. Yi Vang, a local immigrant leader, said the local refugees wanted their children to be able to learn to assimilate from established American children: "It is better to spread them out so that when a Southeast Asian kid has trouble, he is easier to control. We want our children to be with Anglo children in an integrated culture. Lincoln and Franklin schools [where the immigrants are concentrated] have too many Southeast Asians for them to assimilate."

The very fact that Wausau has such a large refugee population is due in part to the rate of immigration being so high in California. A large number of Wausau's refugees settled first in different parts of the country, especially California. But they found California too overcrowded with other immigrants from all over the world, Vang said. They didn't like all the "crime, unemployment, and overcrowding," and the fact that the schools there were filled with a cacophony of languages. Vang said refugees in California and other places heard about Wausau's good schools and the chance to learn English and assimilate into an American culture.

Latino immigrants are not having much luck at all in getting an education where English is predominant. According to the National School Board Association, Latino students in California and Texas are more segregated than blacks in Mississippi and Alabama. In fact, Latino students nationwide now are the most segregated ethnic group in American schools.

As new immigrants pour into the school districts already laden with previous immigrants, the increasing concentration is strongly related to negative educational outcomes, Chapa and Valencia maintain. The dropout rate rises, the number of college preparatory courses diminishes, and the average college admissions test scores decline. The Census Bureau found that only half of Latinos over the age of twenty-five had completed high school. That is a dropout rate 144 percent higher than for all other Americans.

The humanitarian nature of the U.S. immigration program is suspect when one considers the cavalier consideration given to the immigrants themselves. The system looks a bit like a caricature in which middle-aged rich men idolize very young women and marry them as "trophy" wives who, as they age, are cast aside for the next batch of eligible women reaching their twenties. Like year-old cars in the showroom when the new models are unveiled, "last-year's-model" immigrants seem quickly forgotten as attention is focused on the "new-model" immigrants asking to come in next.

As a humanitarian policy, immigration offers no clear-cut evidence that current U.S. levels are particularly helpful to the rest of the world—and on balance, they could even be harmful to Third World countries. That weak or nonexistent international benefit hardly seems a justification for the harm immigration is doing to the vulnerable members of American society.

4

Engineering a Disaster

In 1958, Senator John F. Kennedy wrote a little book with huge consequences. Largely ignored at the time, *A Nation of Immigrants* eventually helped change the direction and very nature of the country. Together with historical events that Kennedy could not have foreseen, the book revived the age of mass immigration that had been declared dead and buried in 1924.

As a result, nearly every aspect of American life in the 1990s is different. Nobody had intended to transform the nation in this way. The revival of mass immigration was totally unintentional.

Of the two great questions of immigration policy—"Who should come?" and "How many should come?"—Kennedy had begun a debate only about the "who." He wrote in his book: "The clash of opinions arises not over the number of immigrants to be admitted but over the test for admissions."[1]

Virtually all policymakers agreed that the pattern of low immigration set by the Immigration Act of 1924 should continue with little change. What motivated the reformers—including Kennedy—was their opposition to provisions of the law that reserved most of the limited annual immigration slots for Northern Europeans and barred all but a few Asians from the opportunity. Each country was given a quota representative of its population in the United States as of the 1920 Census. The idea was that immigration should not be an instrument to change the ethnic balance of the United States. Presidents Truman and Eisenhower unsuccessfully tried to change the quota system during their terms. Kennedy first had called for the changes as a senator from Massachusetts in 1959, and then did so again in 1963 as president.

Reformers, who sought to give all nationalities an equal opportunity at immigration, promised that they weren't renewing mass immigration. But that is precisely what they did in the way they reworked the proposal in 1965.

Congress rewrote immigration law in the national wave of emotionalism that followed Kennedy's assassination in 1963. A new edition of *A Nation of Immigrants* was published within a year of his death. Some seized upon the book as a blueprint for how a grieving nation could honor its slain leader. *Newsweek* magazine suggested that reforming immigration law would be as worthy and lasting a memorial as something in marble, and far better than the "oceans of empty rhetoric [that] have been spilled in ineffectual tribute since November 22."[2] President Lyndon Johnson evoked the memory of Kennedy in a State of the Union address as he urged enactment of immigration reform. Passage of the Immigration Act of 1965 essentially was a legislative tribute to Kennedy, according to former senator Eugene McCarthy of Minnesota, who co-sponsored the act with fellow Democrats Philip Hart of Michigan, Robert Kennedy of New York, and Edward Kennedy of Massachusetts.

Reformers also appealed to Congress to bring immigration policy in line with the new civil rights ethos of the country. The civil rights movement to end legalized racial discrimination had culminated with the Civil Rights Act of 1964 and the Voting Rights Act of 1965. "Everywhere else in our national life, we have eliminated discrimination based on national origins," Senator Robert Kennedy said before the immigration vote. "Yet this system is still the foundation of our immigration law." Many regarded the reform as necessary symbolism to change the image of the United States abroad. During our Cold War against the Soviet Union, we wanted to demonstrate that we were friendly to the underdeveloped world.

The high immigration and resulting tumult that we have today is not what John Kennedy or his supporters had sought with immigration reform. But it nonetheless is what the 1965 memorial by Congress wrought.

* * *

The proposals to reform immigration laws did not enjoy popular support. A Harris Poll before the vote in 1965 found the public was opposed by a 2 to 1 margin. Americans were happy both with the relatively low number of immigrants and with who they were. Immigration since 1924 had been immensely successful, and the newcomers were unusually popular with natives. Why mess with a successful formula, the public seemed to be saying.

During the debate over the new law, members of Congress and the Johnson administration repeatedly guaranteed the public that immigration numbers would not rise—at least, not by very much. "It is a limited measure, since it does not make any substantial increase in the number of immigrants who can enter each year," McCarthy said on the Senate floor.

The immigration level in 1965 was almost exactly the level it had been in 1925, the year after Americans overwhelmingly had persuaded Congress to put an end to the age of mass immigration. The national consensus that the United States should be a post–mass immigration country had included most leaders of business, religion, labor, academia, and social work. They agreed that, like most nations, the United States no longer had need of immigrants to settle open frontiers or to help build an infant nation; the population was mature.

That consensus continued to hold during the debate in the 1960s. *A Nation of Immigrants* did not contest the legitimacy of concerns about the country's capacity for handling large numbers of immigrants: "We no longer need settlers for virgin lands, and our economy is expanding more slowly than in the 19th and early 20th centuries." Kennedy wrote that his proposals "will have little effect on the number of immigrants admitted."[3]

Pressed about how many additional immigrants might come under the law, Senator Robert Kennedy surmised that perhaps another five thousand would come from Asia and the Pacific during the first year. But those additional numbers would "virtually disappear" within a few years, he said. Representative Emanuel Celler, a Democrat from New York and chief sponsor of the legislation in the House, reassured the public that while he was changing the intent of the 1924 law to restrict certain *types* of people, he was not changing that law's intent to restrict the *number* of immigrants. Similar promises were given by all the chief sponsors, as well as by Labor Secretary Willard Wirtz, Secretary of State Dean Rusk, and President Johnson.

Senator Edward Kennedy promised: "The bill will not flood our cities with immigrants. It will not upset the ethnic mix of our society."

For forty years, U.S. immigration policy had been based on the premise that the age of mass immigration was dead—that it had no role in the modern American nation. In passing the Immigration Act of 1965, no supporter advocated a change in that premise, which had limited immigration to an average of 178,000 a year since 1924.

The year after the 1965 immigration bill was enacted, however, 323,040 immigrants arrived in the United States.

In 1967, 361,972 came.

In 1968, 454,448 came.

And the numbers continued to rise.

* * *

When results of legislation vary from promises so quickly and so drastically, one has to wonder if the sponsors were engaged in a widespread conspiracy to lie to the public or if they simply didn't know what they were doing.

Eugene McCarthy today insists that the reformers meant what they said in pledges not to increase the level of immigration. But in their rush to pass the "Kennedy memorial" and appease conservative opponents who threatened to block it, reformers put provisions into the bill that inadvertently created huge loopholes. Conservative Democrats—many of them the same people who had opposed the Civil Rights Acts—feared that Kennedy's proposal to remove the national origins quotas would flood the United States with immigrants from the Third World. They came up with something of a trick that would allow the United States to say that it had no quota discrimination against any country but which, in actuality, would bring about the same mix of immigrants as had been coming. The trick was "family reunification." While the reformers had wanted a priority on picking immigrants by skills, the conservatives insisted that the priority be on an immigrant's family connections to Americans.

The conservatives, of course, were totally wrong in their projections about how family reunification would work. They thought that since nearly 90 percent of Americans were of European descent, most of the relatives would come from small European families. Congress didn't seem to realize that family reunification primarily would bring in relatives of the large groups of Asian and Caribbean refugees and Latin American workers who had been allowed into the country during the last decade. In addition, successive presidents allowed vast numbers of people fleeing Communist countries to move permanently to the United States as a Cold War policy enacted with no thought for the dramatic consequences.

Neither the liberal reformers nor the conservative opponents wanted immigration numbers to rise. But for all their promises, nobody thought to put an overall cap on how many immigrants could come annually, nor did they limit the number of refugees the president could bring in permanently each year. That made it possible for the family reunification provision to lead to an immigration program today that bears almost no resemblance to the reformed policies that John F. Kennedy and his supporters sought.

By establishing family reunification as the priority of immigration for the first time in U.S. history, Congress provided a method for each refugee or recent immigrant to begin an almost endless chain of family migration: A man sent for his wife and minor children, and later sent for adult children and brothers and sisters, who brought their spouses, children, and parents, who brought their other adult children, who sent for their spouses, who sent for their parents, and so on.

* * *

That the Immigration Act of 1965 had unintended consequences was not out of the ordinary in congressional machinations. The art of legislating is one of constantly correcting and modifying. Congress meets every year during most months. It has plenty of opportunity to correct its mistakes or to adjust to changing conditions.

But as the size of the legislating mistake grew by the year, Congress did nothing to correct it. The labor economist Vernon Briggs decries the "appalling indifference by policymakers to the unexpected consequences of their actions," and attributes it to the fact that nobody ever did a careful study of how increases in immigration might affect Americans, particularly in the job market. "Mass immigration" was allowed to reemerge for the first time since 1924, Briggs say. His textbook on labor and immigration defines "mass immigration" not just by its size but by the fact that the numbers are set without regard for their effect on wages, employment, and social stresses.[4]

By 1969, it was clear that the 1965 act contained some mistakes. They were turned over for study to a bi-partisan commission appointed by the leadership of the Senate and the House and by President Richard Nixon. The Commission on Population Growth and the American Future was charged with looking at immigration as part of a much larger task of determining whether it was in the nation's best interests to continue to grow as in the past. In an ambitious two-year study, the so-called Rockefeller Commission (named for its chairman, John D. Rockefeller III) concluded that "in the long run, no substantial benefits will result from further growth of the Nation's population, rather that the gradual stabilization of our population would contribute significantly to the Nation's ability to solve its problems. . . . We have looked for, and have not found, any convincing economic argument for continued population growth. The health of our country does not depend on it, nor does the vitality of business nor the welfare of the average person."[5]

By the time the report was released, the American people already had moved to a fertility rate low enough to allow for population stabilization in a few decades. But the commission members could see that the increasingly high immigration levels would not allow that to happen.

The commission was divided about immigration. The majority of the 24 members voted to recommend that annual immigration be frozen at 400,000 (less than half the volume in the 1990s). A sizable and vigorous minority pointed out with accuracy that Americans never would enjoy the benefits of population stabilization within their lifetime if 400,000 immigrants a year continued to arrive. They called for reducing admissions by 10 percent a year for five years until the annual level was closer to the 1925–65 average of 178,000. Despite the split, the commission's members from corporations, unions, government, environmental, women's, urban, and ethnic groups were in agreement that immigration, at a minimum, had to be capped at no higher than 400,000.

The report to Congress and the president was issued in the midst of Nixon's troubles with the Watergate scandal. Chances for acting on the calls to stabilize and cap immigration were lost as Nixon resigned and the new president and Congress struggled to stabilize the government itself.

In 1978, total permanent admissions of foreign citizens surpassed 600,000 for the first time since 1924.

That same year, Congress created another bi-partisan blue-ribbon panel: the Select Commission on Immigration and Refugee Policy, chaired by Theodore M. Hesburgh, the president of the University of Notre Dame and a previous chairman of the U.S. Civil Rights Commission. After three years, the sixteen-member commission concluded that immigration was "out of control," and that the nation could not avoid dealing with "the reality of limitations." It agreed with the Rockefeller Commission that immigration had to be capped. Its preferred level: 350,000. The longer mass immigration was allowed to continue and America became more and more congested, the lower the reformed level of immigration would need to be.[6]

* * *

By the time the Hesburgh Commission reported, the lobbies for maintaining the accidental immigration flood had control of Congress. For thirty years, no efforts to cut immigration numbers back toward the original intent of the sponsors of the 1965 act have succeeded because of the power of two groups: conservative business interests; and a liberal coalition of religious, immigrant, and civil liberties organizations.

At the time of the 1965 debate, the groups were not well organized to promote mass immigration and had not developed such strong advocacy views. As immigration rose, so did the two advocacy groups' enthusiasm for high numbers. By the end of the 1970s, their lobbying against immigration reduction was so forceful that the Hesburgh Commission felt compelled officially to try to discredit it. The commission warned that the public's interests were being subjugated by the lobbying appeals of business, immigrant organizations, and religious groups. The commission explicitly stated that it rejected the arguments of those special interests about the need for high immigration.

"If it is a truism to say that the United States is a nation of immigrants, it is also a truism that it is one no longer. . . ." Hesburgh stated.[7] In saying that, while advocating 350,000 immigrants a year, he obviously did not mean the United States should stop taking immigrants. But he was reaffirming the consensus of the nation since 1924—and agreed upon by John F. Kennedy and the Congress of 1965—that this no longer was a nation of *mass* immigration. In other words, immigration numbers had to be set according to their effect on the American people.

Polls showed that a large majority of Americans agreed with the Hesburgh Commission's recommendation to reduce legal immigration toward more traditional levels. But the appeals of businesses, immigrant organizations, and religious groups won the day in Washington. Congress never seriously considered turning back, stopping, or even slowing down the ever-increasing numbers of immigrants coming through the unintended loophole of the 1965 act.

What Americans have had to live with are the *results* of the 1965 act. The Hesburgh Commission and other advocates for reductions have in effect been asking for a return to the *spirit* and *intentions* of the 1965 act.

The *Saturday Evening Post*, one of the most outspoken opponents of the 1965 Immigration Act, had insisted for years that the proposed reforms would result in a major increase in numbers. In 1957, it had editorialized: "To open wide the floodgates of immigration could well depress our standard of living to a dangerous level without making more than a dent on the world problem of overpopulation. Is it wrong for us to consider first the interest and welfare of the Amerian people?"[8]

The chapters that follow focus on the interests and welfare of the American people after thirty years of unprecedented and unintended immigration.

5

Shooting the Middle Class

Before the 1970s, black and white American workers in Miami's construction industry earned middle-class wages, had middle-class benefits, and lived middle-class lives.

That was before Washington inadvertently aimed mass immigration at America again and began shooting the legs out from under the country's middle-class economy.

Cubans poured into Miami during the 1970s and overwhelmed the local labor market. Immigrant firms formed and hired the excess workers at lower wages, which allowed the new firms to underbid many of the unionized native construction companies. Immigrants "penetrated the industry and contributed to deunionization and a decline in wages," so the sociologists Guillermo Grenier and Alex Stepick concluded in one study. By the mid-1980s, Miami construction unions found that immigrants had taken away most of their bargaining power. Unions were forced to accept wage cutbacks and to give up their right to strike. Cuban firms, mostly non-union, with wages lower by about a third, had captured more than half the construction market. The erosion has grown worse under the steady flow of more foreign workers from Nicaragua, Cuba, Haiti, and elsewhere. Small new subcontractors have exploited the surplus labor and underbid even the more established Cuban firms. Grenier and Stepick found that many of the firms no longer paid time and a half for overtime, and paid wages in cash so as not to have to make appropriate deductions. Jobs that provided a middle-class lifestyle before mass immigration became little more than minimum wage labor.[1]

Thus, the American middle class shrinks. The economic law of supply and demand has not been repealed; it is a law that needs no official enforcement. Once the federal government pours large numbers of foreign workers into American communities, the free-market economy takes care of the rest, converting surplus labor into lower wages and worse working conditions than otherwise would exist.

"In general, an increase in the number of potential workers will tend to reduce prevailing wage levels," the U.S. General Accounting Office stated after issuing a study on illegal aliens in 1988. "This would occur whether the increase is the result of the growth of the native population, legal immigration or illegal immigration."[2]

* * *

For at least two decades, the U.S. government has waged war on the American middle class in numerous ways. Whether or not the war is deliberate or just the result of colossal mismanagement, immigration policy has been a crucial weapon in carrying out the thus-far-successful attack.

By the 1950s, the United States had become an overwhelmingly middle-class country and as such the envy of the world. For truth be told, the appeal of America in the world's eyes has not been that it's an easier place for the extraordinary individual to rise to the top, but that it gives the ordinary person a better chance in life. Since mass immigration was curtailed in 1924, an additional 20 to 30 percent of the U.S. population had moved into the middle-class ranks by the 1950s. The American culture of that time was militantly middle class.

Much has changed since then. Between the election of President John F. Kennedy in 1960 and the Census of 1990, the middle-class portion of the U.S. population has thinned by 8 to 15 percentage points. Increasingly, wages for full-time jobs won't support a middle-class lifestyle. By 1979, 12.1 percent of all full-time workers were paid wages too low to keep a family of four above the poverty line. By 1990, the proportion was half again as high, at 18 percent.[3]

Nearly everybody is in agreement that something very different and negative has happened to the U.S. economy since 1973. On the pessimistic side, the economist Timothy Smeeding declared after a University of Michigan study, "What we are looking at is a permanent decline in the size of the middle class."[4] The erosion of the middle class has spawned scores of books and fueled myriad political campaign platforms. But no consensus has emerged about how to fix the problem. We can, however, shed some light on the matter if we consider what has happened to the middle class in relation to the increasing looseness in the U.S. labor market.

The Jerome Levy Economics Institute of Bard College showed how the middle class has been shrinking when it estimated the average hourly wages for different educational groups in 1973 and 1988 (adjusted for inflation). While incomes were increasing for the top of the upper class, the compensation for everybody else was declining. Wages, even for college graduates, were dropping on average—by 3 percent for women and by 5 percent for men.

Wage depression between 1973 and 1988 was most pronounced for Americans with less education:

- for workers with some college education, wages went down 6 percent for women and 11 percent for men;
- for workers with only a high school diploma, wages went down 7 percent for women and 17 percent for men;
- for workers who dropped out of high school, wages went down 10 percent for women and 22 percent for men.

As bad as those averages appear, they mask much worse circumstances for the mostly under-thirty Americans who had less than ten years of work experience. In all but one of those gender and educational categories listed above, wage depression for the young workers was between 50 and 150 percent worse than the average for their entire category.

The biggest shocks from the rapid deterioration of U.S. wages may have come between 1990 and 1992 to some men in the middle of their careers. The U.S. Bureau of Census reported that for the men age between twenty-five and fifty-four who lost full-time jobs and were able to get new full-time jobs, their average earnings declined a whopping 20 percent. And their loss of standard of living did not take place over a fifteen-year or generational period but, in essence, overnight.[5]

Such declines in earnings have driven large numbers of formerly middle-class workers out of the labor market. Perhaps 1 million or more prime-age workers—mostly men—have stopped looking for jobs since 1989.

Nonetheless, no matter how far wages fell over the last two decades, Congress resisted cutting its annual importation of competitive foreign workers—and, instead, continually increased the numbers.

Overfilling the labor pool with immigrants is a federal policy change that is a part of what the sociologists Frances Fox Piven and Richard A. Cloward describe as a "war against labor" that has created a historic shift in how income is distributed. Businesses reaped the spoils of war, they say: "The simultaneous growth of poverty and wealth was unprecedented in the 20th century."[6]

The richest 1 percent of Americans always have earned an enormously disproportionate share of the income. But now, according to the Congressional Budget Office, the top 1 percent earn almost the same amount as the middle 20 percent of Americans combined! That proportion represents a doubling for the top 1 percent since the early 1970s.

Concentration at the top is so great that the Catholic bishops in the United States issued a pastoral letter in the 1980s containing a warning that sounded more appropriate for a Third World country: "In our judgment, the distribution of income and wealth in the United States is so inequitable that it violates a minimum standard of distributive justice."[7]

The growing disparity was especially evident between those who have college degrees and the majority of Americans who do not. In 1979, the income gap between an average white male college graduate and an average white male high school graduate was 49 percent. That gap had grown to 82 percent by 1994, forcing many of the high school graduates out of the middle class.[8] Those who defend the growing gap say it is caused by the country's increasing need for skilled workers and the declining need for lower-skilled workers. Yet, Congress every year imports hundreds of thousands of lower-skilled workers to add to the glut at the bottom of the labor ladder.

By 1995, Edward Wolff, an economics professor at New York University, could state that "We are the most unequal industrialized country in terms of income and wealth, and we're growing more unequal faster than other industrialized countries."[9] Several conservative commentators rushed to the defense of inequality, pointing out that the fact that some Americans are getting richer doesn't mean they are doing so by making other Americans poorer. Labor Secretary Robert Reich conceded that there is nothing necessarily wrong with some Americans getting rich, but pointed out that "if we have economic growth and most Americans don't enjoy it, we're not succeeding as an economy."

Immigration is closely tied to two of the fundamental trends behind the fact that the U.S. economy is not succeeding for the average

American worker. First, much less new wealth is being created in the United States because output per worker is not increasing nearly as fast as during the middle of the century. And second, of the small amount of new wealth being created by productivity improvements, very little is being shared with the workers; the owners of capital are keeping most of it for themselves.

The abnormally high level of immigration since 1965 has contributed to the productivity problem by substantially boosting U.S. population growth and the size of the labor force. Growth in population lowers the amount of capital investment per worker, which makes it more difficult to increase the productivity per worker. Robert M. Solow of the Massachusetts Institute of Technology was honored with the Nobel Prize in part for his development of an economic model that explains why high population growth tends to impoverish a country. He has shown that immigration since 1965 has moved the United States away from the stable or very-slow-growing population style of other advanced economies and toward the fast-growing population trends of Third World nations.[10]

Although the improvement in U.S. productivity has been far less than in previous decades, per capita productivity has continued to rise. But while productivity rose between 1977 and 1992, the average wage fell.[11] "Productivity improvements are going into corporate profits, not workers' pockets," Reich lamented.[12]

The results should not be surprising. When labor is in surplus, pressure is reduced on corporations to share with employees the rewards of their increased productivity. Federal immigration actions constantly engorge the labor supply. The ensuing juxtaposition of anemic wages and robust profits feeds Americans' increasing alienation toward economic and political institutions, Treasury Secretary Robert E. Rubin has suggested.[13]

* * *

The labor glut during this period of unprecedented immigration not only has retarded and depressed wages, it has helped make it possible for corporations and the government to slash benefits to middle-class workers.

The portion of newly hired workers with access to pension programs dropped by 12 percent between 1979 and 1990. Over the same decade, new hires who got health benefits dropped by 35 percent. Piven and Cloward say that nearly four-fifths of all strikes in the 1980s were staged not for higher wages but to protect health benefits. In April 1975, 81 percent of all unemployed Americans got unemployment benefits. By October 1987, only 26 percent did, the lowest amount since the program was begun in the Depression.

More and more Americans are being stripped of their benefits and security under a transformation of the labor market in which companies are eliminating full-time jobs and replacing them with temporary or part-time employees, day laborers, and employment services. *The Washington Post* found that this trend in the Washington, D.C., area, for example, was encouraged by the ready supply of immigrant workers.

Piven and Cloward decry the shift during the 1990s of some 30 million workers into jobs outside the regular full-time workforce: "While some are well-paid freelancers, most contingent workers are women and minorities clustered in low-wage jobs with no benefits."[14]

Along with deteriorating wages and benefits have come deteriorating lifestyles for current and former members of the middle class.

Many families have had to sacrifice having a full-time homemaker or parent at home as they moved to two full-time, paying jobs just to stay in the middle class. Over the last twenty years, the portion of married women who work for pay has risen by 50 percent. For many women, the shift into paid work has been eagerly sought and an essential element in their self-fulfillment. For others, it has been an unwelcome shift forced by household economic realities. For all, it has involved some sacrifice. But all of that extra work by women has not increased the median household income. Wages have fallen so fast that the nationwide loss has canceled out the additional income new women workers have brought into their households.

Lower wages, less leisure time, reduced parenting hours, slashed benefits, and mounting economic insecurity have taken their toll in the communities where American workers live. The damage is especially evident where immigration has most affected the labor supply.

In a 1995 study, Tulane University demographer Leon Bouvier and Scipio Garling of the Federation for American Immigration Reform looked at life in selected cities with less than 7 percent immigrants, and compared them with same-sized cities with populations that were more than 25 percent immigrant. The findings were startling.[15]

Even though they had the same population as the low-immigration cities, the cities with high immigration

- had a 30 percent longer commuting time,
- had 40 percent more people living in poverty,

- had 60 percent more high school dropouts,
- had twice as many violent crimes,
- had twice the level of unemployment,
- had more than twice the welfare dependency,
- had more than seven times as much crowded housing as defined by the Census Bureau.

In a separate exercise painting much the same picture, Rice University economist Donald Huddle created something he called a Misery Index. It measured negative changes in the wage rate, in the ratio of labor force participation to population, and in the fraction of the past year worked. "Declines in these measures mean less work and lower earnings and hence more misery for the unskilled native work force," Huddle says. He found that the metropolitan areas with the highest immigration also ranked the highest on the Misery Index.[16]

* * *

There is no doubt that the plight of the American middle class has deteriorated seriously since mass immigration was renewed. But the answer to whether immigration was a significant cause of the deterioration or merely a coincidental force during the same time period has been highly contested among scholars and public policy officials.

Immigration is not the only economic force that has pummeled the United States during the last three decades. Hundreds of thousands of middle-class jobs have been lost in America's electronics, machine-tool, steel, textiles, and auto industries. Blame is variously placed on: (1) U.S. corporations that had not invested enough profits to stay ahead in research, development, and new plants and equipment; (2) unions that pushed labor costs above what the productivity of workers could support; (3) the Federal Reserve Board and others who pushed interest rates to exceptionally high levels; (4) the foreign oil cartel countries, whose rapid increases in energy prices sent shocks throughout the economy; and (5) Congress and presidents who ran up gigantic foreign debt to finance federal deficit spending, lowered trade barriers, and exposed U.S. companies to a level of international competition virtually without precedent.

In response to all those economic factors, U.S. companies restructured, cutting their workforces permanently in the process of streamlining and becoming far more efficient. They emphasized cognitive skills for the remaining jobs and dramatically reduced the demand for lower-skilled workers. Such workers previously had been able to earn wages and salaries that moved them at least up into the bottom tier of middle-class living. But with demand for their services down, the law of supply and demand drove wages down.

In that complicated mix of economic traumas, it is not easy to determine how much of the depression of American workers' wages is the result of increased immigration. We'll tackle that question a little later. For purposes of determining how many immigrants to bring in the future, however, one need merely answer a much simpler question: Given that many other forces are depressing wages and undermining the middle class, will immigration make the situation worse or better?

The commonsense answer would seem obvious: Adding still more lower-skill workers through immigration surely would be harmful to natives and would increase inequality in this country. One can observe that happening in local communities across the land. Yet, the abundant on-site evidence has not been enough to convince one major group: most of the economists who are quoted in the mass media.

Throughout the 1980s, most economists who were interviewed by the news media about immigration said they could not find a large negative effect of immigration on American workers. Their comments often were frustrating to experts in other disciplines who criticized the economists for avoiding case studies and relying too heavily on computer models. While many sociologists and anthropologists studying specific jobs in specific local communities—such as construction work in Miami—had no difficulty in finding the negative effects of immigration, the economists couldn't prove the existence of the problems with their econometric models. As the Stanford economist Paul Krugman has written, "Economic theory is, in essence, a collection of models: simplified representations of reality, which inevitably leave out some aspects to focus on others." Academic economics remains a "primitive science," similar in stage of development to the field of medicine around 1900, Krugman says.[17] In many ways, the economists have tried to *simulate* reality while experts in other disciplines have *looked* at reality.

Nonetheless, the experts usually cited in news stories about immigration have been economists. A common sentence in many media stories about immigration—especially in business-oriented journals—goes like this: There is a virtual consensus among economists that immigration has had at most a minor negative effect on American workers.

Such a consensus, which never existed, appeared to be real in part because of surveys of selected economists by pro-business think tanks and publications. Cornell University's Vernon Briggs, who has studied the effects of immigration on U.S. workers since the 1970s, says the views gathered in such surveys are not much better than educated guesses because the economists are asked to comment on something that is not in their area of expertise. Few who are quoted in the media have actually conducted studies of labor economics or immigration, Briggs maintains.

One of the economists most quoted by advocates of high immigration, however, has done a lot of pertinent study. George Borjas of the University of California-San Diego published his mixed findings in 1990 in the book *Friends or Strangers: The Impact of Immigrants on the U.S. Economy.* Immigration advocates continue to quote the parts of that book to show he still did not find conclusive proof of major negative impact on jobs. But Borjas also noted that nobody yet knew the full impact of the massive numbers of lower-skilled immigrants who had come in the 1980s.

Borjas continued his research and later found that he agreed with some of the criticisms that had been made of economists' work in the 1980s. The problems with earlier studies were numerous:

· Most relied on data from the 1970s when immigration was far lower and did not reflect the cumulative effect that had gained full momentum in the 1980s. The 1990 Census provided sharply different data. Simply plugging the new data into computer models produced much-changed verdicts about the effects of immigration.

· Economists have tended to look at wide metropolitan areas—or larger regions—so that sharp negative effects in particular neighborhoods tended to get averaged or washed out in the broad statistical analysis.

· Most previous studies failed to account for the fact that many of the native workers who were hurt by immigrant competition no longer could be measured because they had moved from the city being studied.

· And they failed to account for the lost opportunities for natives who remained in other areas of the country but who would have moved to higher-wage cities if not for the immigrant influx there; thus the costs of immigration were spread out to other cities and states.

Once Borjas updated his data and methods, he came up with very strong conclusions about the impact of immigration—conclusions which tended to match the street wisdom of people who live in the communities where immigrants settle and work. Borjas's bottom-line computation is that recent immigration may be responsible for one-third of the growing economic inequality in America.[18]

He has not backed away from his original contention that immigration on balance is a net plus for the U.S. economy—about $7 billion a year. But the balance entails big winners and big losers among American natives. As it turns out, immigration causes a gargantuan redistribution of wealth, from the workers who compete with immigrants, Borjas says.

Immigration helps the owners of businesses and the employers of gardeners, chauffeurs, and nannies to pocket an extra $140 billion a year. But immigration also causes native workers to lose about $133 billion a year in depressed wages, he maintains. That explains why a small, but affluent and powerful, segment of the population continues to press for high immigration and can't understand why most Americans don't like it, Borjas wrote in the *National Review,* one of the few conservative publications to editorialize against maintaining high immigration for the benefit of the wealthiest Americans.

Immigration turns out to be a perverse federal Robin Hood scheme that takes from middle-class workers and gives to the country's most affluent.

Journalists and politicians today who repeat the claims about a "virtual consensus of economists" not finding negative effects from immigration are copying lines from pre-1990 Census newspaper clippings and are failing to note the chorus of economists now finding very real reasons for concern.

According to some experts like Robert M. Dunn, Jr., the damage from immigration should be self-evident. The professor of economics at the George Washington University noted in *The Washington Post:* "If the United States faces an unlimited supply of labor from the south at a wage of about $5 per hour, incomes of less-skilled Americans will not increase even if economic growth in the country accelerates. . . . If Washington wants to increase incomes of low-wage Americans and reduce the growing inequality of U.S. incomes, it must severely restrict the inflow of unskilled workers from abroad. . . . When supply-siders and other 'free market' economists argue for open immigration policies, it ought to be remembered that they usually reflect the views of owners of businesses, who benefit from the abundance of low-wage labor that immigrants provide."[19]

Even Stephen Moore, of the libertarian, pro-business Cato Institute, now acknowledges that immigration depresses wages. In occupations dominated by immigrants, "the wage rate probably is lower than it would be if immigrants weren't available," he recently wrote. To Moore, though, the harm to American workers in those occupations is worth it: "Yes, some people may be adversely affected, but the other people who use the now cheaper goods and services also benefit. Overall, the presence of immigrants means the economy will do better."[20]

One of the most common arguments against the existence of wage depression—repeated by many journalists and think-tank analysts alike—is that wages in many high-immigration cities are higher than wages in many low-immigration cities. That is true. Such comparisons, however, don't particularly measure anything of relevance. In most cases, wages already were higher in those cities before the latest wave of immigrants arrived, which is one reason why the immigrants settled there. We learn much more by tracking how wages have changed over a period of time in which immigrants arrived in high or low proportions. When scholars have done that, the link between immigration and wage depression again appears quite clear.

In a study described in the *Journal of Economic Geography,* a multidisciplinary team of scholars provided the kind of comparison that truly reflects some of the change caused by high immigration. The Walker-Ellis-Barff study looked at wages in each sample city before and after a period of immigration. It found that the average wage increase (not factored for inflation) was 26 percent lower in high-immigration cities than in the average U.S. city—and lagged a whopping 48 percent behind wage increases in low-immigration cities. Even this kind of comparison tends to understate the wage-depressing strength of immigration because it doesn't measure the effects from the many American workers who are driven out of immigration centers. By leaving high-immigration centers, American workers keep wages there from being as depressed as they otherwise would be. By moving to low-immigration cities, the fleeing American workers keep wages there from going up as fast as they otherwise would.[21]

Immigration advocates often focus on another version of comparisons meant to prove that the importation of foreign workers doesn't depress wages. They point out—correctly—that some of the worst black poverty in the country is in cities with hardly any immigration and that it is much worse than in cities like Los Angeles that are teeming with immigrants. That must prove that immigration improves the economic conditions for black Americans, some suggest.

But for decades—long before mass immigration was unleashed on it—California had been a place where black Americans could enjoy considerably higher living standards than in the rest of the country. Immigration didn't cause that, because immigration was not a significant factor then. The California Department of Finance found that during the 1980s, under the heaviest immigrant influx of the state's history, California blacks lost much of their economic advantage. While the poverty rate among California blacks was about 14 percentile points better than for other American blacks in 1980, the Californians had lost about half that advantage by 1990. California Latinos had held similar economic advantage over Latinos in the rest of the country and, like the blacks, lost much of it under the tidal wave of 1980s immigration.

In Los Angeles, where the majority of workers are black and Latino, the Walker-Ellis-Barff study found serious wage depression coinciding with high immigration. Los Angeles wage increases lagged 31 percent behind Birmingham, Alabama, and 47 percent behind Pittsburgh, two low-immigration cities that were studied.

* * *

This country's economic history should dispel any doubt that high immigration tends to lower the wages of the working class and to increase inequality in a society. In his presidential address to the American Economic Association in 1955, Simon Kuznets laid out a theory about rising and falling income inequality in capitalist societies. Many economists since then have sought to quantify the factors that, in different countries and different decades, have depressed earnings for the lower working class while increasing the wealth of the affluent and skilled.

Immigration has proven to have been a major factor in past increases of inequality. Delivering the Kuznets Memorial Lecture at Harvard in 1991, Jeffrey Williamson showed how economic inequality in America was greatest from 1820 to 1860 and from the 1890s until World War I. Those periods coincided with the two previous major waves of immigration.

According to Williamson, the occurrence of high immigration and high levels of economic inequality at the same time was not happenstance: increased fertility and immigration foster income inequality. Despite having democratic institutions, abundant land, and a reputation as a workingman's country, America during those periods of nineteenth-century immigration surges was a land of jarring inequality.

The economist Peter H. Lindert noted in his book *Fertility and Scarcity in America* that American inequality has lessened when immigration was curtailed. When World War I abruptly cut off most immigration to the United States, the huge gap between rich and poor closed incredibly fast: "Within three years' time, pay gaps dropped from historic heights to their lowest level since before the Civil War." But just as quickly, inequality grew as soon as mass immigration resumed after World War I, so that later in the 1920s, "income looked as unequal as ever," Lindert said.[22]

Once Congress curtailed immigration in 1924, the middle class grew again and inequities receded to historic low levels by the early 1950s. America finally had become a paradise for the common workingman and woman.

Lindert found it peculiar that America would have such a robust march toward middle-class equality during a period that included widely varying external events, such as the nation's deepest depression, a sudden wartime recovery, and moderate postwar growth: "This timing suggests that the explanation of this drop in inequality must go beyond any simple models that try to relate inequality to either the upswing or the downswing of the business cycle."[23]

In the egalitarianism of the era after the 1924 curtailment of mass immigration, the economic bottom of society gained on the middle, and the middle gained on the top. The closing of the gap in wages had as much of an effect in enlarging the middle class as did all the transfer taxes and programs of President Franklin D. Roosevelt's governmental activism combined, according to Lindert and Williamson.

Several factors caused the fluctuations in inequality during U.S. history. But "the central role" has been played by the change in labor supply—through immigration and fertility—claims Lindert. Both Lindert's and Williamson's calculations found that decreased immigration and lower fertility between 1929 and the Korean War were responsible for about one-third of the decrease in American inequality.

The rise of powerful unions during that period also played an important role in moving larger and larger numbers of laborers into the middle class. But Lindert concluded that the unions were able to gain their power because low immigration and low fertility kept the size of the labor force smaller while the demand for labor remained high. Not surprisingly, unions have withered in power during the wave of mass immigration since 1965.

A tightened labor pool not only makes employers pay more for scarce labor, it is a great stimulator of a country's creativity. The economist Harry T. Oshima reported in 1984 that when immigration was restricted in the mid-1910s and again in the mid-1920s, employers were forced to raise wages. That induced the employers to press for major advances in mechanization. The resulting new technological applications of gasoline and electric machines made it possible to mechanize enough unskilled operations and hand work to release many workers into more skilled jobs. Growth in output per worker hour was phenomenal. That made it possible to raise wages still further. Because of the increasing demand for skilled workers, American parents realized they would need to spend more money to help each child gain a better education. This contributed to lower birth rates, and thus to slower labor-force growth, and thus to tighter labor markets, and thus to higher wages, which pushed manufacturers to push the skill levels of their workers up even further. In this cycle of productivity and wage gains—each feeding on the other—the United States became a middle-class nation.[24]

That cycle has been broken for many years now. Immigration is high. Productivity growth is low. The middle class is shrinking. If you want to see the attributes that made the United States such an economic powerhouse in the middle of the century, look at Japan. It has almost no immigration. It has a very slowly growing population and labor force. It has a very high rate of machinery investment, which multiplies the productivity of the country's workers. In a paper for the National Bureau of Economic Research, J. Bradford DeLong explained that all those are characteristics that make a country an economic winner: A low rate of growth in the number of workers means that a country does not have to divert its capital to provide for new workers. Instead, capital can be used to increase the productivity of the existing workforce. While the United States has been spreading out its capital investment to provide jobs for millions of immigrants over the last thirty years, Japan has continued to concentrate its investment on increasing the productivity—and thus the wealth—of its native workers.

The long trend toward a middle-class society in America first began to stall in the 1950s after the U.S. fertility rate skyrocketed. Although fertility has receded to economically healthier levels since the early 1970s, immigration has skyrocketed, and America has been moving backwards toward greater inequality—just as it has during every major period of increased immigration.

One need only look to Argentina this century to see the possible perils of waiting too long to scale back immigration. During the late twentieth century, most observers have tended to lump Argentina with other Latin American countries, their economies characterized by small economic elites, a vast class of impoverished citizens, and a weak middle class. The economist Carlos Diaz-Alejandro wrote that some modern commentators have even classified Argentina with less developed nations such as India and Nigeria. Such comparisons would have been thought ludicrous just eighty years ago, he said: "most economists writing during the first three decades of this century would have placed Argentina among the most advanced countries—with Western Europe, the United States, Canada, and Australia. . . . Not only was per capita income high, but its growth was one of the highest in the world."[25]

How did Argentina cease to be one of the world's richest countries? That puzzle was the challenge for Allan M. Taylor, the Mellon Fellow at the Harvard Academy for International and Area Studies and the Department of Economics at Harvard. "More compelling and mysterious examples of failure than the ruination of Argentina are hard to imagine," Taylor said in a 1992 paper published in the *Journal of Economic History*. He concluded that a key factor for Argentina's economic disintegration was the continuation of high European immigration to Argentina after the United States, Canada, and Australia began ending their eras of mass immigration early this century.[26]

No single explanation could account for such a sustained and deep economic demise, Taylor said. But a crucial factor surely was the country's remarkably low savings rate, as compared to Australia, for example. Taylor linked the low savings rate to the high rate of immigration and the high fertility rate of the immigrants. Both immigration and fertility were higher than in Australia and contributed to Argentina having higher consumption and lower savings, Taylor found. The country made up the shortfall of capital for a while by heavier reliance on foreign capital. The differences in Argentina's circumstances—with their roots in the difference in immigration rates—left the country much more vulnerable than the other advanced nations to international events. Argentina's rich, middle-class economy was not able to survive.

Although the United States was spared Argentina's sad fate, it and other countries that had received large numbers of immigrants early in the century suffered more severe depressions in the 1930s than did European countries that had not received immigrants, according to Timothy Hatton and Jeffrey Williamson. If immigration to the United States had not dropped drastically, the U.S. Depression would have been far more severe, they maintain.[27]

Hatton and Williamson say that until recently many economists have greatly underestimated the power of immigration to slow down productivity, depress wages, and increase inequality. With newer research showing that high immigration caused all of those negative trends in the past, there is no reason to suspect that high immigration is not contributing to those trends in the 1990s. As for those economists who have not yet found the link between immigration and present economic trends, Hatton and Williamson suspect that they "have looked for evidence in the wrong place."[28]

* * *

Some immigration advocates argue that the lessons from the past may not apply today because of the very new phenomenon of the "global economy." According to them, the heavy importation of foreign labor and the declining wages are almost inevitable results of the workings of the global economy. Without the massive numbers of immigrants, the United States might be even less competitive and suffer even greater wage declines, they suggest.

Such off-the-mark ranting would be humorous if it were not influencing so many policymakers and analysts. Historians generally date the beginning of the truly global economy to the 1840s. That is nearly 160 years ago. International trade is barely more significant in the 1990s than in the 1890s, the economist Paul Krugman pointed out in his *Peddling Prosperity: Economic Sense and Nonsense in the Age of Diminished Expectations*. While trade fell for many decades earlier this century and then played an increasingly large role during the 1960s and 1970s, trade grew very little as a share of the total U.S. national product during the 1980s. A modest number of Americans have jobs that depend on so-called global competitiveness. In 1991, for example, only 10 percent of the U.S. product was in exports. Krugman states that 76 percent of all U.S. output consisted of services and that most services are insulated from global competition. The celebrated economist from Stanford University argues emphatically that the stagnation of U.S. living standards is not largely due to a failure to compete in the global economy:[29] "Although we talk a lot these days about globalization, about a world grown small, when you look at the economies of modern cities what you see is a process of localization: A steadily rising share of the work force produces services that are sold only within that same metropolitan area."[30]

The fate of U.S. workers is in the hands of American policymakers, not some faceless global economy. But according to the "inevitability" crowd, the United States cannot compete in this thing called the new global economy unless it opens its labor markets up to the global workforce. This line of reasoning is especially embraced by some enthusiasts of free trade. To many of them, it is intellectually inconsistent to sing the praises of free trade and the free movement of capital and information without also advocating the free movement of workers.

Such thinking, however, is disconnected from the roots of the modern free-trade movement. Henry Simons, a pioneer advocate of free-market economics at the University of Chicago, never would have linked free immigration to the benefits of free trade. "Free trade may and should raise living standards everywhere," Simons said. But major cross-border movements of workers would do the opposite: "free immigration would level standards, perhaps without raising them anywhere."[31]

Another noted pioneer free-market economist, Melvin Reder, cautioned about the dangers of loosening borders back in 1963, when President Kennedy introduced his immigration reform. Reder's warnings were prescient. He said free immigration would cause per capita incomes between nations to equalize, mainly by leveling the incomes of workers in industrialized countries down toward the low wages in the Third World. Substantial increases in immigration would especially injure labor competitors of immigrants—notably blacks, recent immigrants already here, and "secondary earner" workers such as married women, young people, and the aged.[32]

David Griffith, an anthropologist at East Carolina University, has supervised recent anthropological teams that have validated some of Reder's warnings. They studied the inner workings of a number of low-wage plants, primarily in the American South, that have experienced a rising presence of foreign workers. Griffith says many corporate chiefs have gained knowledge from their overseas operations to assist them in exploiting workers in the United States. The captains of industry can best institute the global ways of treating workers in U.S. operations when they have immigrants in their workforce. Immigration provides workers who are "cheaper, more desirable and more exploitable than native workers in advanced capitalist economies," Griffith maintains. Advocates of foreign workers appreciate their docility in the workplace. The docility is not so much because the immigrants are content with their working conditions as because they have a fatalistic philosophy and do not expect improvements. Griffith describes how most foreign workers in the United States have acquired their work philosophy from the peasant conditions they knew in their home countries: "The history of any peasant region is written in droughts, unjustified taxation, forced recruitment for labor or war, crop failures and misguided agrarian reforms. Such hardships both generate suspicion and pre-adapt people to austerity, which in turn breed fatalism and acceptance of current conditions. Workers with fatalist attitudes tend to be difficult to organize for collective bargaining, if only because they perceive that peasants—or rural peoples generally—tend to be the last to benefit from revolutionary change."[33]

The pool of international competitors to the American worker is so deep as to come close to the meaning of "limitless." It includes not just adult peasants but children, too. In 1995, reporter Molly Moore discovered an eleven-year-old boy, Dinesh Devran, in Dewari, India, "crouched before a loom in a dim, oven-hot mud hut, where he knots carpets 10 hours a day—his sweat the interest payment on loans taken by his family." When Dinesh was nine years old, his father sent him to the factory to pay off loans. Unless U.S. immigration and trade policies protect them, American workers must compete with Dinesh, who earns about 12 cents a day making carpets sold in the United States. There are 55 million child laborers working away from their parents in India alone. The International Labour Organisation estimates that as many as 200 million children between the ages of ten and fourteen worldwide are working in jobs that are dangerous, unhealthy, and inhumane.[34]

The dubious rewards of competing with Third World workers can be seen in El Paso, Texas. In a study for the Center for Immigration Studies, David Simcox showed how El Paso during the 1970s and 1980s met many of the conditions of what the business community considers to be success: Manufacturing employment grew steadily even as it was stagnating in the nation as a whole. Industries such as leather, apparel, primary metals, and miscellaneous manufactures—industries that were withering in other states—experienced flourishing investment in El Paso. The city's service employment also had rapid job growth.[35]

But all that economic growth has been on the basis of a Third World strategy involving a heavy influx of immigrant workers. U.S. businesses have taken advantage of the labor surplus and the lower expectations of the workers by investing in low-wage industries. Business activity has grown, but the plight of El Paso's workers has grown steadily worse. Per capita personal income in 1989 ranked El Paso the lowest of the nation's seventy-five largest cities. Unemployment continually has ranged from 1.5 to 4 percentage points higher than the U.S. average. Income inequality in El Paso is even worse than in the country as a whole.

University research teams that have studied how foreign workers have changed the U.S. plants where they work discovered that foreign workers often teach their employers how to exploit other workers from their own cultural and national backgrounds. With enough immigrants in a plant, managers can begin to lower working conditions toward global standards for native workers as well. Of special significance has been the education that multinational firms have gained in Third World countries about "de-skilling" jobs, Professor Griffith says. Jobs are broken down into extremely simple and repetitive tasks; businesses don't have to worry much about rapid employer turnover because it takes so little time to train each new worker. This has made it easier for companies to run a steady stream of foreign labor—with little or no knowledge of English—through their U.S. plants. "In the process, the people on the floor of the plant are robbed of the dignity of having an opinion on the way the plant is run or the line arranged," Griffith concludes. "Nothing challenges the employee's intellect; he or she cannot take much comfort in the idea that nearly 'anyone' can perform his or her job."

This global economy business ideology that has reduced many U.S. workers to little more than mindless robots also has begun to eliminate the concept of businesses as citizens of their local communities. Griffith recounts a conversation with a plant manager of one of the largest meatpacking companies. The manager explained that when his company was formed, "we were determined from the start to get the highest return on invested capital for our stockholders; we weren't going to do any of this goody two-shoes stuff with the community." Indeed, Griffith says, the manager's company had reorganized local labor markets with imported labor, at the expense of the local communities in terms of unemployment, social welfare costs, crime, and other factors.[36]

Sociologists Piven and Cloward say the government and corporate elite in America shored up profits by closing plants and moving capital to lower-wage regions and to other countries; by breaking workers' unions; by lowering wages; and by speculating in real estate, corporate mergers, and leveraged buyouts. Other industrial nations, however, responded to the so-called new global economy by promoting increased investment in plants and equipment; by starting additional labor market policies that included the retraining of workers of buffeted industries; and by emphasizing innovation in technology. And the other countries did not try to compete with low global wages by importing massive numbers of Third World workers.

The approach in other industrialized nations "apparently worked, at least for a time, not only to shore up profits, but to sustain wage levels and maintain stable class relations," Piven and Cloward suggest.[37] While the portion of workers protected by collective bargaining agreements plummeted by nearly 60 percent in the United States, only three other industrialized nations experienced drops in unionization—and those drops were marginal.

The cruelty of America's recent economic trends is represented not just in middle-class workers who lose income and jobs but also in those who lose their chance to climb into the middle class. This is especially evident for young Americans. They desperately need the entry-level jobs that immigrants are so prone to take. If young adults don't get started on the economic ladder by the time they are twenty-five, they may end up defeated and alienated. Just how desperate the situation has become is revealed in a recent survey of all Americans aged sixteen to twenty-four who were not in school, the military, or in prisons. The rate of joblessness for those young adults who actually were available for work was around 35 percent for white and Hispanic males. And that was the good news. The jobless rate was about 50 percent for white females, nearly 60 percent for black males, and more than 65 percent for black and Hispanic females. Congress and the president annually import more than 1 million foreign workers while large chunks of the nation's young adults can't grab hold of the first rung of the mainstream job ladder.[38]

* * *

In *Boiling Point* (1993), the conservative analyst Kevin Phillips laid out his argument for why the United States should re-embrace a dynamic middle-class ethos. The peak periods of inventiveness, power, and prosperity for nations, he said, almost always have also been periods when the middle class has triumphed over established elites. Phillips urges a turning away from the glorification of elitism that began to rise after the election of John F. Kennedy and that predominated during Ronald Reagan's 1980s, when leaders flirted with an elitist philosophy that "celebrated investors, entrepreneurs and the rich while neglecting the interests of a middle class."

The U.S. government's recent lack of interest in expanding—or even preserving—the country's own middle class raises frightening parallels with two previous great powers: Holland and Great Britain. The golden eras of the Netherlands in the seventeenth century and of Great Britain in the nineteenth century were dominated by an assertive middle class. The downfall of both coincided with a growing infatuation by their monied class with foreign investments at the expense of investments in industry at home. Preceding the decline of both great powers, Phillips points out, was a loosening of restrictions on immigration and a growing reliance on foreigners to perform the country's work at various levels:

> The Dutch traded all over the world, and, in turn people from almost everywhere came to make their fortunes in Amsterdam. Some were poor . . . but many were more prosperous or even rich . . . by 1650 no less than one-third of Amsterdam's population was foreign-born or of foreign extraction. So it was not surprising, during the 1700s, as Dutch investors and financiers sent their ships to Surinam and Java, invested in huge chunks of British government debt, and wooed borrowers—from the Prince of Mecklenburg-Strelitz to the Empress of all the Russias—that the monied classes were in no hurry to rebuild the decaying towns and industries. . . . Grand international exposures do not whet concern for the low and middle order of one's own nation. . . .[39]

Phillips says the same pattern emerged in the United States during the 1980s as massive immigration increased the prosperity and power of the rich, and as the government—like that of Edwardian England early this century—did not take corrective action to stop the declining purchasing power of the ordinary citizen.

Michael Lind of the liberal *New Republic* sees mass immigration almost as an opiate to which American leadership elites become addicted. They revel in their ability to gain inexpensive foreign servants to tend their kids, their lawns, and their houses. They profit from investments in industries able to cut their labor costs. Foreign workers even serve to relieve the white elites of guilt about the squalor in which millions of Americans must live. Lind writes in a scathing indictment: "The daily sight of hardworking immigrants in jobs that underclass blacks and poor whites spurn, and folkloric anecdotes about Vietnamese Westinghouse scholars and valedictorians, confirm the suspicion of members of the white overclass that the native-born poor, those Appalachian coal miners and ghetto residents, are really just lazy, compared to Juan the doorman or Mrs. Lin the laundry lady."[40] Furthermore, as Katharine Betts explained in *Ideology and Immigration,* those with the most money, power, and education can use immigration as a way to distinguish themselves as morally superior to the masses of middle-class and poor citizens whom they can label as pro-vincial, selfish, and even racist for opposing the importation of foreign workers.[41]

For members of an elite class with no major interest in the fate of their fellow citizens, mass immigration can seem like the perfect na-tional policy.

* * *

For those Americans of any class who would like their government to help reverse the middle-class slide and resume assisting the working poor to climb into the middle class, one simple solution jumps out: Tighten the labor supply.

"I consider labor shortages wonderful," says Vernon Briggs. "I've never known anything bad to come from a labor shortage, and what we are doing with our immigration policy is keeping the labor markets in constant surplus rather than letting shortages work."[42]

Despite rapid population growth during much of its history, the United States typically had an economy that was expanding faster than its population. The degree of labor scarcity "encouraged experiments with labor-saving approaches and technologies, which in turn led to higher productivity, higher wages and a mass market that is still the center of the world trade," argues former Assistant Secretary of State Lindsey Grant.[43]

Talk of labor shortages in the 1990s, however, is a bit premature. The United States has such an immense surplus of workers that if all immigration could be stopped tomorrow, it might be years before the labor pool contracted to anything resembling an actual shortage.

In 1994, the Jerome Levy Economics Institute of Bard College tackled the seemingly intractable problem of American workers who cannot find a way into the middle class. It focused on the millions of Americans who apparently lack the intellectual capacity, the drive, or some other ingredient to hold more than a lower-skilled job. In the 1950s and 1960s, such Americans—if they were hardworking and thrifty—still could aspire to a middle-class lifestyle. That is much more rare today. The Institute sought to answer the question: What will happen to young people with low reading and mathematics test scores? Are such people consigned to a life of unemployment and low wages, or are there paths by which some fraction will find a degree of financial security?

Their report stated that the labor market for unskilled workers probably will continue to deteriorate. Acknowledging that there is no simple solution to the problem, the Institute concluded that the best way to promote an environment where academic underachievers have at least some opportunity for upward mobility is to reduce the size of the unskilled population.

Immigration policy offers the cheapest and quickest way to tighten the labor supply. "Sharply restrict immigration of unskilled workers into the country," the Institute's public policy brief recommended.

Labor shortages almost always do wonders for the economic conditions of workers, even in macabre circumstances, as John Larner noted in his account of massive death from famine and plague in fourteenth-century Italy: The labor supply was so reduced that wages and working conditions rose considerably after the plagues and "did much to better the lot of the poorer classes."[44] The same thing was happening during the 1980s in the few parts of the United States where immigration was low and labor markets were tight. In a study for the Brookings Institution, Richard B. Freeman found that tightening the labor supply had disproportionately positive effects on youth employment and an even greater effect on black youth. It appeared that a 1 percentage point drop in an area's jobless rate raised youth employment by 1.9 points, and black youth employment by a hefty 4.3 points. Freeman points out that "Local labor market shortages greatly improve the employment opportunities of disadvantaged young men, substantially raising the percentage employed and reducing their unemployment rate. . . . Labor market shortages also significantly increase the hourly earning of disadvantaged youths, particularly blacks."[45]

Freeman discovered that disadvantaged young men in tight local labor markets in the 1980s defied all national trends. Their economic position improved substantially, despite the socialpathologies afflicting them and the changes in the national economy that pushed income down for most other lower-skilled Americans.

Newspapers' business sections in the 1990s are filled with proof that the law of supply and demand continues to govern the labor market. In Indianapolis, which has had little immigration to swell its labor supply, labor shortages prompted the mayor to raise the minimum wage employers must pay if they want tax abatements for job-creating projects. One article announced in 1995: "Starting this year, employers seeking such breaks have to pay average hourly wages of $7.50 in the inner city and $9 in surrounding townships, up from a flat $7 last year. The city's 3.9 percent unemployment rate is among the lowest of major U.S. cities."[46]

In Nashville, where unemployment hit an all-time low of 2.1 percent in December 1992, employers were crying and workers were exulting over sharp rises in wages. "We can't get anyone here to work for the minimum wage," said Gaylord Entertainment's vice president of public affairs. The Galleria restaurant in the Radisson Governor Inn had to raise wages for waiters by more than 70 percent. And the head of a franchise that operates twenty-eight Burger Kings complained: "Our average wage has skyrocketed more than a buck an hour in six months." Some breakfast-shift employees were being paid up to $8.50 an hour. The shortages were especially driving up wages for entry-level jobs. And that is great news for young adults who have had such a difficult time getting a foothold on the job ladder in recent years.[47]

Labor shortages strike terror in many business executives, even though businesses in places like Nashville and Indianapolis remain profitable and secure. "We are at a breaking point and approaching a crisis," said the chairman of NationsBank Corporation. "Companies here are scared to death that they'll have to jack up pay to keep their workers," said the business development director of the West Alabama Chamber of Commerce in Tuscaloosa. "It's not like there are thousands and thousands of workers available at any price."

Secretary of Labor Robert Reich, however, points out that a labor shortage "rarely means that workers cannot be found at any price. Its real meaning is that desired workers cannot be found at the price that employers and customers wish to pay." There always are many people who are working part time who would prefer to work full time if given the chance or offered the right conditions. There also are so-called marginal workers who lack the training or have other qualities considered by employers as less than optimum. During a labor shortage, employers may be forced to figure out ways to hire those less desirable workers.[48]

A major group of workers whom employers tend to treat as undesirable are those with disabilities. Four years after Congress passed the sweeping Americans with Disabilities Act, the number of disabled people in the workforce had barely changed, according to a survey by the National Organization on Disabilities. Only 31 percent of disabled people age sixteen to sixty-four were working either part time or full time. Employers were choosing foreign workers over the disabled.[49]

Retirement-age Americans represent an even greater pool of potential workers if labor-market conditions tightened. A Harris Poll found one in seven retirees would prefer to work if a job were available.

Costs do not have to go up during a labor shortage. Increased labor costs usually prompt innovations to gain more productivity out of each worker. During a labor shortage, every willing American worker counts and is taken seriously. The "most direct means of remedying a labor shortage is to offer better wages and training," Reich says.

There are enough American workers to do everything if U.S. businesses would be willing to hire them. But the U.S. government gives businesses another option, which Reich notes is usually cheaper. They can avoid offering better wages and training for American workers and instead—as Nashville businessmen announced they intended to do—recruit foreign workers.[50]

That foreign alternative creates an economy in which millions of Americans can be cast aside as no longer needed. It is not an economy in which everybody who works hard and plays by the rules can earn a middle-class living. But it is the kind of economy we have today.

6

Jobs Americans *Will* Do

Steam rises from the big hog slaughterhouse of Storm Lake, Iowa. The plume catches the gaze of American-born workers watching traffic from a nearby gas station. "This was a completely different town in 1980," says Ted Kramer from the middle of the group gathered around a cowhide workglove display. The cars passing by are filled with Laotians, Mexicans, Thais, Vietnamese, Somalians, and Central Americans. Like kill plants across the country, the one here relies on immigrant labor.

The tasks of disassembling America's hogs, sheep, and cattle are nasty, tedious, and risky. They look like jobs most Americans would rather not do.

In damp conditions surrounded by animal offal, meatcutters often stand in a single place, making the same cuts, all day long, trying to keep up with the fast-moving line while not being struck by the lifeless livestock or slashed by knives, their own or their co-workers'. "Workers have little time for idle conversation or even work-related discussion, as carcasses whiz by at four hundred or more an hour," explains Donald D. Stull, a University of Kansas anthropologist and noted expert on the industry. In a recent year, more than 126,000 people nationwide labored in the red-meat slaughter industry at relatively low wages. Stull says the rapid, continuously repetitive tasks frequently lead to hand, arm, and wrist disorders, the most common being carpal tunnel syndrome. David Griffith of East Carolina University says workers report that they feel like "old used up pieces of machinery after occupational injuries: 'used up and tossed out the door.' "

For a worker, meatpacking is the most dangerous industry in America.[1]

The foreign workers sacrificing their own bodies as they carve up those of large animals are prime examples of what immigration advocates mean when they say the U.S. economy depends on the importation of workers to "do jobs Americans won't do."

What galls the natives gathered this morning in the Mid-Town Service Station in Storm Lake, however, is that the immigrants at the slaughterhouse are doing jobs these Americans *once did*. Every Iowa man in this station used to work at the hog plant. Every nasty part of the killing and butchering process throughout this country was done by a native-born American, not that many years ago. And Americans prized having those jobs.

Before the immigrants started coming fifteen years ago, "the local people lined up to get jobs in that plant," growls Richard Krout from behind the gas station's cash register. He adds, "But now the bastards [the meatpacker corporations] won't pay up." A group of scholars writing for the *Aspen Institute Quarterly* stated that the meatpacking industry has "broken unions, initiated internal and international labor migrations, taken advantage of ethnic, gender, regional and legal-status differences among workers and revitalized methods of labor mobilization and labor control resembling peonage and servitude."[2]

With the cushion of an unending stream of fresh immigrants, the industry slashed the pay, sped up the lines, and allowed safety conditions to deteriorate back toward the level described by Upton Sinclair in his famous exposé, *The Jungle* (1906). Surveying the workplace of today, Professor Stull says conditions are alarmingly similar to the ones described in the book that shocked the nation.

* * *

Every time somebody points to a job and declares that it depends on immigration because it is beneath an American to take, it is important to ask how that job became so unattractive. Until Congress began flooding the United States with immigrants after 1965, all jobs were filled overwhelmingly—and often almost exclusively—with native-born American workers. In the United States, there were no "jobs Americans won't do."

Many observers—including some highly educated ones—have

made the mistake of looking at foreign workers performing lower-skilled tasks today and assuming that, if not for them, there would be no one to do the jobs.

Reason, a libertarian magazine, displayed this distortion on its cover for April 1995. Across a drawing of the head of the Statue of Liberty hung a sign: "Closed for Business." Next to it, the cover story promotion stated: "An Economy Without Immigrants: The real-world consequences of shutting out foreign workers." Inside, the author detailed the number of foreign-born persons in various fields of work. "Who is going to pick the lettuce and tomatoes?" the article asked. "Who is going to design the computers? And, of course, the questions don't stop there. Without Ethiopians, who will be the parking attendants in San Jose? Without Haitians, who will drive Miami's taxis? Without Filipino nurses and Pakistani doctors, who will care for the ill in inner-city and rural hospitals? Without Mexicans, who will build houses in North Carolina?"[3]

The author and editors revealed a common misunderstanding of three key aspects of the labor market and immigration:

1. Shutting off immigration would not mean that recent immigrants would leave their jobs. Nobody is proposing to ship away the foreign-born persons in this country—except perhaps for the small percentage of them who are illegal aliens. Even if all future immigration were shut off tomorrow, all the immigrants already working here would still be working. Any resulting change in the workforce would be gradual.

2. In many cases, so-called immigrant occupations already have Americans working alongside foreigners. There are plenty of unemployed Americans who might take those jobs if they began opening up after a halt in immigration, especially if the workplace culture once again became American- and English-speaking. That was demonstrated in 1995 when immigration agents conducted massive arrests of illegal aliens, removing thousands from plants in six southern states. Within days, the majority of those vacant jobs were filled with American workers. "That says something about the oft-heard claim that illegal workers take only the jobs legal workers don't want," said Doris Meissner, head of the Immigration and Naturalization Service. Tens of millions of dollars in annual income was transferred overnight from aliens to Americans. If there were plenty of Americans to take the jobs illegal aliens had, one has to assume there would be even more willing to do the work that legal immigrants do.[4]

3. For other "immigrant jobs," there may not be a sufficient number of Americans who would take them as they now exist because the pay and working conditions are so deplorable—the meatpacking industry being a notable example. The presence of immigrants keeps those wages and conditions from improving to the point where Americans would take the jobs. Without the availability of new immigrants, though, employers would have to make innovations and improvements in their employment, and in doing so, most would find enough Americans to keep their business running. "You hear the myth so much that immigrant farmworkers take jobs Americans won't do, that Americans won't clean the streets, clean the rooms, wash the dishes," says economist Marshall Barry of the Labor Research Center of Boston and Miami. "But that isn't true. If you pay right, Americans will do everything."

Like many immigration-advocacy organizations, *Reason* magazine opposes cutting foreign admissions, fearing that the action would cause increases in the wages of janitors, busboys, waitresses, cooks, maids, nannies, farmworkers, and all sorts of other laborers. To Americans with a more populist perspective, of course, raising wages would be great news. It would be a comforting thought that the people doing those jobs would not have to risk poverty at every turn. The rest of us might have to pay a little more for some goods and services, but we would be living in a more just society, as well as one in which more people were able to pay their own way without welfare or draining other social services. It is possible, however, that we might not end up paying anything extra for the privilege of living in a society where lower-skill workers earn a decent wage. A study by two Princeton economists, David Card and Alan Krueger, provides some insight. When New Jersey raised its minimum wage by nearly 20 percent in 1992, the scholars had a case study on their hands. In New Jersey restaurants, for example, they found that the higher pay did not cause prices to rise. Using better personnel practices that reduced turnover and improved productivity, the restaurants offset the higher wages.

Robert Kuttner commented that the study seemed to show that the employers could have been paying higher wages all along; "they simply chose not to, given that enough workers were available at the lower wage."[5]

Denying businesses their stream of cheap new foreign labor would jolt many of them out of a counterproductive complacency about worker productivity, and market forces would drive today's so-called immigrant jobs to improvement back to being "jobs Americans *will* do."

A journey across the country may be the strongest rebuttal to claims that large numbers of tasks wouldn't get done without immigrants. If indeed the occupations filled by foreign workers in high-immigration areas can be done only by foreign workers, then that should be true throughout the United States. But, as my two sons were surprised to learn when they were younger, it is not true. Living on the East Coast, where immigration is higher than the American average, both of them became accustomed to certain types of service and manual labor jobs being filled primarily by immigrants. So when we ventured inland—a hundred miles usually was far enough—they consistently were surprised to find English-speaking, native-born Americans in every one of those so-called immigrant jobs: convenience store clerks, fast-food workers, blacktoppers, busboys, motel maids, landscapers.

That was especially apparent one night in Lexington, Kentucky. We had pulled off the highway in the midst of a dazzling summer lightning storm and sought shelter at an all-night gas station. The other customers looked as seedy at 3:00 A.M. as we did. After paying the middle-aged woman at the cashier island in the middle of the store, we went to a concession booth at the back and asked a young man to make submarine sandwiches for us, spreading the mustard freely over the freshly baked bread. "Well, Dad," my eighteen-year-old son said as we sat down at a little table, "I guess there are two Americans who will get up at four in the morning to butter the bagels." Looking at my sub, I was puzzled at first. Then I realized he was referring to an exchange I had had a few months earlier on a TV program. A New York City advocate of high immigration had insisted that without foreign workers, the residents of that city would not have anybody to get up at 4:00 A.M. and butter the bagels. My immediate retort was that Americans are quite capable of getting up at 4:00 A.M., but that many businesses on the coasts have become so addicted to cheap, compliant foreign labor, they may have ceased to try to attract American workers. Without access to a lot of foreign workers, the Lexington, Kentucky, gas station had to offer whatever it took to attract Americans to do the job. And it worked. Americans will do the jobs if they don't have to compete with people who are accustomed to degraded Third World conditions.

"The most amazing thing about current immigration policy," comments Peter Brimelow, senior editor at *Forbes* magazine, is that "it serves no economic purpose. It does nothing for Americans they could not do for themselves."[6]

* * *

The importation of hundreds of thousands of foreign workers each year is worse than unnecessary: It ruins good occupations; it rewards callous business management; it penalizes businesses with a strong sense of corporate citizenship; and it creates sweeping changes for communities that never request them and seldom approve of them. At the most basic level, it changes the lives, the aspirations, and the very identity of many individual Americans.

Perhaps no industry reveals that sad spectacle any more dramatically than the meatpacking industry of the last three decades.

When Ted Kramer moved to Storm Lake, Iowa, in 1959, he figured out quickly that the top-status work in town was at the hog plant. "After awhile, I went to the plant every morning to try to get on. When I did, I never had seen such paychecks in my life! Things really looked up for us. We had guys with a college education who worked there because the pay was so good." From the 1950s until everything changed in the early 1980s, people held on to their slaughterhouse jobs like gold. And they pulled strings to get their relatives and children into the plant. Because nearly all packing companies offered handsome pay and benefits, no company had trouble remaining profitable while treating its workers well.

Today, jobs have so deteriorated that it is difficult to keep workers—whether native-born Americans or immigrants. Stress-related disorders and injuries drive many workers off the jobs within months. The companies expect it. They have designed their plants for high turnover and may even encourage it, according to the *Aspen Institute Quarterly*. A recent turnover rate in the packing plants of southwest Kansas, for example, was between 6 and 8 percent every *month*. That annual rate of 72–96 percent a year was considered low in the industry.[7]

Driving a lot of the turnover is an incredible rate of injuries. Meatcutters are injured 400 percent more often than workers in the average U.S. industry. The annual injury and illness rate affects an incredible 44.4 people out of every 100 full-time workers.[8]

The current injuries and the worker turnover astound the former meatcutters gathered at Mid-Town Service. As they talk of bright futures that never came and of a present that "isn't what it used to be," they bear witness to the unrelenting power of mass immigration. They say they never saw unsafe working conditions as they exist today. Some scoff at the injury rate, suggesting that it proves the foreigners aren't any good at their jobs. "They don't know how to use a knife," one says. But another interjects, "The company doesn't train them right, not like we were trained."

"I worked there for thirty-four years," says Joe Kennedy, a grizzled retired man who has just entered the station. "I remember two guys the whole time with carpal tunnel."

"Sometimes you'd see a strained back," says Kermit Hendricks, who now drives a truck.

"I don't think they care if they run through those immigrants," Mark Young says. All agree that their strong meatcutters union in the past made certain that working conditions stayed safe and that everybody was trained properly. "You have to keep your knife sharpened right. Nothing is harder on an arm than a dull knife," Young says.

"It took awhile, but once I got the knack of keeping the knife sharp, the job wasn't nothing to it," Hendricks agrees.

"In thirty years, I never found the knack," Richard Krout mumbles as he leaves the cash register for the storage room. Ted Kramer turns toward Krout's disappearing figure and says admiringly, "Don't let him fool you. There goes one of the best knives there was."

Mark Young is getting nostalgic. "I miss most of the people there. You could leave your tools and knife lying around and never lost any. You never locked a vehicle in the company parking lot. Now they can't do any of that."

Kramer stares back toward the hog plant: "There wasn't a better production crew in the United States than what we had."

Like veterans of ancient wars, the former meatcutters speak of camaraderie and pride now bathed in a valiant glow. Their own knives long ago sheathed, they recall their prowess at sharpening and wielding their tools of battle. They speak of lives that might have been if they had not been run out of their jobs, and about the town that once was and is no more.

When the anthropologist Donald Stull says nothing much has changed between Upton Sinclair's *The Jungle* and the slaughterhouses of today, he doesn't mean that nothing changed in between. In fact, for decades the meatcutters across America worked and lived great middle-class American lives. The jobs didn't maim them. And the pay allowed workers to buy houses and cars, to take vacations, to raise families, and to retire on a decent pension.

"What was nice was that the head of the household worked and the other half could stay at home and take care of the kids," one man says.

But all of that in Storm Lake came crashing to an end in 1981, when changes in the industry resulted in some five hundred of these Iowa men losing their jobs and only a fraction of them being hired back later at half-wages to work with immigrants. A lot of the old meatcutters spent years after that just doing pick-up jobs by the day, says Mark Young, who has farmed with his father-in-law ever since. "I never have made as much money as at the plant." The consensus of the men here is that very few of the native workers ever again matched their earnings. The town's population size remained fairly stable as natives left in about the same numbers as the incoming foreign workers. Such a significant cut in wages for hundreds of jobs works its way through all parts of a town's economy. Downtown merchants saw a significant change in spending patterns and, through the years, in the whole culture of commerce. Most jobs in a town are created to serve the small fraction of people who actually produce something that leaves the area and to serve the other people in service jobs. When the value of the manufacturing jobs plummets, that sends ripples throughout the local economy.

Unsurprisingly, the foreign workers in Storm Lake encounter a lot of bitterness among some of the natives. Mark Young, though, appeals for understanding, suggesting that the immigrants are just looking for work like everybody else. The culprits, he says, are the state and federal government leaders who make decisions based on what is best for big business: "This immigration is damned good for big business. There's nothing better than cheap foreign workers."

* * *

Immigration has a long history of turning jobs into—or keeping them as—ones nobody but a desperate foreign worker would be willing to accept.

Consider Kansas City a century ago. Laborers in the sprawling slaughterhouses had organized to force improvements. The labor force was filled with freed slaves and Americans of English, Irish, German, and Swedish backgrounds. As again is true in the 1990s, the work was dangerous; a consumer often got a shoulder roast at the expense of permanent damage to the shoulder of a poorly paid laborer who butchered it. When the packing houses balked at demands for reform in 1893, the workers went out on strike.

Because of the mostly open immigration policies of the time, Kansas City industries didn't have to pay any attention to their workers. During a time when Booker T. Washington was eloquently pleading with industry personnel managers to "cast down their bucket" where they were and to hire underemployed black Americans, the meatpackers were sending recruiters to Europe—especially the Balkans—to find strikebreakers. New waves of Croatians, Serbs, Dalmatians, Slovenians, Herzegovinians, and Bosnians poured into the "West Bottoms" area of Kansas City and crushed the strike.

American workers were driven out of the industry.

The immigrant strikebreakers were rewarded with the lifestyle the American workers had refused. Most lived in "The Patch," a labyrinth of substandard shacks behind the slaughterhouses, and in the floodplain of the Kaw River. Many such as Milovan Yovetich were single men who shared beds with other men. He counted himself lucky, although he had to sleep with two other men in a boarding house, because he had the spot next to the wall and could not be pushed out during the night. It was not unusual for whole families including children to work just to survive. Earning 3 or 4 cents per hour, the meatpackers performed hard manual jobs from early morning until late at night. With little time for leisure and not much more for sleep, their lives were centered in the few blocks around the slaughterhouses.

Upton Sinclair noted that in order to maintain those conditions as much as possible, the industry continuously brought in more foreign workers—thanks to President Cleveland's veto of immigration restriction legislation in 1897. In Kansas City, the flows came from Poland, Greece, Russia, Italy, Japan, and Mexico, as well as from families in the Balkans.

It was nearly impossible to organize labor in those conditions. In 1910, a federal commission studying immigration reported that an "exceedingly small proportion" of employees in Kansas City were affiliated with labor organizations. One survey found less than 1 percent of the slaughterhouse workers connected to a union.

By vetoing new restrictionist legislation, Presidents Taft and Wilson would ensure that immigration continued to keep conditions so bad that packing-house work remained a job most Americans wouldn't do until after 1924.

Over the next few decades, however, the meatpacking industry would prove that the dominance of immigrants in a job category at any given time does not mean that Americans won't take the jobs in the future.

Meatcutters began to live a little higher on the hog after Congress sliced annual immigration numbers in the 1920s. Without a virtually unlimited supply of foreign labor with which to intimidate their workers, the packing companies slowly were forced to offer decent working conditions and pay. And with a heavy dose of ingenuity, the companies found it possible to do so and remain profitable.

Labor organizing moved swiftly, and improvements were made even during the Depression in the 1930s. "I started at the plant in 1935," says Marvin Goldsmith of Storm Lake. "It was before the humane killing; I stuck pigs while they were still squealing. The union came in June 1937. I was drawing 47 1/2 cents an hour. It went up to 75 cents just like that."

The struggle was hard and sometimes violent. But the low-immigration, tight-labor, booming economic conditions of the 1940s made it possible for Americans to eat their steak and pork chops without any guilt that their good diet depended on worker exploitation. The unions gained a hold on nearly the entire meatpacking industry, guaranteeing one of the best wage and benefits packages of any industry.

"I worked forty years," Goldsmith says. "The industry was good to me. I cut two-thirds of a finger off once and fell and broke a wrist, that's all. For years, I had six weeks of vacation each year. But we put in lots of hard hours. I honestly can say I didn't take home a nickel that I didn't earn."

As the country entered the 1960s, the meatpacking industry was providing solid middle-class wages and a boost to the middle-class economy of scores of communities, notably Philadelphia, St. Louis, Memphis, Omaha, Sioux City, Kansas City, Wichita, Fort Worth, and Los Angeles.

Phil Stough, circulation manager of the *Storm Lake Pilot-Tribune,* says that when he graduated from high school in 1969, the meatcutter jobs at the Hygrade hog plant were the social fabric of society: "Hygrade was the college for high school students. They said, 'My dad works there, my future is secure,' because they could become a meatcutter, too."

Kay Larson, a librarian in Spencer, Iowa, remembers that when she was a girl, "we always looked at the kids with parents in the packing plant as the rich kids."

A chain of national events that began in the 1960s would ensure that by the 1990s nobody would look with envy at anybody working in a meatpacking plant.

* * *

In 1960, the year John F. Kennedy was elected president, the IBP meatpacking company was founded. Originally called Iowa Beef

Processors, it turned the industry upside down with its innovations and eventually acquired nearly one-third of the national red-meat slaughter market.

IBP and other new firms that later followed its tactics sought ways to take the market from the old established packers of Armour, Swift, Wilson, and Cudahy. The new packers slashed their costs and simplified the process by shipping boxed beef instead of hanging carcasses, eliminating highly paid butchers in the middle. They built new, more efficient plants, locating more of them near the rural areas where livestock raising was concentrated. The old companies had to follow suit to compete. In the process, tens of thousands of jobs eventually were eliminated.

All of that was in line with the workings of a free, capitalist market system in which entrepreneurs constantly search for cheaper methods of production and distribution to enable them to increase their sales.

If it had stopped there, the workforce would have been reduced by about a third but there still would have been 130,000 meatcutters earning great middle-class incomes. The new efficiencies and reductions in workforce helped the productivity of each remaining worker to rise by 2.8 percent each year between 1967 and 1982. That was nearly a half percentage point above improvements in all U.S. manufacturing, and should have supported pay raises, or at least protected previous gains.

But the new companies wanted to drastically reduce the wages. If they could do that, they surely would be able to take market share from the huge packing companies which had controlled the industry for decades and which were locked into major, high-wage contracts with the unions.

At first, the new companies could lower wages on some of their jobs by using another standard free-market device: They placed plants where there were pockets of rural underemployment and where residents were willing to work for lower, non-union wages, especially in states like Kansas and Nebraska with laws unfavorable to union organizing.

The new companies soon ran into problems, though. There wasn't anywhere close to enough surplus labor in those potential sites to make it possible to move much of the industry away from the urban areas. Recruiters found it was not easy to entice American workers to move to new states for low non-union wages. And the many existing plants in rural areas like Storm Lake already were unionized. The wages of most workers in the industry continued to rise along with their per capita productivity.

Up to this point, the free-market system was operating in a normal way, with labor and new entrepreneurs and the other owners of capital jockeying for their best position within the established boundaries of the American economy. Supporters of the system claim that it produces the most overall good for society, balancing benefits and incentives for consumers, for business, and for workers. But the federal government brought in an outside force that would change all the rules of business and tip the tables against the old companies and against American workers.

Congress in 1965 inadvertently came to the rescue of the union-busting, wage-lowering strategy of the new meatpackers. The 1965 immigration law had a major impact on the direction of the meat-processing industry by creating surplus labor pools with spiraling family chain migration and massive refugee resettlement operations.

The state of Iowa ran one of the most aggressive Southeast Asia refugee programs in the country. In a devastating lack of insight into the way labor markets always have worked in this country, the Iowa government failed to see that with its refugee program it was importing a foreign labor force large enough to undermine its own citizens, especially in eliminating the middle-class meatcutter jobs in Storm Lake, Spencer, and many other Iowa cities. The growing number of Southeast Asian refugees eagerly took meatcutter jobs at half the wages and at reduced benefits while working faster lines with much less attention to safety. They were especially valued by industry because—with minimal skills, education, and English—they had few alternatives and were unlikely to quit and go back to their home country, says Janet Benson, an anthropologist at Kent State University.

The Southeast Asians changed the labor market in the small towns of Iowa. David Griffith found that they created their own recruiting networks and began to set the terms by which new workers moved into plants through such conditions as posting bonds, giving kickbacks, or providing sexual favors to personnel managers.

"The use of immigrants was a blatant and obvious attempt to undercut the labor movement," says historian Ken Cox of Northern Iowa University.

During the 1970s, the old packing companies were in a bind. Washington's new immigration policy and the upstart challenger companies were forcing them to lower their workers' wages, regardless of whether they wanted to.

Over in Storm Lake there were few immigrants. But the Hygrade plant there had to compete with plants that had many. Ted Kramer recalls that during the 1970s, "we had to fight every contract because

Hygrade would say that over in Dakota City and South Sioux, IBP was paying half the wages." Even though some plants had unions, the presence of a lot of immigrants had sapped them of much aggressiveness or clout.

Up in Austin, Minnesota, the changing conditions caused the paternalistic Hormel Company to change its community personality. According to the team of scholars led by Robert A. Hackenberg writing for the Aspen Institute: "The Hormel family, company executives, supervisors, line and clerical workers earned annual salaries within a few thousand dollars of one another. Their children played together, learned together, celebrated rites of passage together. George Hormel and his family lived in Austin, participated in community events alongside the women and men who bloodied butchers' aprons in his plant. Hormel's union-negotiated wages and incentive programs allowed line workers and bosses alike to live in Austin's middle-class neighborhoods."[9]

But beginning in the 1960s, Hormel realized it would have to begin demanding wage concessions if it was to survive the competition of the wage-cutting companies.

The federal government—through its immigration program—was having the opposite effect one normally expects from government. Usually, citizens look to their government to set up systems that provide incentives and rewards for behavior that benefits the people, and disincentives for behavior harmful to the community of citizens. At least, we expect the government not to rig the free market against the ordinary man and woman. As long as all businesses have to play by the same rules, such governmental incentives and disincentives tend to enhance the public good without restraining commerce.

Mass immigration turned those incentives and disincentives upside down: It was rewarding companies that offered low wages and poor working conditions to American citizens. And it was penalizing companies that provided for a middle-class lifestyle. By providing unending labor-force and population growth for thirty years, immigration has rewarded sweatshop owners, land speculators, unscrupulous developers, and other environmental marauders, while disadvantaging business owners who have tried to be caring employers and good corporate citizens. In highly competitive industries like meatpacking, "good" employers were forced to adopt the practices of "bad" employers if they were to remain in business.

Although the pursuit of profit within our economic system generally is considered good for the public, businesses sometimes need help from the government to enable them to avoid behavior that would harm the public. The automobile-plating industry in Grand Rapids, Michigan, during the 1960s provides a helpful illustration.

The Grand Rapids platers were abominable polluters of the Grand River, turning it into a nearly lifeless stream of heavy-metal wastes. Owners of some of the plants happened to be avid trout fishermen. Of course, they had to go to other streams far away from their plants to find any trout. By the 1960s, heightened environmental consciousness caused some of the owners to feel bad about what their plants were doing. But they couldn't just unilaterally "do the right thing," recalls Roger Conner, who led the major environmental activist group of the area. "They were in a highly competitive market. There were no surplus profits. The companies were pitted against each other. Any plating company that voluntarily equipped itself with pollution-control devices would increase costs significantly and simply put itself out of business. The only way they could put on pollution controls was if all their competitors were required to do the same at the same time."

Thus, some businessmen were great promoters of federal regulation that would force them—and all their competitors—to install pollution-control devices. Such federal coercion would allow them to do the right thing for the environment and their community without risking their business competitiveness.

For decades, laws that limited the flow of foreign labor into the country had a similar effect on American industries. Since no one company could lower labor costs by importing immigrant workers, all had to compete with each other for a rather static pool of American workers, bidding up wages and benefits in the process while finding innovative ways to increase the productivity per worker. Federal immigration law kept the playing field level in a game that enabled larger and larger portions of Americans to earn middle-class wages. Under that system, U.S. corporations could do the right thing for American workers and communities without jeopardizing their profits.

With the 1965 Immigration Act, Congress changed the rules without intending to. The availability of an unending stream of cheap foreign workers drives working conditions down and makes it impossible for any plant manager to offer decent conditions that are much better than at any other plant. Each plant must compete with all others. No plant can veer far from the lowest common denominator set by the other plants.

Without immigration, the managers still would remain under intense competitive pressure. But if they had to raise wages to draw the needed number of American workers, they wouldn't go out of business, because all other plants would be doing the same.

Inevitably, the question arises whether an industry can keep paying middle-class wages now that global competition is so much more intense. If not allowed to use foreign workers and to slash wages, might not an industry have to move its plants overseas to keep from being run out of business by foreign companies?

"There have been whole conferences on whether meat processing might move offshore," says industry expert Donald Stull. "The consensus has been that for beef and pork, and for most chicken, they aren't going offshore."

The reasons are fairly simple. The primary cost is the animal, and slaughtering needs to occur near where the animal is raised. Cattle are traumatized when they are shipped more than 150 miles; they release enzymes that darken meat and make it less marketable. So, American farmers are not going to ship cattle and hogs to slaughterhouses in other countries.

How about other countries raising and slaughtering livestock and shipping it here? First, it is important to remember that most countries depend on the United States for food. Secondly, the price of labor in the United States would have to rise greatly before it would justify the extra shipping costs for most processed meat from other countries, except perhaps for Canada and Mexico. Of the two, only Mexico has low enough labor costs to provide a competitive advantage. But Mexico lacks the transportation system that would make it possible to do large-scale beef processing for the United States, Stull says. "The cheaper labor in Mexico doesn't save enough to make up for distance and poor transportation to where Mexico grows the beef."

In short, global competition did not force the industry to slash the pay of meatcutters and would not likely preclude raising wages now to attract American workers if Congress were to declare a moratorium on future immigration.

* * *

Every four years for two decades, presidential candidates have tromped across the state of Iowa and have listened to complaints about the loss of middle-class jobs. They have heard the laments from communities that have lost their packing plants or had the jobs converted from middle-class wages to incomes that often require public assistance for the workers' families. No state has been more scrutinized for the kind of local problems that might relate to national policy.

Yet, discussion of immigration policy has been negligible. Physicians might see the candidates' deficiency as being a faulty "differential diagnosis."

There is a saying in medicine that you never make a diagnosis that you don't think of. With a technique called "differential diagnosis," doctors list all possibilities of what might be causing a problem for a patient. Then they work at eliminating or proving each possibility. But that results in finding the true cause only if the true cause is one of the possibilities on the list.

For one societal problem after another for the last thirty years, Americans' governmental officials have made up their own lists of possible causes. Almost never has the increased level of immigration gotten on the lists.

In the autumn of 1977, for example, when the old meatpacking companies were closing or threatening to shut down plants all over Iowa, Congressman Berkley Bedell called on the U.S. Department of Agriculture to launch an investigation into what was going wrong. Secretary of Agriculture Robert Bergland came to a conference in Sioux City to address questions from worried Iowans. Nobody talked about immigration policy.[10]

To all the politicians, the loss of a middle-class way of life for the Americans who had been meatcutters was a mystery. They apparently thought it was an inevitable result of some unstoppable force of modern economics. It seems never to have occurred to them that a simple passage of legislation cutting back annual immigration could have had immeasurably positive effects for their constituents. They held the power of solution in their hands but apparently didn't know it.

They couldn't make a diagnosis or offer a cure that they didn't think of.

* * *

Atop the western edge of the tall bluff that holds downtown Kansas City, Missouri, a large statue of a Hereford steer perches on an eight-story-high red pillar. It gazes down at the expansive floodplain home of the famous Kansas City stockyards and meatpacking industry. "Some busy days, 60,000 or more head of cattle clambered out of the rail cars in Kansas City's stockyards; cattle trains sometimes stretched to the horizon, waiting to unload," in the words of *Kansas City Star* writer Charles R. T. Crumpley.

President Eisenhower dedicated the "Hereford on the bluff" on 16 October 1953, saying it was a "tribute to the faith of the pioneers and the determination of the men who have carried on to establish the Hereford breed as leader in the beef cattle world."

In 1960, the "Hereford on the bluff" looked out over the Kansas county of Wyandotte with eleven meatpacking plants, including all of the Big Four old packing giants. The high wages of their workers multiplied through the local economy, making nearly everybody a little more prosperous. A confident *Kansas City Star* that year proclaimed the livestock business "one of the brightest spots on the metropolitan Kansas City industrial scene." The unloading, holding, and slaughtering of thousands of animals filled the air with what some called "the smell of money." To the *Star,* industry trends suggested that Kansas City would "continue along with Omaha, Sioux City, St. Joseph, Denver and several others as a major center of the livestock trade and meat processing."[11]

None of that proved true. IBP was created that year, and the *Star* had no way of knowing how its innovations would transform the industry, nor could it foresee the passage of the immigration changes of 1965.

By 1976, all of the Big Four had closed down their Kansas City operations.

By 1987, the "Hereford on the bluff" looked out over a dilapidated, grown-over, animal ghost town in the floodplain. Wyandotte County had *no* meatpacking plants left.

Wyandotte historians say that during special weather conditions, the century of blood, fat, and manure that seeped into the ground there still sends out some of that famous Kansas City smell of money. But pungent symbolism is all the county gets; there is little sign of actual money like what the meatcutters were able to spread around. Annual per capita income in the county was within $600 of the national average in 1969, but lagged behind by more than $5,000 in 1990.

Because of industry restructuring, much of Kansas City's loss may have occurred even without the national presence of a massive foreign workforce. But the workers who lost their jobs in Kansas City could have followed the jobs to their new locations. To run all those new rural slaughterhouses without immigrants, the companies would have had to offer employment attractive enough to entice unemployed urban workers to move. Wages would have been more likely to remain near their old level. And the unions and middle-class incomes in the rural towns that already had packing plants might have survived.

But there was a massive flow of foreign workers, and the corporations had no need of the workers cast aside. The changes in the meat-packing industry were disproportionately damaging to old urban centers and to black workers. The United Packinghouse Workers of America (UPWA) for decades had been the most progressive union in America in terms of openness to black workers, according to Herbert Hill of the University of Wisconsin. During the strike in Waterloo, Iowa, in 1948, for example, the union had black leaders. Because of the large black presence in union membership and leadership, the meatcutters unions were leaders in the civil rights movement.

Albert Browne remembers his dad, who was white, going out on a wildcat strike at the Waterloo plant because of the firing of a black man: "They realized they were in it together." After 1965, native-born American workers, black and white, were increasingly "out of it together."

There was no hiding from the aggressive battle to drive down wages in the packing industry.

In 1977, Spencer Foods in Spencer, Iowa, warned workers that if they didn't accept a wage freeze, the company would have to shut down. They didn't, and it did.

In Storm Lake, Hygrade threatened to close operations in 1978. Then in 1981 it did so, citing refusal of local workers to accept pay cuts of $3 an hour.

When IBP announced it would reopen the old Hygrade plant as its own, local bands met the company officials as they arrived in town. "In my opinion this is going to have one of the most positive effects on Storm Lake that has ever happened in our community," said Jim Haahr, chairman of a city committee that wooed the company. "Above all I am thrilled for the hundreds of people who do not have jobs and who will have an opportunity to work again." The local newspaper led off its coverage: "There is hope in Storm Lake now—hope that the coming of Iowa Beef Processors to the city will mean jobs for the unemployed, increased sales for recession-ridden businesses and a new outlook for the people of the area."

The real outlook was not so hopeful, though. The new jobs would pay only around half the wages of the ones just lost. After a year of unemployment since Hygrade's shutdown, however, more than 1,000 local residents stood in line when IBP started taking applications for the 350 jobs it was offering for startup.

"A lot of us who worked at Hygrade applied for half-wages," says Richard Krout, who has been ringing up the cash register at the gas station ever since. "IBP fooled us. All along they said they were going to use local people. But the Laotians and Vietnamese came almost immediately. A few years later the Mexicans started."

There was no excuse for bringing in foreign workers into plants across Iowa, says Professor Ken Cox: "We had plenty of Iowans without jobs to do those jobs. In some towns, they may have been a little slow to take them because of their pride in wanting a better wage."

Rubbing salt into open wounds, the state government gave companies incentives to hire refugees over natives, the former meatcutters complain. The state subsidized part of the wages of refugees. Mark Young had personal experience with that: "My church was looking for help for the Vietnamese. So I hired them for my hog farm. The state sent me a check for 50 percent of their wages for six months. That's quite an incentive for a company to hire an immigrant instead of a local person."

In addition, the state gave some tax breaks to refugees. "When those Laotians come in here to buy cigarettes, they don't want a pack without a state stamp because they use it to get refunds," says Ted Kramer at the gas station. Kermit Hendricks claims that the foreign workers who took the meatcutters' jobs paid hundreds of dollars less in sales taxes than the locals had to pay on their products. "We end up paying for them to take our jobs," he says. In addition, house-owning immigrant families double up and triple up in their houses, and thus pay only a third to a half the property taxes per capita that natives do to cover the cost to expand infrastructure and schools for the newcomers.

In some towns, native workers were able to hold on longer. They saw what became of their former colleague cutters in other towns and determined that the stakes were high enough to violently defend their lifestyle. Workers in Dakota City, Nebraska, conducted several long strikes. In 1982, the union called a strike when the company asked for a four-year wage freeze. The strike resulted in the use of company strikebreakers and in violent confrontations between the strikers and the Nebraska State Police and National Guard. But the Dakota City workers were fighting against immigrant-driven economic forces that were almost impossible to beat. A year later, the union signed a contract that reduced workers' pay.

The new companies weren't so small any more. Bringing cheap immigrant labor into small towns across Kansas and Nebraska, they built enormous new plants as their lower labor costs allowed them to take larger and larger shares of the market from the old unionized firms.

IBP set the standard, proving to be "startlingly anti-labor, slashing

wages below the old packers' scales, then confronting strikes by transforming its plants into walled fortresses, complete with housing for
strikebreakers so that they never had to leave the area and face angry
picket lines," writes Hardy Green, author of *On Strike at Hormel.*[12]

The old companies slashed wages or declared bankruptcy. Wilson
Foods Corporation filed for Chapter 11 bankruptcy in order to abro-
gate its labor contracts. Then big conglomerates took over the meatpacking operations of Wilson, Swift, Armour, Morrell, Hygrade, and
Cudahy. Some slashed the pay of existing workers after taking over;
others laid off union workers and reopened with non-union labor. In
Columbus Junction, Iowa, workers voluntarily took pay cuts to help
save the Rath plant, but it was closed in 1984, to be replaced by new
low-wage plants.

Some of the companies had been poorly managed and may have
gone under on the basis of the new restructuring and efficiencies alone.
But the ability of the new companies to hire foreign workers at low
wages while the established firms were locked into high-wage contracts was a critical ingredient for most firms.

The human tragedy of the whole industry was played out on national television, in the national press, and through an award-winning
documentary in the form of the 1985–86 strike at Hormel in bucolic
Austin, Minnesota. With most of the old high-wage packing industry
in shambles, the workers at Hormel staged a last-ditch battle to save
the middle-class, meatcutter lifestyle. But they were crushed by the
power of Hormel, by the state of Minnesota—which ordered the National Guard to protect strikebreakers entering the plant—and even by
their own national union, which argued there was no chance for success.

Paul Larson, a veteran union organizer who is retired in Waterloo,
says that, regretfully, the national union officials were correct that the
writing was on the wall against the Hormel meatcutters. It had been
scrawled by the 1965 Immigration Act and the refusal of every Congress and president since then to stop its destructive power, he says. No
company could remain a good employer to its workers in the old style
as long as Congress provided its competitors with all the exploitable
foreign labor it could use.

The old-line packers are gone, replaced by the new Big Three—
IBP, Excell, and ConAgra Red Meats.

The meatcutters "can no longer hope to earn incomes that once
elevated them to solid middle-class status," scholars stated in the
Aspen Institute Quarterly. "No longer can communities expect food-

processing personnel departments to meet their labor needs with workers native to the community."[13]

During the campaign for the 1996 Iowa presidential primary, candidate Phil Gramm of Texas encountered a bit of embarrassment over IBP's assertive support for him. Reporters noted the low wages paid at IBP plants. "Almost all the applicants I get, one of the parents is working for IBP," a county welfare worker near IBP's plant in Perry told one reporter. Gramm's wife, a member of IBP's board of directors and a former economics professor, defended the low pay, saying, "Wages of labor, like other prices, are determined in a market."[14] Nobody pointed out, however, that the scales in the Iowa labor market had been tipped against workers by the heavy hand of federal immigration policy. The market could set wages near or below poverty level only because of the actions of Congress in changing the supply of workers.

An assistant personnel director of one meatpacking corporation notes that of 1,400 retired meatcutters out of a plant in Dubuque, Iowa, not one of them has a child in the industry. A few aggressive corporations and a detached federal government with a careless immigration policy had succeeded in making it possible to say once again, with considerable accuracy, that tens of thousands of meat-processing tasks are jobs Americans won't do.

* * *

While immigration was helping to drive meat-processing jobs out of the middle-class economy, it was forcing workers in the fruit and vegetable industries into outright poverty.

If Americans are to maintain their appetites at mealtime, they must be kept ignorant of—or be able to turn a blind eye to—the new realities of U.S. food production. As David Griffith and Ed Kissam have concluded, "poverty, injury and inhumanity are now common features of putting food on America's table."[15]

It may be that most Americans already know that and believe that such shabby treatment of 1 or 2 million food industry personnel is the regrettable compromise necessary to enable 200-plus million residents to continue their inexpensive but incredibly varied diet.

Nothing, it sometimes seems, is more effective in throwing Americans into retreat from considering immigration restriction than when they are asked: "But who will pick the lettuce and tomatoes?" So ingrained is the idea that field work *must* be degrading and underpaid that many Americans apparently assume the only way to bring in the crops is to import foreign laborers who are willing to be exploited.

Although a very small percentage of all foreign workers actually labors in agriculture, concerns about manual field work tend to dominate public policy decisions that set the number of immigrants each year. No matter how compelling immigration restriction may otherwise seem, soemphatic have been the agricultural scaremongers that it is difficult to escape the visions of fruit and vegetables rotting in the trees and fields while the American table is robbed of its interest and variety.

At the root of all such reasoning is the belief that farmwork is a job that Americans would not do in the past, won't do now, and will never do in the future. To shuck the subconscious, the emotional, and the mythological husks that disguise the truth of the matter, we need to answer two basic questions:

First, If immigration were halted, would the crops get picked? And second, Would the present farmworkers in this country be better off or worse off if immigration stopped?

The short answers are these: The sorry plight of farmworkers would improve dramatically if Congress shut off immigration. And the crops would still get picked—although farmers and the government would need to make great improvements in labor coordination.

Despite all the concern expressed about some imagined threat of a farmworker shortage, the country is awash in people willing and eager to toil in the fields. That became clear to the bi-partisan U.S. Commission on Agricultural Workers that was jointly appointed by President Bush and leaders of Congress. Perhaps the most telling findings in its 1992 report were these:

- During the peak season, the United States has slightly more than 1 million farmworker jobs.
- Approximately 2.5 million people residing inside our borders are farmworkers.

That is close to the estimate of labor economist Marshall Barry, who says, "We have three farmworkers for every farmworker job that I have looked at."

Anyone who believes in the law of supply and demand would fear that such an imbalance would lead to atrocious wages and working conditions. That is precisely what the Commission on Agricultural Workers found: Since 1977—when the conditions of farmworkers routinely were described in news features as heartbreaking—real income has dropped every year except in 1986. Farmworkers now find work during fewer weeks of the year; they work shorter weeks when they do get jobs; and they make less money per hour. Half the workers have incomes below the poverty level, even accounting for jobs they find outside agriculture.

Farmworkers are falling over each other at the worksite hiring lines. "A frequent complaint of workers interviewed in the commission-sponsored case studies was that there was not enough work to go around," reported the U.S. Commission, which was dominated by representatives of growers but also included a representative of labor and experts from government and academia. "Because most employers have had no difficulty attracting and retaining workers, there has been little incentive for them to increase benefits or generally improve working conditions for farmworkers," the commission concluded.

The flooding of the agricultural labor market infuriates Marshall Barry, who began studying farmworkers in the 1960s and was a chief analyst in helping Caesar Chavez win his famous labor-organizing effort with the workers in Coca-Cola's Florida citrus groves. "The news media loves to write about farmworkers," Barry maintains. "More Pulitzer Prizes have been for writing about farmworkers than any other, I think." But while Congress has used immigration to ruin the gains earned by farmworkers in the 1960s and 1970s, the journalists have looked the other way, Barry says. "Real wages of citrus workers went down by two-thirds, from 1967 to 1988. To argue that Americans won't do the work while you are cutting the wages in real terms seems to be at least inconsistent. But when somebody makes an irrational argument again and again it becomes conventional wisdom and very hard to refute."

One of the abiding immigration myths was repeated by *Reason* magazine in 1995: "Throughout most of American history, there's only been one group willing to consistently take on [farmworker jobs]: recent immigrants."

To most Americans from the vantage point of the last thirty years, that statement probably appears reasonable. But although new immigrants occasionally made up an important minority of the agricultural workforce in the past, their dominance in the fields is a recent phenomenon that got its impetus only during World War II. When the war broke out, the bulk of farm labor still was being done by established American residents, according to *Working Poor: Farmworkers in the United States.*

Growers tried to use the labor shrinkage during the war to break the government's resistance to major importation of farm laborers. At first, they were thwarted as "twilight bands of townspeople, soldiers on special leave, vacationists, high-school students and college girls temporarily increased the ranks" and successfully brought in the harvests, reported the *Monthly Labor Review* in 1945.[16] As Wayne Rasmussen wrote for the U.S. Department of Agriculture in 1951, growers during World War II didn't face a real shortage of workers, but they had lost the surplus labor conditions of the Depression that had allowed them to keep wages low and working conditions poor.[17] The U.S. Department of Labor was so adamant against starting a foreign agricultural worker program that it recommended that all public documents supporting the idea of a farm labor shortage receive department review before release.

But by the middle of the war, the growers won permission to start channels for foreign workers, and nobody has been able to stop them since, even though the president's Commission on Migratory Labor in 1951 recommended more reliance on a better-paid domestic farm labor force.

Congress guaranteed agribusinesses an unending supply of cheap labor when in 1965 it opened the way for hundreds of thousands of immigrants to enter each year.

Today, it is difficult to imagine that the agricultural industry did not have to be run on the backs of immigrants. By recalling the previous era when Americans did the work, we can gain some assurance that the domestic labor market will find a way to bring in the crops in a post-immigration era. In his refreshing examination of manual labor, *How to Tell When You're Tired,* the lifelong manual laborer Reg Theriault describes an eighty-year period of American nomads picking fruit in the West. He was born into that group, which called itself "fruit tramps." He grew up in the lifestyle and later left college to reenter that field of work, which he described as hard but rewarding, both socially and economically. But after the government began allowing agribusiness to import foreign workers, the American fruit tramps found it more and more difficult to secure enough work. When given the chance to become a longshoreman, Theriault took it. At that point he describes what to most Americans must seem an amazing hold the fruit tramp life continued to have over him:

> After I began longshoring, for the next sixteen years I would slip away from the waterfront each summer and return to fruit tramping. Eventually I took my three sons with me and they got jobs on the packing sheds, too (also lying about their ages,

of course). But fruit tramping as we had known it was obviously doomed. A way of life that began with the century was not going to last it out. Imported labor and new, genetically engineered fruit and vegetables were doing it in. Aliens, in America only to work provisionally (or perhaps here illegally), are docile employees and sell their labor cheap. They have become the corporate farmers' choice.[18]

In all industries that once were filled with native-born American workers but now are considered to offer only immigrant positions, it is important to ask: What if the government had not changed its immigration policies and provided the option of choosing foreign workers over American workers?

Because immigration policies were changed, agricultural working conditions are so bad that dramatic stories about migrant work are a staple of newspaper and TV reporters every year. This has been true for thirty years. The focus almost always is on ways to require improved working conditions. It is a focus on the symptoms of the problem of a surplus labor market. Despite some improvements in housing resulting from all the media attention, the incomes of the workers have grown worse during all of the media exposure. Until the attention is turned to immigration's underlying role in the conditions, no reform is likely to be sufficient or lasting.

* * *

In a ramshackle neighborhood on Virginia's seaboard, residents bunch together under a street lamp and talk about life at the bottom of the American job ladder. The majority of them are the forgotten Americans, struggling to eke out a living in jobs which immigration advocates commonly say Americans won't do.

"This is a working community; it's not a welfare community," Ruth Wise emphasizes. But the available jobs—mostly in agriculture, poultry processing, restaurants, motels, and seafood plants—are almost totally in industries heavily penetrated by immigrant workers nationwide. A growing number of foreign workers compete directly with the natives here, and already have taken over virtually all agricultural jobs. Wage rates vary by region but are closely connected as part of a national economy. Businesses here cannot allow wages to be out of line with those of competitors in other parts of the country which hire even more immigrants in order to lower wages, says Professor Griffith, an expert on the low-wage economy.

Gradually drawn to the impromptu discussion under this street light after nightfall, these are not people easily sidetracked by appeals to immigrant traditions. These are African Americans whose ancestors had been tending the fertile coastal soil here long before the arrival of most other Americans' ancestors. On average, most residents of this black community probably are twelfth- to fifteenth-generation Americans. Yet in the closing years of the twentieth century, most still have not achieved the basic essentials of a modern American lifestyle.

Poverty for black residents in Northampton County is such that some express envy of migrant workers who are provided workcamp shelter "with running water and indoor toilets." During a two-hour discussion, residents periodically wander off into the darkened backyards to visit the outhouses that serve as toilets for more than 25 percent of all black-occupied housing units in the county. This county suffers from especially high infant mortality, poverty, teen pregnancy, and a disparity in incomes.

Burley Rogers, his name on his workshirt, says some agribusinesses in the area now "hire only Mexicans. They used to hire schoolkids and other African Americans, but then they said they didn't work well enough, not as good as Mexicans. Now, they don't hire any locals." Others in the group shake their heads at what they see as the impossibility of competing with foreign workers who will accept lower pay and harsher—even "slavelike"—working conditions. Ruth Wise snaps that it isn't right to expect black workers or any other Americans to have to compete at that level: "Why should we have to work like slaves? We've been slaves."

But black Americans systematically have been rooted out of farmwork by the relentless "Latinization" of the fields, according to Monica Heppel, who was director of research for the U.S. Commission on Agricultural Workers.

Heppel has a special perspective on the changes immigration has brought to the nation's black farmworkers. In 1979, she did her doctoral dissertation on agriculture in Northampton and Accomac, the two Virginia counties known as the Eastern Shore—the narrow strand between the Chesapeake Bay and Atlantic Ocean. She lived in the farm labor camps. At that time, black workers—including migrants based in Florida—made up about half the workers in the fields and nearly all the workers in the sheds where they packed cucumbers, potatoes, green beans, and other vegetables: "I don't think I saw a Mexican working in a packing shed, except down by Cheriton in a sweet potato factory." The agricultural industry was profitable while using American labor.

In the mid-1990s, it is difficult to imagine such a workforce on the Eastern Shore. Since 1979, immigrants from Latin America have taken over the Eastern Shore's fields and packing sheds. "Now, you have an industry where it would be very hard for a local black to get a job," says Heppel, who is currently director of the Inter-American Institute on Migration and Labor and a professor at Mount Vernon College in Washington, D.C.

"You get this switch in the workforce that seems to happen overnight," Heppel says. "But you get this culture that once it takes hold, U.S.-born workers lose out. Crew leaders used to be black, so all the instructions were in English. Food in the camps was black food. Now, labor camp food is Mexican. Now, the language of the field is Spanish. There are so many ways for the employer to discourage native workers. They will give them the worst rows to pick; they'll give the immigrants the first pick on the trees and give the natives the second pick. Natives will quit. Then the word goes out to natives, 'Don't work there because the good work goes to Mexicans, etc.' Then the employers can say, 'See, the locals don't show up.' "

The results feed the racist inclinations of many observers, who then say that the low-income, rural black residents have become too lazy or too uppity to do agricultural work, necessitating high immigration, when in fact it was the high immigration that drove black farmworkers from the fields.

Marshall Barry points out that as late as the 1970s, black Americans made up the overwhelming majority of the hired farm labor force in the East. Today, workers from Latin America and the Caribbean are the overwhelming majority. While he continues to speak for the improvement of conditions for the immigrants who now hold the farm labor jobs, he lashes out at the intellectual leaders of this country—especially those posing as liberals—who allowed "the absolute destruction of America's black farmworkers, the descendants of slaves, only because they were competing against foreign workers who didn't require as much pay."

The U.S. Commission on Agricultural Workers in its 1992 report offered western New York as an example of the rapid transformation. In 1985, black Americans still dominated the fields. Latinos do so today. "Between 1965 and 1992, Mexican workers succeeded in establishing footholds in virtually every important perishable-crop production region in the country," replacing and displacing black Americans, Chicanos, and others, according to Professor Griffith.

Now it is the Latino farmworkers' turn to survive the threats from immigration. One problem with an immigration-driven economy is that no group ever gains security. Each group of foreign workers that supplants an established population is in turn supplanted by a later immigration. Having nearly eliminated black Americans from farm work, federal policymakers now continue an immigration flow that is making life miserable for Latino farmworkers.

"I'm seeing things differently here than in prior years," says Bonifacio Mazariegos, a farmworker in Rochester, New York. "There was more work, but now work is very scarce. There are many people, and the people in charge of the farms are very hard to work with. One puts up with it because one has no choice."

The Reverend Arturo M. Fernandez, director of Casa de Amigos Center in Visalia, California, says he can see the increase in poverty and in the social problems of his farmworker clientele over the last decade. There is such an overabundance of labor that workers accept conditions they wouldn't have considered a few years ago. The special U.S. Commission that investigated conditions learned of desperate workers even picking grapes for free around Fresno, California, in the hopes that they would be noticed and hired. Increasingly, farmers turn over recruitment and workforce discipline to private labor contractors, who tend to be immigrants themselves. Maria Carmona, a farmworker in Coachella Valley, California, told of gaining work through one: "He would threaten us before we would start work. He would say, 'The one that would like the work and the conditions, enter. If you don't like it, you can leave.' . . . And because we were lacking work, we had to start working there. . . . For three days of work, I received $42."

The labor contractors, even more than the farmers, seem to prefer workers who have as little experience in the United States as possible; they are easier to control and to cheat, according to a book based on research by Jeronimo Camposeco, Anna Garcia, Max Pfeffer, David Runsten, and Manuel Valdes Pizzini. They found that established Mexican-Americans who spoke Spanish, and theoretically should have been compatible with the Spanish culture of the fields, nonetheless were "discouraged from farm labor" because they were U.S. citizens. The farm labor system favors the new immigrant at the expense of the old immigrant: "Simply, citizenship has become a liability for them [established Mexican-Americans] in terms of finding work in agriculture. Their status as citizens affords them powers and rights that impeded the current 'efficiency' of the agricultural labor process—an efficiency based on disinformation, unequal power relations between workers and their employers, and a variety of 'kickbacks' and expenses borne by farmworkers for the privilege of working."[19]

In Ventura County, California, the veteran Mexican-American

labor force in the citrus industry was able by 1980 to win many collective bargaining agreements and major improvements in pay and benefits. But private labor contractors used the rising abundance of more recent Mexican immigrants to underbid, causing the veteran Mexican-Americans to lose all of their contracts and eventually to dissolve their unions, according to the U.S. General Accounting Office.[20]

Nowhere may immigration's devastating effect on American Hispanics be more stark than in what Texans call "the Valley"—the American towns and agricultural plantations along the Mexican border near where the Rio Grande empties into the Gulf of Mexico. The Mexican-American population there had provided the labor for nearby plantations and for long-established migrant treks through other states. But "the constant influx" of new Mexican workers into the Valley is disrupting all that, especially by keeping wages low for most Mexican-Americans already living there, according to Robert Lee Maril in a major report for the University of Notre Dame Press.

Many established Mexican-Americans have given up their attempts to work on the migratory route where they face discrimination because they are citizens and where more recent immigrants continue to bid wages further downward. Out of 305 metropolitan areas ranked, the two in the Valley are among the worst five in terms of unemployment. While the poverty rate for Hispanics nationwide is exceptionally high, Mexican-Americans in the Valley live in poverty at double the national Hispanic average. "A virtual flood of new poor from Central America" has only added to the Valley's massive problems, Maril said.

Maril identified immigration and high birth rates as important reasons why the Valley's Mexican-Americans are among the poorest people of the entire country. He suggested there still is some hope that the residents of the Valley could rise to a truly American standard of living if fertility and immigration can be cut: "Fewer jobs would need to be created for those entering the labor market, fewer classrooms erected, pressures on social services would diminish, and limited natural resources could be stretched further."[21]

But in one of its supreme gestures of hostility to Hispanics and farmworkers, the U.S. Congress continues policies that allow substantial flows of immigration into the Valley and which trap the Mexican-Americans there in powerlessness and poverty.

*   *   *

Despite appearances, Congress doesn't really keep immigration high just so it can be cruel to some of America's most vulnerable residents.

But Congress doesn't pay a lot of attention to them because its ear is captured by the agribusiness lobby with its repetitive warnings that without immigration the growers may end up having crops ready to harvest without enough workers to do so. The growers have some legitimate concerns. They have huge investments that are almost totally at the mercy of a migrating, seasonal workforce which nobody has any guarantees will actually show up when needed. Although there is a gargantuan national oversupply of farmworkers, there continue to be a number of instances of local labor shortages for specific crops, confirmed the U.S. Commission on Agricultural Workers.

But immigration is a mighty blunt solution to sporadic local shortages, and it comes with lots of negative side effects. The commission said the answer for the farmers is in much better labor management by them and by the government.

"People have a tendency to look at the workers as the problem—that they won't stay," said Heppel, the commission's research director at the time. "But it is reasonable to say, 'Look at the employers, they haven't been changing. They haven't had to go ahead and recruit workers because the government has provided through immigration.'"

The commission said the country has plenty of Americans who will do the farmwork; there is no need to further supplement the farmwork force with foreign labor. But to meet agricultural needs without immigration, the commission recommended the following changes:

- Many farm operations are "characterized by organization inefficiency" so that the workers' dissatisfaction and turnover increase employer costs and reduce farmworkers' earnings. Farmers, on their own or with other farmers, need to diversify their crops so they can provide steady work over longer periods of time. Workers will be much more likely to be around when a crop must be harvested if they feel a loyalty to the operation—and especially if they can settle down near the operation year-round.
- To keep farmworkers dependable, employers should offer better benefits, and employees must be placed under the full protection of unemployment insurance programs and under state workers' compensation statutes.
- The U.S. Department of Labor should play a much more aggressive role in matching farmworkers to jobs so that they and the growers are protected from lost earnings.
- Governmental agencies should create a major program to educate

growers, packing-house operators, labor contractors, and worker organizations in better management techniques.

The 1992 recommendations are not a lot different in concept from those by a commission appointed by President Theodore Roosevelt. Its famous *Country Life Report,* issued in 1909, expressed worries about the seasonality of work for farm laborers and the uneven predictability of the labor supply for employers. It called for a system of better labor management: "The best labor, other things being equal, is resident labor. Such reorganization of agriculture must take place as will tend more and more to employ the man year round and to tie him to the land. The employer bears a distinct responsibility to the laborer, and also to society, to house him well and to help him to contribute his part to the community welfare."[22]

Nearly ninety years later, that commission's ideal of farm labor might finally come true if Congress would give it a chance by cutting off or lowering immigration. Even now, many farmers already are pioneering employee relations that point the way to how the country could have a stable labor force of American farmworkers.

For some like the Van Kesteren Farms on Virginia's Eastern Shore, it amounts to a few simple management techniques and a basic commitment to American workers. Driving up the road to the company's big spinach packing house at the end of a workday, a visitor immediately notices the complexion of the workers in the cars headed for home: They are all local black residents. It is a throwback to a couple of decades ago and a surprising sight in an area where nearly all other agribusinesses use immigrants while a large segment of the native black population lives in underemployment and poverty.

For JoAnn Van Kesteren, daughter of the founder of the business, hiring local workers is a matter of fairness: "We don't use immigrant labor. We have so many local people who need jobs. We have eighty-six local laborers on the payroll right now."

To her brother Steve, it is a matter of tough conservative principles: It doesn't make sense to bring immigrants when that just increases the number of natives on the welfare rolls.

The Van Kesterens grow, harvest, and package spinach, selling it for fresh-produce retailing, not frozen foods. So it is important that the spinach still be crisp when it leaves the farm. They must be sure that the farmworkers move it quickly from field to market once it is ready for harvest. The incentive to ensure the workers are on the job when needed is a bonus of 50 percent more pay for every hour of every week in which the worker shows up every day requested and is not tardy. Workers get the lump-sum bonus at the end of the six-month season.

Loyalty and dependability are the rewards to the farmers, JoAnn Van Kesteren says. "There's a great deal of loyalty. Only a handful of this spring's workers are new hires. Some of these guys have worked as long as my dad's been here." These definitely are jobs Americans will do.

Bixby Orchards in Michigan needed a more complex overhaul. Paul Bixby added peaches, plums, strawberries, sweetcorn, asparagus, melons, cabbage, cauliflower, and summer vegetables to his standby of apples and cherries. Instead of worrying whether he could get the fifteen to twenty pickers he needed for the old eight-week harvest, he now has a steady group of eight to ten workers who can get around forty hours a week of work ten months of the year.

A. Duda & Sons of Florida created a dependable force of farmworkers on a much larger scale. The personnel manager estimates a 95 percent employee return rate each year for Duda's three thousand workers. Farmworkers stand in line to get the few new open slots because the business offers health and life insurance, a retirement plan, a day-care center, and paid holidays.

With enlightened business practices like those, nobody has to worry about who will pick the lettuce and tomatoes. The bottom line is that every agricultural job that will need to be done in the United States can be done by an American worker—either native-born or foreign-born—as far into the future as anybody can see. There is no need to bring any more foreign farmworkers.

Concerns that treating farmworkers with dignity will drive the price of food unacceptably high have no basis in reality, argues Philip L. Martin, a professor of agricultural economics at the University of California-Davis and a member of the U.S. Commission on Agricultural Workers. One first has to remember that foreign-born laborers work with only about 20 percent of all the food harvested in the United States (most is handled mechanically). Congress is running an immigration program that impoverishes a couple million seasonal farmworkers and their families, and yet the effect for the average American family is that the food bill is just slightly lower than if the farmworkers were paid enough to rise above poverty.

Because of the huge oversupply of farmworkers, it probably would be a while before the labor market got tight enough to start pushing wages up appreciably, even if all immigration were stopped immediately. But there isn't much to worry about in terms of prices, Professor

Martin says. The wages paid to farmworkers typically account for only about 10 percent of the retail price of a number of crops. In other words, farm wages could be doubled and poverty among farmworkers could be virtually eliminated while adding only about 10 cents to the cost of a head of lettuce.

In actuality, Martin and others say, the price of food probably wouldn't go up at all. Tighter labor markets would encourage more mechanization to keep prices down. Tomato farmers claimed in the early 1960s that their industry would not survive if a program for temporary guest farmworkers was halted. But when it was stopped, the farmers mechanized in a manner that quadrupled production and led to the price of ketchup and other tomato products dropping for consumers.

Monica Heppel acknowledges that if wages go up significantly, it may not be possible for mechanization to make all crops economically viable to continue growing in the United States. The technology may be some time in coming that would allow mechanization for some labor-intensive crops, she says. Thus, it may become uneconomical to continue to produce them in the United States. "We probably are going to lose the California avocado industry. So what?" Farmers simply will switch the use of their land to other crops when the ones they currently produce can be grown and shipped from other countries cheaper than they can be grown here, she explains.

As the U.S. Commission on Agricultural Workers stated, there is no future in American farmers trying to compete with Third World countries on the basis of their low wages. The ability to compete is and will be based on America's "advantages of a highly-developed infrastructure, high-quality produce and the ability to offset higher labor costs with greater productivity." Immigration has merely retarded some of the agricultural industry's movement to better technological and organizational practices.

Still, with hundreds of millions of laborers around the world willing to work for less than $10 a day, the fear is that some American industries—manufacturing and agricultural—could not compete globally if they didn't have access to immigrants who will work for less money than American workers. Without foreign workers, many U.S. companies might close down their plants and move operations to Third World countries, warn some immigration advocates.

On the surface, it doesn't seem like much of a threat. If the conditions of employment are so dismal that Americans won't work at a plant, it is difficult to see much gain in keeping it on American soil. As

Nathan Glazer questioned in the *New Republic,* why should the most advanced economy in the world try to hold on to industries whose method of operation is to compete with low-wage, underdeveloped countries?[23]

Immigration advocates, though, claim that when immigrants work in Third World conditions in the United States, they often make it possible for American workers to retain middle-class jobs in the same company or in supplier companies. If those substandard jobs disappear in the United States, so will some middle-class jobs, the reasoning goes.

The General Accounting Office gave some credence to that claim in a preliminary report in 1987. It referred to "segmented labor markets," in which some jobs in a business were kept at such abominable conditions that nobody but an immigrant would take them. The GAO used the example of a restaurant paying abysmal wages to busboys and dishwashers. By working for those wages, immigrants might reduce employer costs enough to allow the restaurant to reduce meal prices, which might increase the number of customers, which might result in the hiring of more Americans in the better-paying jobs of chefs and waiters, the GAO reasoned.[24]

William E. Brock, who was Secretary of Labor at the time, sent a fiery retort to the report. He said the GAO's hypothesis about the benefits of immigration in a segmented labor market was farfetched and did not begin to counterbalance the losses American workers suffer due to low-wage competition from immigrants. The GAO defended the concept of segmentation, but revised the first section of its report to state that it is rare that American workers are in a truly segmented labor market in which they benefit from immigrants taking jobs at very low wages.

Even if the segmented labor market worked to preserve jobs for a lot of Americans, one questions whether the United States really wants to base its economy on a class of semi-slave workers. Arguments for high immigration today resemble the justifications made by southern businessmen for the retention of slavery 150 years ago. Without that source of cheap labor, they said, large numbers of free whites would lose their jobs or at least their prosperity because of the collapse of agriculture that surely would follow. Likewise at the turn of the century, the textile industry claimed that its better-paying jobs for adults would be jeopardized if it was not allowed to continue to fill many of its positions with children working for minuscule wages.

In both instances, when the federal government did the humane thing—abolishing slavery and child labor—the results proved that the government also had taken an action that improved economic conditions for nearly everybody. Elizabeth Koed of the University of California-Santa Barbara notes that the South's long reliance on slave labor "slowed the progress of technology and the development of skills that would be needed to compete" in the ensuing industrial revolution. After child labor was outlawed, the voice of the industry, *The Textile World Journal*, expressed gratitude for the action: "It can be stated without fear of effective contradiction that . . . the labor of children under 14 years of age is not only inefficient in itself, but tends to lower the efficiency of all departments in which they are employed. . . ."[25]

Newspapers in recent years are filled with reports of the rising business practice of using foreign labor—both legal and illegal—in near-slave conditions. Occasionally, the employers of immigrants succeed in actually reestablishing slavery. In August 1995, for example, federal officials uncovered a business east of Los Angeles using more than sixty workers from Thailand to make clothing for some of the nation's best-known department stores. In a barbed-wire compound, the immigrants worked seven days a week for as little as 50 cents an hour. "This really is slave labor inside the United States," Labor Secretary Reich said. "We are witnessing the development of a third-world economy—both workers and employers—in the very midst of the first-world."[26]

Former Colorado governor Richard Lamm is confident that the American economy and middle class would be better off without cheap foreign labor. He feels no threat from businesses that say they will have to move to another country if they are not allowed to match deplorable Third World working conditions: "If a company cannot afford to run a healthful and safe plant, we shouldn't allow them to run an unsafe one. We should let them close. We'll be better off without them. Letting go of dying companies and industries may cause some economic dislocations in the short term. But in the long run it will contribute to the health of our economy."[27]

The immigrant-importing, low-wage strategy of industries like agriculture, clothing, meat processing, motels, restaurants, custodial services, retail sales, and more and more of the construction trades is an immoral distortion of free-market principles. The strategy is based on the premise that immigration should be used to hold down wages for American laborers making as low as $5,000 or $10,000 a year simply to lower prices for other Americans who average $25,000 or more a year. What ethical basis can a society claim to make those at the bottom of the economic ladder pay to make life more comfortable for those at the top?

If the United States stopped its importation of cheap foreign labor today, one wonders how long it would be before analysts generally could look back on our present immigration flows as being as unnecessary, embarrassing, and economically damaging as we now consider the country's past dependence on slavery and child labor.

7

Foreign Skills
We Don't Need

America's young people, who study diligently and aim high, often arrive at their moment of opportunity in adulthood to find the federal government has placed a high-skilled foreign worker in their way. Some earn their college degrees only to discover that their field is glutted with immigrants and that they must take a job lower than that for which their education prepared them. And among Americans who are able to move into the advanced careers of their choosing, the danger always looms that their company will replace them with imported foreign workers willing to offer high-tech services for less money.

Congress turned up the competitive pressure on America's bright students and professionals in 1990 by nearly tripling the allotment for importing highly skilled and professional immigrants—up from 54,-000 to 140,000 each year. Businesses also were given the right to temporarily import another 65,000 professionals each year for up to six years.

In the opinion of many people, the problems of immigration can be solved without cutting the very high current flow if the government ensures that every immigrant is educated and highly skilled. As individuals, the foreign workers entering in skills categories are an attractive lot. They are middle class, they are less likely to use welfare or commit crimes, and they hold good jobs. But their presence brings very real consequences to skilled American workers, and perhaps more significantly, to Americans who aspire to professions.

The skills part of our nation's immigration program is based on a supreme lack of faith that "the kid next door" in America is capable of being trained and motivated to perform the country's most challenging tasks. The federal policy of summoning tens of thousands of skilled immigrants a year is driven by belief on the part of powerful leaders in Congress and the business community that in a country of 265 million people: (1) there are not enough entrepreneurial Americans; (2) there are not enough American professionals; (3) there are not enough brilliant Americans to provide the country with necessary innovation; (4) there are not enough smart American young people who could be persuaded to seek higher degrees in education; (5) there are not enough Americans with the international savvy to keep the United States competitive in the global economy; and (6) there are not enough American workers to keep the Social Security system solvent. Let's examine these beliefs separately.

1. NOT ENOUGH AMERICAN ENTREPRENEURS?

The idea that immigrants have an exceptional capacity for starting businesses is deep-seated. To listen to some immigration advocates, one might think that few new businesses would ever be started by native-born Americans if immigrants did not lead the way. Donald Lambro, chief political correspondent of *The Washington Times,* exemplified this almost beatific view of immigrants in 1995: "More often than not they end up building enormously successful enterprises and creating jobs, from Farah slacks to Wang computers. Immigrants remain one of America's greatest economic and cultural strengths, helping to ensure that we will remain a land of everlasting opportunity and growth."[1]

In fact, more often than not immigrants don't start any kind of business. And of the ones who do, most muddle along in mediocrity just like most Americans who try their hand at entrepreneurship. Some immigrants come from cultures with a high degree of entrepreneurial tradition, but many do not. The 1990 Census found that immigrants as a whole are *less* likely than native-born Americans to go into business for themselves.

Although it is commonly suggested that immigrant businesses are necessary to provide Americans with jobs, immigrant-started businesses are not particularly helpful to American workers. They are notorious for hiring primarily, and often exclusively, other immigrants. American workers—especially black Americans—seldom benefit. Neither do native-owned businesses because immigrant businesses typically buy from suppliers that also are immigrant-owned.

2. NOT ENOUGH AMERICAN PROFESSIONALS?

One out of four researchers at IBM's Yorktown Heights laboratory is foreign-born. Two out of five researchers at Bell Labs are immigrants. Americans who enter hospitals encounter tens of thousands of foreign-born nurses, therapists, doctors, and technicians. When the White House needed assistance in 1995 to install and maintain a correspondence system, it sought out a minority-owned business. It might seem that no U.S.-born minorities were available, since the White House contracted with Mastech Corporation, a company owned by two Indian immigrants who have brought 900 of their 1,300 workers from India.[2]

The tendency when looking at all those foreign-born professionals is to think that if they were not here, the jobs they hold would go vacant. It is a mistaken assumption, though. Ethnic networking often is the reason so many foreign-born workers are at the same plant or laboratory. Each immigrant hired tends to help other immigrants of the same nationality to gain employment, too. Some top corporation executives who are unfamiliar with their personnel operations look around their plants, see a lot of immigrant workers, and falsely conclude that there were no American workers available to fill the positions. The U.S. Commission on Immigration Reform, chaired by Barbara Jordan, reviewed the importation program for skilled immigrants and determined that the level was far too high. It recommended a reduction in skilled slots, and suggested that a special tax be levied to discourage companies from recruiting skilled foreigners.

The Jordan Commission recommendation stirred a public spectacle of horrified reaction from the National Association of Manufacturers, from immigration lawyers, and from America's preeminent business publications. And editorialists for numerous major general-circulation newspapers, while less hysterical than the direct spokespersons for business owners, expressed great puzzlement about why the United States would cut skilled immigration and risk losing its ability to compete in the global high-tech economy.

That so many members of Congress and the news media gave credence to the business titans' cries of alarm illustrated how little they knew about the lives of wage-earning American professionals. Because the Jordan Commission had taken time to talk to real, live American engineers, scientists, and commuter programmers, it knew that the United States has the opposite of a high-skills shortage; it has a glut. And it knew that federal immigration policy for twenty years has been making life miserable for many of those Americans who studied hard, aimed high, and prepared themselves for scientific endeavors. To the various associations of American professionals it has been fairly clear what U.S. industries have been doing: The pro-immigration lobby clamors for foreign professionals because they work for less and help depress wages for American professionals.

Consider engineers. The largest single category of employment-based immigrants is engineering, in direct defiance of the American Engineering Association (AEA), which has been asking Congress for more than twenty years to cut the importation of engineers in order to allow Americans in the profession the opportunity to pursue their careers. During a time of defense and corporate downsizing, two major recessions, stagnant engineering wages, and record levels of engineering unemployment, Congress has allowed U.S. industries to import record levels of foreign engineers, often by securing permanent residency for foreign students as they emerge from U.S. colleges. "The universities attract foreign graduate students with the promise that they can ultimately get a green card," says David C. Lewis, an AEA official. "This self-destructive policy—that throws away the nation's investment in the best of our young people and their future—must end."[3]

The greed of some U.S. industrialists to earn additional profits at the expense of American workers may have reached new heights in 1990. The pro-immigration lobby persuaded Congress that despite the overcrowded engineering and scientist labor markets of the time, the nation was facing a severe shortage of engineers and scientists in the near future. Congress responded by nearly tripling the size of the skilled-immigrant category that already had caused so much damage during the 1980s.

The increase in skilled immigration since 1990 has been devastating to engineers, according to the Institute of Electrical and Electronics Engineers (IEEE). "The only shortages that occurred were shortages of jobs for American's technical professionals, to the point where U.S. electrical-engineering unemployment reached its highest level in history (in 1994)," says Joel B. Snyder, chairman of the IEEE. Since 1990, 146,000 U.S. engineering positions have been eliminated, the IEEE estimates. These would have been tough times for engineers even without the federal government's insistence on flooding the market with foreign engineers. "Not only have engineering jobs been harder to come by—especially for new graduates and older engineers—but many pay a lot less than they did a few years ago." The American Association of Engineering Societies found that the real purchasing power of all engineers' salaries reached a twenty-year low in 1994, with entry-level wages particularly hard hit.[4]

The legislative proposals of 1995 and 1996 that so angered many industrialists would make only small cuts in skilled immigration. The cuts would not even lower the admissions back to the very high level of the 1980s.

Among the professions especially hit by the 1980s level and the increases in admissions since 1990 has been the field of computer science. A group of programmers finally organized themselves in 1994 as an organization called "SoftPac." Relying on data from the Bureau of Labor Statistics, SoftPac estimated that about 40,000 new positions opened up in the U.S. software industry in 1994 while the federal government gave software employers permission to import 30,000 foreign programmers. That didn't make for a very happy graduation present for the 51,000 computer science majors completing their education at U.S. colleges that year.[5]

Susanne O'Brien of SoftPac is discouraging her son and his friends from entering computer or engineering professions because she believes most of the work in the future will be sent overseas or be given to foreigners who will work in the United States for much lower wages than Americans will accept. Larry Richards, SoftPac executive director, points out that while government and industry have colluded to fill the domestic labor market with foreign professionals since 1990, the number of unemployed computer scientists and engineers doubled. Not surprisingly real wages have declined. All of that will eventually create the conditions Congress in 1990 had sought to avoid, Richards contends: There really will be a shortage of Americans in the computer and engineering professions because fewer and fewer Americans will find any incentive to study for them.[6]

Norman Matloff, professor of computer science at the University of California-Davis, sees firsthand the heartache of American students who cannot find jobs after graduation: "The University of California is investing millions of dollars in training students for careers in computer science. Yet this investment is often going to waste. The computer industry fills many technical positions with foreign nationals, shunting American graduates of the University of California into nontechnical positions, if hiring them at all."[7]

Industry officials counter that American programmers often don't have the specific skill needed for a new task and that companies like to be able to scout the whole world for somebody who can step right in and do the job. Critics, though, say the companies overdefine their job requirements. Studies have shown that a company can throw a new technology at programmers and that, in one month, the workers reach about 80 percent of their full productivity, achieving 100 percent within four months. Although Microsoft's lawyers were among the army of lobbyists who climbed Capitol Hill in 1995 to protect their foreign worker programs, the company's founder, Bill Gates, has said that Microsoft doesn't look for specific knowledge in a programmer "because things change so fast, and it's easy to learn stuff. You've got to have an excitement about software, a certain intelligence. . . . It's not the specific knowledge that counts." A modest amount of retraining could make valuable employees out of the 20,000 programmers laid off from the defense industry. Instead, many are working as pizza deliverers and security guards while computer companies import tens of thousands of foreign programmers.[8]

U.S. businesses get permission from the government to import professionals by stating that no American is available for the job. A casual observer undoubtedly would ask how that can happen when tens of thousands of American professionals are looking for work. The answer is that U.S. businesses have the services of very creative immigration lawyers. "Really good immigration lawyers know how to write a job description that only one person can fill, and yet looks reasonable," according to Joan Fitzpatrick, a University of Washington law professor who specializes in immigration. After an extensive review of Labor Department records, the *Seattle Times* concluded that the claims of Northwest firms that they couldn't find available American professionals were mostly pretense. "Some employers just don't want to hire an American," wrote reporters Eric Nalder and Paul Andrews. "The sponsored foreign applicants have significant advantages, including the backing of a U.S. company and the best immigration-law advice that money can buy. The U.S. citizen has only a resume." The

Northwest firms apparently believe that foreigners will work harder and for less money. During a recession economy while thousands of Americans were being rejected for skilled and professional jobs in the Northwest, the federal government allowed local businesses to bring in hundreds of foreign workers for salaries paying as much as $100,000 a year.[9]

Not all industries are acting maliciously toward American workers when they hire foreign workers instead. For some, it is just incompetence. Professor Matloff notes that many computer companies have set up clumsy personnel procedures that inadvertently ignore qualified Americans whose applications are already in house. The companies computerize their personnel procedures; when a department needs a new programmer, it specifies exactly the skills required; the computer scans applications for exactly those skills, often failing to find Americans who have listed everything needed; the company then sends out a call through the immigration network to find its employee. The problem, Matloff says, is that the computer doesn't recognize that many of the American applicants who have failed to list the exact list of qualifications being sought have similar skills that make them capable of quickly learning the task at hand or perhaps even of performing the task immediately. Computer programmers are trained to be flexible, constantly learning new skills. Corporations that overspecify jobs consistently fail to tap into that flexibility as they shun unemployed American programmers in favor of turning to the foreign labor recruiters for help.

Of course for other corporations, the preference for foreign workers is no accident; they are looking for people who will work for less money and put up with worse working conditions. As a former manager in the computer industry, with former students reporting back to him and with a wife in the industry, Professor Matloff gains insight into the hiring process. One man who had immigrated to the United States from Russia fifteen years ago interviewed for a position with a software firm in New York. He was surprised that almost all of the technical staff were from India or Russia. The employer told the man that the company would sponsor him for immigration. When the man explained that he already was a naturalized U.S. citizen, he was told the company was no longer interested in him. A young woman from China was hired by a Silicon Valley computer firm that worked its programmers ten hours a day with no overtime pay or compensating time off. Once there, she said, she noticed that the company rejected applicants who were citizens or who had permanent resident status. The 1990 Census data revealed that foreign-born computer professionals in Silicon Valley worked for nearly $7,000 less than did natives of the same age and level of education.

"Our nation benefits greatly when employers bring truly exceptional foreign talents to the United States, and this facet of immigration law should be retained," Matloff says. "But at the same time, this view should not be extrapolated to foreign-born computer professionals in general. The vast majority are of ordinary abilities, hired into positions in which they perform ordinary work."

The U.S. Department of Labor agrees that the chief attraction of thousands of skilled foreign workers is that they will work for less than Americans in the same field. And in the cases where Americans may not be available, Labor Secretary Robert Reich says, the importation of foreign workers is just a means to circumvent the costs of training Americans to take the jobs.[10]

Business spokespersons don't totally deny that many of their colleagues are trying to cut costs. With skilled people able to demand premium salaries, it is understandable that employers would look abroad for lower-cost professionals, said the chief executive officer at Diamond Multimedia Systems, a maker of computer accessories. An immigration attorney told the *Wall Street Journal* that companies also go abroad because they can't find Americans with the right "attitude," which often is a euphemism for a willingness to put up with working conditions unacceptable to Americans.[11]

"Greed is the reason they're doing this; anybody who says it ain't greed is smoking rope," said John Morris, whose Houston consulting firm lost its largest customer because he wouldn't provide low-cost foreign programmers. In Hollywood, movie technicians complain that they are being replaced by cut-rate foreign workers. Physical therapists are being imported by the thousands, many of them to work for less than one-fourth the prevailing wages of Americans. The federal government's policies make a farce of admonitions to the country's youth to get an education and acquire a skill so they can play an important role in America's increasingly high-tech economy.

Gloria Jenks especially feels the contradiction between the government's words and actions. She was one of some 250 computer specialists and assistants fired in 1994 by American International Group, an insurance company which replaced them with workers fresh from India. "We went to school for these skills, and someone else comes in and takes them," Jenks told CBS's *48 Hours*. She recalled being summoned to a hotel along with others from her Livingston, New Jersey, plant. They learned not only that they were fired but that they would have to stay sixty days to train their immigrant replacements if they were to receive severance pay. The American workers had been earning salaries between $40,000 and $80,000. CBS reported that the immigrant replacements were making roughly half that amount.[12]

"The incentive is money—not quality, not skill and not a company's health; it is not due to re-engineering or downsizing or merging," claims Linda Kilcrease, who also lost her job at AIG. "Because it is at the expense of employees who built the companies, it is greed and worse." She noted in a press conference at the U.S. Senate that AIG did not need to slash salaries to remain profitable. It is 26th in the Fortune 500, first in its industry, and 34th in *Business Week* Global list.[13]

In fairness to businesses, most of them are not so ruthless as to throw Americans out of work to make room for lower-wage immigrants. Many indeed do find it difficult at times to locate available employees in their city with the precise training they seek, although they sometimes are more likely to recruit in a foreign land thousands of miles away than in another region of the United States. The National Association of Manufacturers cited a survey in 1995 which found that one-fourth of the small businesses contacted feared a shortage of qualified workers. To the national business leaders, that was proof of the need to open the doors to more immigrants. But to educators and job-placement professionals, that should have been a wonderful challenge to help Americans move up the ladder to take higher-skilled jobs. America has no shortage of jobless people looking for work or employed people seeking to make themselves more economically valuable to an employer. When we look at the unemployed and underemployed populations of Appalachia, the inner cities, the rural South, and elsewhere across the country, have we forgotten how in America talent and good ideas often pop up in unexpected areas? Why are we so eager to import talent without ever having made the effort to find the bright American kids whom society has never fully developed?

It is unconscionable for the federal government to allow immigration of skilled workers to dampen two types of free-market pressures: one that encourages Americans to prepare for expanding vocations, and the other that pressures governments and businesses to provide the necessary tools to prepare Americans for emerging jobs. Without those pressures, too many boys and girls will continue to wend their way through high school with no particular idea of how they will contribute to society and no special appeals from the outside to learn the skills that the economy needs. The immigration enthusiasts cannot seem to imagine that the American kid next door could possibly be trained to do the skilled jobs being given to immigrants. While social critics, politicians, and newspaper editorialists moan over America's unmotivated youth and talk of the need to shape up and work harder, the nation's immigration policies rig the game against the young.

3. NOT ENOUGH BRILLIANT AMERICANS TO INNOVATE?

Even if the kid next door could be educated to be a skilled or professional worker, immigrants are needed to provide the cutting-edge thinking that will keep Americans in business, according to many leaders. For example, Run Unz, a California computer entrepreneur and former Republican candidate for governor, fears disaster if the number of skilled immigrants is cut: "Silicon Valley, which is home to my own software company, depends on immigrant professionals to maintain its technological edge. A third of all the engineers and chip designers here are foreign-born, and if they left, America's computer industry would probably go with them."[14] Ken Alvarez, vice president of Sun Microsystems, said that a reduction in skilled immigration would block the best talent and "kill" his company.

Professor Matloff finds the rhetoric unconvincing, maintaining that America's major technological advances in the computer industry "have been made by native talent." Listening to the industry lobbyists, one would think that immigrants are dominant among the top innovators. But look at these statistics:

- The Association for Computing Machinery (ACM), the nation's main computer science professional society, lists 132 top computer scientists in the United States. Fewer than 10 percent are immigrants.
- Of the thirty-nine scientists honored by ACM for software systems work, only one is an immigrant.
- There is not even one immigrant among the seventeen scientists honored by ACM for advances in computer hardware.

Despite such evidence of Americans' abilities, many immigration enthusiasts doubt that native-born Americans can continue to provide the necessary brilliance because of the poor showing in graduate schools, as discussed below.

4. NOT ENOUGH SMART AND
MOTIVATED AMERICAN KIDS
TO PURSUE A PH.D.?

To the editorial writers of the *Wall Street Journal,* a "flaccid American culture" and "fair-but-not-great public schools" are not capable of producing professionals of the caliber of immigrants.[15] When the number of skilled immigrants allowed into this country jumped markedly in 1991, the *Kentucky Enquirer* saw that as proof of American inferiority: "If American schools can't provide the educated and skilled workers the nation needs, it will get them from abroad. . . . The new law reminds us . . . of the deficiencies in schooling that, unless reversed, will make the nation increasingly dependent on educational systems abroad for the engineering, scientific and other talents American business needs to compete."[16]

Lobbying Congress for the National Association of Manufacturers, Jerry J. Jasinowski said the United States needed 140,000 skilled immigrants a year to educate and train American workers and to give them a "leg up in the development of cutting-edge technology."[17]

Where are these countries with the vastly superior school systems? Who are these foreign populations with the genetic advantage in intelligence? The fact is that most of the foreign workers who supposedly are so much better trained than Americans were educated in U.S. universities. For the most part, immigrants do not arrive in the United States with a Ph.D. from another country. Rather, foreign students come here on short-term visas, acquire their graduate degrees, and then manage to get permission to stay.

The biggest source of competition to the brightest of Americans comes from U.S. universities, especially the graduate schools. Foreign students dominate many of America's graduate schools. To many immigration advocates, that is proof of the scarcity of American young adults who are capable or willing to study and work at such a high level. Nathan Rosenberg, an economist at Stanford University, is worried about what would happen to the U.S. economy if Congress cut skilled immigration: "About 60 percent of all students earning advanced degrees in American universities in engineering today are foreign. We have benefitted—and we continue to benefit immensely— from this flow of foreign talent."[18]

Other observers, however, say foreign students dominate in many of the advanced degree programs because they have seen that as a way to get a green card. The United States does not actually need the foreign Ph.D. graduates; it already has an oversupply of people with advanced degrees for the positions that require them. The Ph.D. glut is being widely acknowledged in publications such as *Science,* the *New England Journal of Medicine,* and *Scientists,* as well as by organizations such as the Association of American Medical Colleges. "The existence of a serious Ph.D. problem defies dispute," says Daniel S. Greenberg, editor of *Science & Government Report.* "Mysteriously contending that it can't meet its needs with U.S. citizens, industry insists on keeping the doors open, while the big research universities are always on the lookout for foreign superstars. The net effect is a reduction in jobs available to U.S. citizens."[19] Nowhere is that more true than in computer science, where advanced degrees seldom are necessary or even helpful, says Norman Matloff, the professor of computer science. In G. Pascal Zachary's book *Showstopper!* about Microsoft's development of Windows NT, considered to be one of the most complex software projects, the backgrounds of twenty-one key programmers were given. Only four had advanced degrees in computer science. Most did not have any degree at all in computer science. What mattered in that most innovative of Microsoft's projects, as in most computer efforts, was creativity, flexibility, and an energetic love of programming, Matloff says.

Constantly assumed is that the U.S. economy needs every Ph.D. student—foreign or American—who graduates from a U.S. university and that the number of Americans gaining a science or engineering Ph.D. is insufficient. Both assumptions were seriously challenged by a 1995 survey of 13 science and engineering fields, 210 doctorate-granting institutions, and more than 1,000 educational institutions that employ people with doctorates. The survey revealed a shocking state of affairs for Americans who hold a Ph.D. The report by the Institute for Higher Education and the RAND Corporation discovered that "universities in the United States are producing about 25 percent more doctorates in science and engineering fields than the United States economy can afford."[20]

U.S. immigration policy, as it turns out, is no kinder to Americans who obtain their doctorates than it is to lower-skilled American workers who must compete with the flood of unskilled immigrants. The surplus of the Ph.D. supply over demand is 23 percent in geological sciences, 26 percent for chemical engineering, 31.5 percent for physics, chemistry, and mathematics, 41 percent for electrical engineering, and 44 percent for mechanical engineering. These surpluses raise grave questions about a federal program that annually allows large numbers of additional foreign workers with doctorates to settle in the country and add to the surplus.

Young Americans with lower skills by now are accustomed to hearing that they must never expect to achieve the standard of living of their similarly skilled parents. But skilled immigration is putting the most highly educated young Americans in the same boat. William F. Massy of Stanford, an author of the report on doctorates, was asked what he would advise young people thinking about pursuing a Ph.D. degree in science. "I'd tell them, first of all, that they should not expect, as a matter of course, to be able to replicate the kinds of careers that their mentors have had or that I have had," Massy said. "The job market is just too competitive to have any expectation of that."

Massy described an incredible state of affairs. The public is constantly told that its school systems must do a better job in preparing more students for careers in science and engineering. Yet students can hardly be highly motivated to seek such careers when they hear that salaries and prestige are so depressed because of a huge surplus of qualified professionals—a surplus engorged by the federal government through its immigration policies.

If the United States would stop allowing foreign students—except for those of world-class brilliance—to remain here after graduating, the job market for American scientists and engineers would begin to tighten up. After a while, the market might even begin to need larger numbers of American students to fully supply the professional requirements of the country. It is reasonable to assume that far more Americans would seek advanced degrees in science and engineering if they saw they had a better chance of actually getting jobs that required the degrees. What the brightest Americans see today is that they can earn more money pursuing an education in law or business management, fields not nearly so flooded by immigrants.

If foreign students knew that attending a U.S. graduate school would not give them a ticket to U.S. citizenship, far fewer likely would seek their education here. U.S. universities would not like the drop in enrollment. As it stands now, the dominance of foreign students in graduate schools appears to be a great discouragement to the recruitment of American women and blacks, who are woefully underrepresented in the science and engineering professions, according to David North, a former Labor Department official. In his book on foreign-born scientists and engineers, *Soothing the Establishment,* North noted that in 1993, American universities awarded 2,818 Ph.D.'s in the physical sciences to foreign students, but only 41 to black Americans.[21]

Various American commentators have suggested the possibility that racial assumptions underlie U.S. universities' vigorous recruitment of foreign graduate students and neglect of American minorities. Manuel P. Berriozabal, a University of Texas professor, sees a collective decision to deny high-level opportunities to American Hispanics and blacks, many of whom have been turned away from science and engineering programs because of lack of funds.[22] Graduate school enrollments filled with foreign students and bereft of American minorities show that American racism is alive and well, says Frank Morris, dean of graduate studies at Morgan State University, a historically black institution.

Whatever the motivations, the results of current immigration and university graduate school policies are little different than if the policies were based on the belief that American minorities are genetically incapable of being trained and motivated for the sciences and engineering.

"Universities have a clear preference for foreign professionals versus doing what is necessary to develop our own, especially minorities," Morris complains. "Professors have more bragging rights when they have students from Morocco than from South Central L.A. or the Bronx. . . . Funds for the doctoral level go disproportionately to foreign students. Blacks have to borrow."

In research for his book, North found that the few black Americans gaining a Ph.D. in science or engineering were twice as likely as foreign students to be in debt at the end. The key reason was that foreign students are more likely to get grants that they don't have to repay while U.S. students are more likely to get loans. North learned that "the further you are from U.S. citizenship the more likely you are to secure American funding for your graduate studies in science and engineering. This pattern has prevailed for years." Universities not only pay for the education of many foreign graduate students but also for their passports, visas, and travel to the United States.[23]

Why are university graduate schools so eager to have foreign students? It is not international altruism. North said graduate schools use graduate students as a specialized labor market to help the schools perform research under lucrative government contracts. The large presence of foreign students allows universities to pay stipends that amount to lower pay than low-skilled workers get. That leaves more of the government money to pay for university overhead.

One fascinating example of how U.S. graduate schools have come to place so much emphasis on foreign students was provided by David L. Goodstein, a physics professor and vice provost of the California Institute of Technology. He explains in the *Wilson Quarterly* that science schools this century got used to constant growth and failed to recognize that there would come a time of limits. The first Ph.D. in physics was earned shortly after the Civil War; by 1900, about ten a year were being given. The annual number of degrees was about one hundred in 1930 and one thousand in 1970. At that rate of growth, U.S. universities would be awarding ten thousand Ph.D.'s in physics annually and one million per year by the year 2050. Science professors, of all people, should have been able to figure out that the rate of growth was impossible to sustain. In fact, the limit was reached by 1970; the yearly awards of physics doctorates have remained at about one thousand a year.[24]

One problem has been that the economy does not need even one thousand new Ph.D. physicists a year. Smarter American students long ago began figuring out that most Ph.D. physicists could not look forward to a career as a university research professor. In a sign that the free-market system works, fewer and fewer American students since 1970 have sought to become Ph.D. physicists; their choices should have tightened the market for those who did become physicists.

But the decline of American students created a problem for the universities, which wanted cheap labor to conduct the government research that provides a hefty part of the income for many science schools. The universities have kept their Ph.D. numbers up by increasingly turning to foreign students. So the universities crank out far more scientists than are needed for industry, the U.S. government, and for university professorships. The glut works further to the universities' advantage because there is a large pool of scientists willing to continue to work for low wages in postdoctoral research positions for another three to six years. The universities, therefore, gain an even larger low-paid workforce.

All of that throws an entirely new light on the immigration enthusiasts' insistence that the high percentage of foreign students in Ph.D. programs is proof that we need more skilled immigrants. Goodstein said that when the American public fully understands what has been happening, it is unlikely to continue "pumping vast sums of federal and state money into scientific research in order to further the education and training of foreign scientists." In the meantime, federal immigration policies help skew university graduate programs so that they fill up with foreign students who teach undergraduate Americans, which frees professors to work on their research, and who by their third year are "performing difficult technically demanding work at salaries lower than those received by most starting secretaries," in Goodstein's words.[25]

The machinations of the universities would not have such a great effect on Americans if the federal government did not allow such a high percentage of the foreign students to become immigrants. That has brought great changes in America's professions, according to a study by David Simcox and Leon Bouvier for the Center for Immigration Studies. They found that among physicians in the United States, there are many more who were born in India than who are native-born black Americans. The country has one-third more nurses who were born in the Philippines than who are native-born Hispanics. More professors are foreign-born Chinese and Indians than are native-born blacks. People from China and India, not Americans, are getting the best U.S. jobs in physics and computer science.

"Why is it that we, the most powerful nation in the world and the one possessing the greatest system of higher education, use a continuous stream of highly educated foreign-born professionals to fill our needs?" Bouvier asked after finishing his study. "Could we not instead train our own people, particularly minorities, to meet these needs? . . . Our graduate and professional schools must become more aware of their social responsibilities toward our own people. . . . It is time to begin producing a new generation of native-born professionals."[26]

5. NOT ENOUGH AMERICANS WITH INTERNATIONAL SAVVY TO COMPETE GLOBALLY?

Many leaders of industry have argued that the only way the United States can possibly compete in the global marketplace is by bringing in immigrants from around the world to teach U.S. citizens about how to sell goods and services within their home countries' cultures.

It is a strange argument for a multi-ethnic nation of 265 million, when one considers that our chief competitor in the global economy is an island society with very little cultural or ethnic diversity. Japan has needed no immigration to help it figure out how to become a master of world markets in widely diverse cultures.

There no doubt are occasional short-term needs of U.S. industries which can be filled immediately only by some narrowly skilled foreign individual. Labor economist Vernon Briggs suggests that the United States in those circumstances should allow a company to temporarily import that individual. But the term should only be for as long as it takes to train an American to take over.

One of the major reasons corporations have said they need a high level of skilled immigration is that they need to train foreign nationals at the American home office so these people can then go back and run subsidiaries in their home country. Those type of workers have no need for permanent residency or citizenship status in the United States and should not be given any.

Labor groups are justifiably wary of even the temporary foreign worker programs. The strike at Boeing Company in 1995 was precipitated in part by the practice of Boeing bringing in temporary foreign workers to learn skills from Americans. Those workers then were transferred to their home countries, where they taught people to take over work the American workers had been doing there.

In testimony before the U.S. Senate, Robert Reich recommended that temporary workers be allowed no more than three years—instead of six—in this country, stressing: "Hiring foreign over domestic workers should be the rare exception, not the rule."[27]

6. NOT ENOUGH AMERICANS TO KEEP THE SOCIAL SECURITY SYSTEM SOLVENT?

The belief that immigrants must rescue the Social Security system is widely held. It builds on fears that when the baby boomers reach retirement, the ratio of workers to retirees will be too small to support the boomers. Immigration advocates say foreign workers should be brought in to augment payments into the Social Security Fund.

If the scheme is to be at all successful, however, the time to have immigration is after 2010, when the boomers start retiring. Any immigration now is counterproductive, because today's immigrants will retire alongside the boomers, further burdening Social Security. Based on 1990 Census figures, half of all immigrants currently in the United States will have reached retirement age by 2020. Whatever problem faces the United States in terms of too many old people during the next forty years, recent immigrants will make it worse.

So, for the sake of Social Security, immigration probably should be halted until at least 2010. After that, the government could bring in only young foreign workers and only as the baby boomers' need for the new immigrants' Social Security contributions is demonstrated.

Under the current immigration mix, however, rational policymakers would never send for immigrants to shore up Social Security. The Center for Immigration Studies examined 1992 tax payments and Social Security pay-outs of old age, survivor, and disability benefits. It discovered that while native-born Americans paid $19 billion more into the Social Security fund than they took out, immigrants took out more than they paid in. Immigration brings in workers who disproportionately earn too little to pay enough taxes to pay even their own way for Social Security, let alone to subsidize the baby boomers' retirement.

That would change if the majority of immigrants were skilled. But it is doubtful that America's dependency ratio will change enough for the country to have to look to something as broad as immigration to solve any threat to Social Security.

Concerns about the growing size of the retiree population are too narrow. What matters to a country is the ratio of total dependents to the number of people working. Children are dependents, too. There are about twice as many of them as of old people. Old people pay a lot of their own way with savings and private pensions. Children, on the other hand, are totally dependent on the working class—both their parents and all taxpayers—for schools, health care, food, lodging, clothing, and recreation. Immigrants not only add to the number of retirement-age dependents in the future, but their high fertility rates add disproportionately to today's number of expensive, young dependents—a fact well understood by taxpayers in scores of cities that are having to build additional schools to accommodate immigrant children.

When we look soberly at the ratio of the old and young to the working-age population, we see very little change on the horizon if immigration were drastically cut. While the workers would have a proportionately larger retired population to help support, they would have a proportionately smaller population of children to support. Consider these figures:

- The old and the young constituted 39 percent of U.S. population in 1960.
- In 1970, old and young dependents dropped slightly, to 38 percent of U.S. population.
- Because the big bulge of baby boomers has swelled the ranks of

the working-age population, the old and young have been down around the 35 percent level since 1980.

· It is true that the proportion of older people will grow as the Baby Boom bulge moves into retirement. But if the government slows down its importation of high-fertility foreign workers, the proportion of children could go down enough to compensate for the larger population of the old. Under such circumstances, the young-old proportion of population still would inch upward, but only a few percentile points, before leveling off by the mid-twenty-first century at around 39 percent.

· Once any nation's population has totally stabilized, the old and young dependents will constitute 39 percent of the population. That would put the old and young proportion at exactly the level for the United States when John Kennedy was elected president in 1960. American workers had no special difficulty supporting dependents then and should have none in a future of similar dependency.

To the extent the temporary rise in the ratio of retirees poses stress on the working-age population, most experts believe that the problem can be resolved largely through policies that slightly advance the age of retirement and delay the age at which Social Security payments begin. But that may not be necessary. Within the working-age population are possibilities for considerably higher employment without bringing anybody in from the outside. Only about two-thirds of Americans in the 15–64 group have jobs. Thus, when the unemployed working-age Americans are added to the young and the old, each U.S. worker today effectively supports 1.2 non-workers. Simply enticing 2 or 3 percentile of the non-employed working-age population into employment would compensate for the increase in the dependency ratio when baby boomers retire. "If indeed we need more workers, there are ways of improving the ratio," says Lindsey Grant, former assistant secretary of state for population affairs. He advocates bringing down unemployment, finding ways to enlist discouraged workers, and employing the elderly through programs such as shared jobs.[28]

Using our American ingenuity to employ marginal workers would be a welcome change from the devastating social cost of having millions of able-bodied Americans shunned by the marketplace as unneeded.

* * *

No lobbying for immigration is more powerful than the drive by the nation's corporations for easy access to skilled foreign laborers. They are eager to wrap the continuation of skilled immigration in the message of national competitiveness and well-being. For the most part, it is a message based on narrow self-interest rather than the public's interest. Most of the arguments for why 265 million Americans cannot meet U.S. needs are insulting to Americans in general and display a callous disregard for the country's large pockets of underutilized and undeveloped populations.

The plight of bright young Americans victimized by federal immigration policies was highlighted in January 1996 by a startling report on the country's surplus of physicians. The Institute of Medicine of the National Academy of Science issued the report after examining the problem of many American young people spending immense amounts of time, effort, and money to gain their medical education only to find the market saturated with doctors. The chief cause of the problem, according to the Institute's investigating committee, is the immigration of foreign doctors. Even though the United States has been producing all the physicians it needs from its own residents (17,500 medical school graduates a year), the federal government has been allowing more than 22,000 foreign-trained medical graduates a year to enter U.S. residency or fellowship programs. And it has let about 75 percent of the foreign doctors remain here afterwards. Adding insult to Americans' injury, the federal government has been subsidizing this advanced training for the foreign doctors who are crowding out Americans. "We see no reason deliberately to decrease opportunities for young people of this country," the committee chairman said, and the committee urged the federal government to stop glutting the market with foreign doctors. The committee acknowledged that some hospitals, especially in inner cities, have become dependent on foreign doctors, but said a better solution was to offer incentives to American doctors to take those jobs. [29]

The high-level concern and creative recommendations for American doctors should be extended to all Americans whose professions and trades are being filled with foreigners by the federal government. Many business elites don't have much faith in the American kids next door or in the kids' parents ever being able to perform the nation's heavy-thinking tasks. But as the crisis in the physician market shows, the kids next door may already be available to do the heavy thinking and heavy lifting; they may just be waiting for the federal government to get its massive immigration program out of the way.

8

On the Backs
of Black Americans:
The Past

The plight of black Americans faced with the current flood of foreign workers has moved in the same direction it always has gone during high immigration: down.

After decades of steady improvement, the economic and social conditions for many black citizens have significantly deteriorated since the 1970s. The poverty rate of black Americans is triple the rate of all other Americans. One of every three black citizens now lives in poverty. To distinguish them from the majority of black Americans who have managed to hold on to middle-class status, we might call those in poverty the "failed black third."

To the National Academy of Sciences, the "failed black third" is a challenge to the conscience of the nation. "Americans face an unfinished agenda," it stated in 1989 after an expansive study. "Many black Americans remain separated from the mainstream of national life under conditions of great inequality. The American dilemma has not been resolved."

To Leroy Clark, a lawyer with Martin Luther King, Jr.'s, crusade throughout the 1960s, Americans should deal with the "failed black third" for very practical reasons. All of us live more precarious lives because of that concentration of poverty, he says. "From the army of hungry, unemployed black teenagers, come the muggers, drug addicts and gang members who make our cities dangerous."

White Americans realize how bad life is for poor black Americans, according to a report in *American Sociological Review*. But most whites believe that blacks who fail do so because they don't work hard and are unable to delay gratification. The conservative black economist Walter Williams of George Mason University lays the blame largely on bad behavior: "If people would wait until they're married to have children and work when they have children, there would not be a poverty problem."[1]

Even if Williams is substantially correct, that raises a number of questions about the role of government policies that contribute to bad choices, behavior, and attitudes. What if federal policies make it difficult to find jobs—especially ones that pay a family wage and make conventional family life seem possible? What if the federal immigration program has sapped economic hope and created social turmoil by bringing millions of foreign citizens to compete with the "failed black third" in their schools, in their workplaces, and in their neighborhoods?

Perhaps the "failed black third" is really the "sabotaged black third." While the government was purporting to help that segment of the population with myriad social programs, its immigration policies were undermining the benefits. That isn't to say that immigration created the social and economic pathologies of the black underclass. But it may have played a crucial role in stopping black progress in the 1970s and in slowly reversing the progress ever since.

It is easy to believe that is the case because it has happened before—several times.

To review the black side of our nation's immigration tradition is to observe African Americans periodically trying to climb the mainstream economic ladder, only to be shoved aside each time. It is to see one immigrant wave after another climb onto and up that ladder while planting their feet on the backs of black Americans.

Before the Civil War, slaves who gained their freedom and moved north suffered constant setbacks as immigrants pushed them aside. After the Civil War ended, black Americans had barely begun to find niches in industries and trades when the Great Wave of immigration drove them backward. Thus, few black people were able to move into the middle class until after mass immigration ended in 1924. During the tight-labor, low-immigration era of 1940 to 1970, the middle class grew from 22 percent of black Americans to 71 percent! By 1970, though, mass immigration once again was on the upswing. Unfortunately, the march toward equality with whites stalled after that, and the black middle class has been shrinking since.

The connections between high immigration and setbacks for black Americans are far too numerous and detailed to be dismissed as mere coincidence.

DISPLACEMENT:
1820S THROUGH 1850S

When Frederick Douglass escaped from slavery in 1838, he soon discovered that recently arrived immigrants were nearly as tenacious as slavemasters and bounty hunters in trying to keep a black man from freely competing in the labor markets of the North.

The rising tide of European immigrants who began to arrive in the 1820s found a considerable population of skilled free black Americans in the North. Some of the black workers were from families who had been free since the mid-1600s after the first Africans in Virginia and Maryland had worked out their terms of indentured servanthood. Many others had come as slaves and bought their freedom or been released by conscience-stricken owners, especially through wills upon their deaths. And others like Douglass simply had escaped. This modest army of black artisans and domestic workers had managed to stake a tenuous claim on the mainstream economy during the decades of relatively low immigration. But with the rapid increases of immigration in the 1820s and 1830s, free black Americans began to lose ground. Where most of New York City's domestic servant jobs had been filled by free black workers, the majority eventually were occupied by Irish immigrants. And the reason for the shift was not that black workers had moved to higher-skilled and higher-paid jobs. W.E.B. Du Bois later would note that the new immigrants proceeded methodically to drive northern black workers from their jobs of all kinds and to replace them. Violence was not an uncommon instrument.

For eight days in July 1834, for example, the immigrants' antagonism toward free black Americans in New York City boiled over into a full-scale riot, with attacks on black homes and churches. Immigrants feared that the free black Americans would undercut their chances for jobs and wage increases. In fact, it was the free black Americans who were being undercut by the immigrants, as the historian Adrian Cook has pointed out: "Employers preferred to hire immigrants, especially

Germans, who would work long hours for low pay."[2]

Frederick Douglass witnessed the job competition firsthand, even before his escape from slavery. As a teenager he had been transferred by his rural slavemaster to a relative in Baltimore, where he was hired out to work among the immigrant shipbuilders on Fell's Point. He learned the caulking trade at a shipyard that had a number of free black carpenters. The European-American workers at his Baltimore shipyard got rid of the free black workers by taking advantage of a tight deadline their employer was facing in building two large man-of-war brigs for the Mexican government. The white carpenters staged a walk-out, saying they would work no more unless the free black carpenters were fired, which they were. Conditions also grew more strained for the slaves on site, with the whites talking about the "niggers taking the country." Eventually, four of the men attacked Douglass with bricks, sticks, and handspikes, while some fifty others watched and shouted, "Kill the damned nigger! Kill him! kill him!"

Douglass later became a leading orator and author of the abolition movement—as well as an ardent supporter of women's suffrage. A confidant of President Lincoln and holder of several distinguished federal offices, Douglass remained until his death in 1895 an uncompromising proponent of equal economic opportunities for black Americans. He towered over all other Americans in his advocacy of a colorblind, unified national society, and contended regularly with the pressures from immigration to drive black Americans out of the mainstream. Like many other black leaders over the last two centuries, Douglass saw mass immigration as a destructive tool in blocking African Americans from full economic and political freedom.

Douglass escaped to New York in 1838, then moved to Massachusetts. But as immigration continued to increase, the conditions for free black Americans in the North grew worse and slavery in the South was administered more harshly. Douglass would write: "The old employments by which we have heretofore gained our livelihood are gradually, and it may be inevitably, passing into other hands. Every hour sees the black man elbowed out of employment by some newly arrived immigrant whose hunger and whose color are thought to give him a better title to the place."[3]

Rising immigration from the 1820s to the Civil War drove down wages for free black Americans and immigrants alike. Jeffrey Williamson and Peter Lindert's macroeconomic history shows that between 1816 and 1856, the American Northeast was transformed from the "Jeffersonian ideal" to a society more typical of developing economies with marked income inequality and very low wages for laborers.

As badly as new immigrants often were treated by established Americans, even worse treatment was meted out to black Americans by the immigrants. Organizing themselves into trade unions, immigrant laborers helped set the terms of hiring at many urban workplaces. Not only would they not allow black workers into their unions, but they usually would refuse to work alongside them if they were hired. Many firms decided not to hire black workers, or to fire the ones already on the site, because of that refusal on the part of the more numerous immigrant workers.

By the 1850s, for example, free black workers had been driven out of most jobs on the New York City waterfront by the Irish immigrants who had gained control over the trades. Denied work through organized labor channels, black workers increasingly had to resort to gaining jobs by serving as strikebreakers—an unsavory role they had to endure for another century, and one that engendered further hatred from the immigrant workers. Blacks also were restricted in their social life. A gang culture was much in control, with each immigrant group fighting for its own culture, and to determine who could live near them, sell in their neighborhoods, and socialize in their pubs.

It is not difficult to see the parallels with the cities of the 1990s.

INTIMIDATION: 1863

Divisions in the North were especially pronounced during the Civil War. On the abolitionist side were the free black Americans and old established Protestants who joined as Republicans in backing Lincoln's war.

On the pro-slavery side in the North were the Democrats with their solid support from Catholic immigrants. From the strength of the Democratic appeal in northern immigrant cities, suggests the historian Eric Foner, one could question how a society like the North, in which racial hatred ran so deep, could secure justice for the emancipated slaves. And the popularity of the Democrats' pro-slavery stance helps explain how the North, after winning the war, so quickly abandoned the southern blacks.

Surely, the most dramatic manifestation of those northern divisions came on 13–17 July 1863 when New York City immigrants staged a riot so violent and such a threat to the city's continued loyalty to the

Union that five Union Army regiments were ordered directly from the Gettysburg battlefield to suppress it. The riot ostensibly was a protest against a new military draft that appeared to allow the immigrants no way to get out of it. But the main victims of the rioting immigrants were black citizens, more than a hundred of whom were killed, with many more wounded and burned out of their homes.

The episode provides an example of how explosive it can be to continue to pour new immigrants into an already volatile labor market. The historian Iver Bernstein points out that job fears were at the heart of the incendiary social conditions of the time. First, New York already was oversupplied with unskilled foreign workers. Second, the federal government was promoting the importation of still more during the war. "Here it was easy for any group, no matter how well established, to feel threatened by the daily flood of new arrivals," Bernstein says.[4] In the midst of that uncertainty, earlier immigrants were trying to protect their wages and jobs through assertive union activity. Free black workers were seen as a threat to union success because, after being barred by the immigrants from the unions, they made themselves available as strikebreakers. Further, the shipowners had decided just months before the July riot that they would use free black workers to break the Irish workers' strike.

In July, the rioting bands of immigrants—mostly Irish—seemed to focus on the free black population all of their anger at the anti-slavery movement, at the war, at the military draft, and at Protestant Republican efforts to reform the immigrants' use of alcohol, brothels, and so on. The immigrants began grabbing black citizens at random. Crowds surrounded them as if attending an impromptu theater where each member of the gang might perform an atrocity such as jumping on the black person, smashing him with a cobblestone, or plunging a knife into his chest.

Boys ran through the streets throwing stones through windows to identify where black residents lived. Rioting immigrants would pull the black residents from their homes, sometimes beating them and then letting them go, other times not stopping until they were dead. They cut off toes, they burned, they drowned, they lynched, they sexually mutilated, and they did their own version of tarring and feathering. Perhaps the most ghastly of acts occurred when rioters pulled a crippled black coachman named Abraham Franklin and his sister from their rooms. They "roughed up" the sister and dragged Franklin through the streets, finally lynching him on a lamppost. The military dispersed the crowd and cut the body down. But the immigrants, to cheers from the crowd, raised Franklin's corpse up the lamppost again as soon as the soldiers left. When the crowd later pulled the body down, Patrick Butler—a sixteen-year-old Irish immigrant—grabbed the corpse by the genitals and dragged it through the streets to the applause of the crowds.

As is common in outbreaks of anarchy, a minority of citizens were responsible. Many Democrats and immigrants joined Republicans in heroic efforts at keeping the carnage from being worse, although others tended to take the tone of the wife of Democratic Judge Charles Patrick Daly. She indicated great sorrow and outrage over what was done to the black citizens. But she also hoped the episode would "give the Negroes a lesson, for since the war commenced, they have been so insolent as to be unbearable. I cannot endure free blacks. They are immoral with all their piety."[5]

For the moment, it was the Republicans—the champions of the war for emancipation—on whom black Americans depended for protection and support. But although nearly all Republicans were anti-slavery, those who were also anti-immigration were in the process of losing the battle in their party. The ascendency of a pro-immigration ideology in the Republican Party—to serve the party's growing fixation on industrial growth—soon would diminish black Americans' hope for full economic opportunity for at least another century.

CLOSED GOLDEN DOOR:
1865–86

The end of the Civil War opened a golden door of opportunity to black Americans, both those just freed from the chains of slavery and those who long had been free.

In an astounding burst of laws, constitutional amendments, and programs, the federal government sought to ensure full political, economic, and social rights to all Americans. But black Americans, especially those leaving their slavemasters, needed more than rights; they needed concrete means to make a living. Most of them had been farmworkers. Access to cheap or free land, such as that which had helped so many of their white countrymen get their start, would have been a wonderful assistance. So would have jobs that provided opportunity for advancement.

By happy circumstance, both new land and good jobs became available soon after the Civil War:

1. *Land.* Frontier settlement had barely crossed the Mississippi River at that time. Millions of acres of fertile and mineral-rich land lay unsettled to the West. The railroads were looking for masses of people to settle tracts of land along their lines.
2. *Jobs.* Businessmen throughout the country, but especially in the North, needed a new supply of workers for rapidly expanding industries.

If more black Americans had gotten in on the ground floor of both of those developments, they and their descendants would have had remarkably different lives. And all Americans today likely would be living in a much more harmonious and healthy society.

But it wasn't to be. Mass immigration helped slam the golden door shut on equality of opportunity for black Americans after the Civil War. The government allowed the railroads to offer the free land to European immigrants, barring all but a few black natives from settlement. And northern industrialists were allowed to fill their additional jobs with European immigrants.

High immigration solved an immense problem for the defeated southern landed aristocracy. The restoration of the plantation system depended on holding on to the ex-slaves. Eric Foner, the specialist on Reconstruction, says a major priority for both white southerners and northerners was to subdue former slaves into a sedentary agricultural work style in the South. During a brief window of opportunity after the war, many freed slaves made their way to the North and grabbed jobs that they held for years to come. But because of increasingly high immigration, most freed slaves did not get any of the new jobs up north or any of the new land out west.

The unions were an essential force in keeping the ex-slaves out of the North. Nearly all of the unions—dominated by immigrants— barred blacks from membership, Foner says.[6] After the Civil war, for example, the bricklayers' union in Washington, D.C., forbade their men to work alongside blacks. The rule was deemed so important that when four white union men were discovered on the same government project with some black workers, the union unanimously voted to expel them. Frederick Douglass's family was victimized by the unions. Although he achieved great success as an author and journalist, as the U.S. Marshal for the District of Columbia and as the U.S. Minister to Haiti, his four children were lucky to get jobs as clerks and printers. One of the printers, Lewis Douglass, was barred from the printers union and then vilified as a scab for later taking a job at below union wages for the U.S. GovernmentPrinting Office. White printers walked off the job in protest. Frederick Douglass said the union's treatment was like cutting off a man's ears and then claiming that this maiming now gave the right to pluck out his eyes.

High European immigration to the North between 1865 and 1875 not only blocked the jobs to which the ex-slaves might have escaped but it helped shift the northern political balance against Reconstruction. It was the loss of support for Reconstruction in the North that led to the federal abandonment of attempts to force the South to allow full legal rights of citizenship to the ex-slaves. Each year, the Republican Party's power in the North eroded as hundreds of thousands of immigrants entered the country, with most throwing their political lot in with the Democratic Party and its strong opposition to Reconstruction.

In referring to immigrants' participation in the virtual re-enslaving of black Americans, it is necessary to recall that the primary responsibility for the American institution of slavery lay with many of the English Protestants who settled the southern colonies. And it was English Protestants and Deists who were dominant among the founding fathers who enshrined slavery in the Constitution. Nonetheless, the core northern Republican support for the ex-slaves and Reconstruction in the 1870s came from the descendants of the English Protestant settlers. And the European immigrants then streaming into the major cities of the North were much more likely to adopt the anti-black stance of the Democrats.

The intense hostility of the Irish immigrants toward black Americans drew the notice of many writers of the time. Frederick Douglass marveled that a people who could be so warm-hearted and generous back on "their own green island" could so instantly hate and despise black Americans once on U.S. soil. A number of philanthropic merchants in New York City tried after the war to open the job market up to black workers; but the power of the immigrant organizations was too strong. Many cities had similar experiences as the burgeoning immigrant populations were able to form political machines and take control in city governments. Michael Lind has pointed out that the power often was enhanced because the immigrant-controlled political machines were overlaid with the underworld that had come from the old country with the immigrants.[7] Especially in New York City— where an alliance of Irish immigrants and southern Democrats had created the Tammany machine—a strain of white supremacy ran through the new power structure. Before the war, one of the leaders assured the southern states: "If ever a conflict arises between races, the people of the city of New York will stand by their brethren, the white race. We will never suffer you to be trampled upon by those of another blood."[8] The Union's victory in the Civil War and the string of federally legislated civil rights acts for blacks did not stop the power structure's racist actions. Ena L. Farley, in *The Underside of Reconstruction New York,* notes that Tammany minions behaved like the Ku Klux Klan in a reign of terror to intimidate black citizens from voting.

Black residents not only lost their jobs to the new immigrants, according to Farley, "but the immigrants took up residence in city wards where their numerical majority made the black population politically impotent." Across the North in precincts with heavy immigrant settlement, votes on issues and candidates turned against the interests of both northern and southern black Americans. The hopes of ex-slaves in the South were dashed in northern cities that not only were losing interest in equal rights in the South but were creating stronger anti-black systems in the North. New York State, Farley says, "emerged from the postwar deliberations, not with an acceptance of equality for African Americans, but with a definition of and acceptance of the idea of segregation."[9] It is not surprising then that black residents of New York City opposed states' rights and showed a preference for federal protection like that given to southern blacks under Reconstruction.

Cinching the continued economic dependency of black Americans was the presidential political deal in 1877 to allow Republican Rutherford Hayes to become president after the razor-thin results of the election threw it into the hands of a special commission. After the backroom agreement, anti-black Democrats agreed not to block Hayes's election and Hayes agreed to recognize the Democrats' resumption of power in the southern states. Federal troops were withdrawn from the South, Reconstruction ended, and states' rights were reestablished as the dominant principle of government. Northern interests turned from the egalitarian goals of Reconstruction to industrial development. Page Smith says the new states' rights doctrine worked to the disadvantage of common citizens in all regions: "The same doctrine that allowed southern whites to thrust southern blacks back into a slavery in all but name gave free rein to the most rapacious instincts of the new class of capitalists."[10] The northern industries could fill their jobs with new, inexpensive European immigrants, and any efforts to curb the Robber Barons were denounced as infringing on states' rights.

As in many other times, the means of subjugation of black Americans also hurt masses of white Americans. The South was full of impoverished whites who were landless. European immigration in the North blocked job opportunities for southerners who were white, as well as for those who were black. With large pools of white and black cheap labor trapped in the South, employers there had no reason to advance in technology, and the whole southern economy was left in a perpetual state of backwardness, says Gavin Wright in his authoritative life's work, *Old South, New South: Revolutions in the Southern Economy Since the Civil War*. Wright found that unskilled whites were paid just about the same as unskilled blacks in the postwar South: "Owners were able to get white labor at a black wage."[11] The South looked like a conquered, battered subregion for decades, but its loss in the Civil War may not have required that. Rather, the nation's shift to higher importation of foreign workers to the North and West kept the South a low-wage region in a high-wage country, a status it retained until after mass immigration was shut off for several decades after 1924.

Having allowed immigration policies to directly and indirectly lock most black Americans out of advancement, many of the Republicans—who formerly were abolitionists—grew impatient with the black Americans for their lack of progress. They suggested that maybe the government had done as much as was possible to help them. The *Nation* magazine on 1 August 1867 reflected the sentiment of the Republican reformers, saying: "The removal of white prejudice against the negro depends almost entirely on the negro himself." Because blacks were so lacking in the "ordinary claims to social respectability," the magazine reasoned, legislation could not be expected to counteract the natural inadequacies of the race. It was a striking turnaround from the Republican Party's lofty praise of black Americans just a few years earlier during the New York City draft riots; then, the party had lauded black citizens for their positive character, their resourcefulness, and the fact that they seldom asked for charity.

In a cold, economic sense, the steady flow of foreign workers had left the United States—other than southern plantation owners—with little need of the labor of its black citizens. Without economic value, it was easier for black Americans to be neglected by their former champions, the northern Republicans, who no longer fought as hard against the Democrats' efforts to weaken civil rights laws and to pull back on their enforcement.

The dismantling of Reconstruction sealed the fate of most black Americans to live under another half century of extreme economic exploitation, vigilante lynching, and other terrors, and with a status under the law barely above their former conditions of slavery. Immigration was one—although certainly not the only one—of the phenomena that helped kill Reconstruction.

It is difficult to overstate the long-term effect of new immigrants pushing black Americans aside in gaining jobs in new industries after the Civil War. Once the immigrants were in, they generated successive waves of immigrants whom they helped gain employment in the same industries. Gavin Wright says the pattern was reinforced by employers, who left much of the recruitment of new workers to the immigrant networks rather than expending money and energy into recruiting available native-born workers—especially black and white southerners.[12]

Only when World War I cut off the supply of immigrant workers did northern employers have to recruit black workers and learn how to integrate them into their workforce, says the economist Warren C. Whatley, of the University of Michigan. The black workers, particularly from the South, were at an obvious disadvantage. It had been a half century since the end of the Civil War. During all of that time, the waves of European immigrants had been learning the skills of working in the industries through family and ethnic connections. Black workers, though, had been left behind in the technological age. The new Irish and German and other immigrants could not boast a better capacity for industrial tasks than blacks, but for a half century they got the jobs and the experience. If firms during World War I were struck by the black workers' awkwardness with the new jobs, they were likely to attribute that to an inferior group characteristic rather than to the fact that they had been kept out of industry for several decades. Whatley says models of statistical discrimination show that such "imperfect beginnings can have lasting consequences, for even if employers subsequently learn the true abilities of these workers, a rational employer may still discriminate against them in promotion so that their true ability is not revealed to other employers."[13] Since members of groups discriminated against in such ways receive less reward for their job skills, they have less incentive to invest in their own development, thus creating a vicious cycle. Black Americans' decades-late start and the resulting ripples of discrimination from their "imperfect beginnings" hampered their rise inside corporations for years, and doubtless are factors that are behind some of the drags on upward mobility even in the 1990s.

By looking at what happened to black employment in the North when immigration was cut off during World War I, we can gain a glimpse of what might have happened in the 1870s and 1880s had there not been high immigration. In the 1915–19 period of low immigration, between 400,000 and 500,000 black southerners migrated to the industrial belt stretching from New York to Chicago. In Cincinnati, for example, 33 percent of firms had at least one black worker in 1915. By the end of 1918, the percentage was 50. All told, the black share of industrial employment doubled in Cincinnati, as it did in most of that belt of cities; in Detroit, the increase was tenfold. One cannot help but wonder how different American history would be had that black migration occurred fifty years earlier.

The 1865–75 surge in immigration undercut Reconstruction, and the much larger Great Wave that began in 1880 effectively stopped all but a few black Americans from getting in on the industrial ground floor. In 1886, the nation celebrated its commitment to freedom with the inauguration of the Statue of Liberty. That year and nearly every year for almost three more decades, ship after ship sailed past the statue, laden with immigrants whose arrival coincided with the substantial rollback in economic gains many black Americans had struggled to achieve since the Civil War.

That same year, a weary Frederick Douglass, no longer trusting in America's altruism, appealed to the nation's own self-interest in domestic tranquility. The aging author-orator thundered: "The American people have this lesson to learn: That where justice is denied, where poverty is enforced, where ignorance prevails, and where any one class is made to feel that society is an organized conspiracy to oppress, rob and degrade them, neither persons nor property will be safe."

While Lady Liberty's torch of freedom captured the attention of most sightseers and new immigrants, it was her feet that held the most symbolism for America's increasingly forgotten black citizens. Around the feet, Frédéric-Auguste Bartholdi had sculpted the broken chains of slavery. There is no indication that any of the millions of immigrants arriving after 1886 had any thought of helping to re-enslave black Americans; they simply were taking advantage of an invitation from predominantly English-descent industrialists to improve their own economic circumstances. But as mass immigration economically marginalized America's black population, the freed slaves and their descendants felt the country's economic structure and laws steadily reattach most of the old shackles, not to be loosened again—and then only briefly—until World War I, when flotillas of immigrant ships stopped sailing past the statue.

OVERWHELMED:
1895–1924

Frederick Douglass died in Washington, D.C., on 20 February 1895. He knew that many black Americans at the time were not much better off than they had been in slavery. In 1900, for example, 87 percent of all blacks still were farmworkers or household servants in the South.

Words Douglass had written much earlier still stood at his death: "It is true that we are no longer slaves, but it is equally true that we are not yet quite free. We have been turned out of the house of bondage, but we have not yet been fully admitted to the glorious temple of American liberty. We are still in a transition state and the future is shrouded in doubt and danger."

The autumn after Douglass died, Booker T. Washington delivered an impassioned address to a large gathering of industrialists, beseeching them to stop looking to immigration to man their factories. It was a last-ditch effort to give black workers a chance at getting off the plantations and onto the ground floor of industrial prosperity.

The great educator from Tuskegee, Alabama, used the story of a ship that had been lost at sea and had finally sighted another vessel. When the distressed ship signaled that its crew was dying of thirst, the other vessel signaled back, "Cast down your bucket where you are," a salty-sounding suggestion that made little sense. The exchange was repeated three times before the captain at last lowered his bucket and brought up fresh water, for he was in the 200-mile-wide mouth of the Amazon River.

Washington then brilliantly showed the illogic of industries crossing oceans to recruit millions of workers in foreign lands when they were surrounded by vast pools of the very thing they were seeking. "To those of the white race who look to the incoming of those of foreign birth and strange tongue and habits . . . ," Washington cried to the industrialists, "cast down your bucket where you are. Cast it down among the eight millions of Negroes whose habits you know. . . ." He reminded them that black workers had not engaged in the strikes and labor wars so common to the immigrant workers. He asked them to cast down their buckets and hire blacks who "shall stand by you with a devotion that no foreigner can approach, ready to lay down our lives, if need be, in defense of yours, interlacing our industrial, commercial, civil, and religious life with yours in a way that shall make the interests of both races one."

What captured white Americans' attention—and what is most remembered today—was the other part of Washington's speech that essentially waved aside issues such as racial integration and stressed instead the importance of teaching manual skills to the black masses and
of opening jobs to them. The speech turned Washington into America's chief black leader and powerbroker for the next twenty years.
Newspapers in the North and South reprinted the address. President
Cleveland wrote to express his enthusiasm for the speech. In later years
and to this day, many black Americans criticize Washington as an
Uncle Tom because he conceded so many issues of integration and
seemed to accept second-class citizenship. Page Smith points out,
however, that Washington had no alternative. He knew integration
was a lost cause at least for his generation, and was shrewd enough to
press for what was possible: access to better jobs and improved relations with whites by proving black Americans' importance to the overall economy.[14]

If Washington had been successful in persuading white leaders to
stop or even moderate the Great Wave of immigration, that might
have done far more to improve the overall status of freed slaves and
their descendants than any direct integration efforts. In Washington's
words: "No race that has anything to contribute to the markets of the
world is long in any degree ostracized." But it was not to be. A few
philanthropic whites would fund the Tuskegee Institute, and Booker
T. Washington could train any number of black Americans, but the
nation's immigration policy would keep most of the better jobs out of
reach.

The year after Washington's speech, the Supreme Court established the doctrine of segregation for the next half century by declaring
that the establishment of separate black and white facilities did not
violate the Fourteenth Amendment.

In 1897, Congress almost gave Booker T. Washington the curtailment of immigration he had sought. It voted to stop the bulk of the
foreign labor flow. But President Cleveland's enthusiasm for Washington's "cast down your bucket" speech didn't extend to showing any
sympathy for Washington's key concerns. Cleveland vetoed the immi-
gration-restriction bill, ensuring that some 14 million more Europeans
would move into the job line ahead of 8 million black Americans
before World War I cut off immigration temporarily.

The shackles tightened. In 1898, the Supreme Court found that a
Mississippi plan to take the vote from black citizens was not unconsti-
tutional. With most of their rights stripped away, black Americans suf-

fered even more intensely from the wave of foreign workers than they had earlier. Black losses in the North were exemplified by Steelton, Pennsylvania. Steel production had begun there in 1866. Freed slaves from Virginia and Maryland used their newly won freedom of movement to apply for jobs. During that brief period of industrial opportunity after the Civil War, many northern free black workers and southern freed slaves grabbed jobs—especially in towns distant from the immigrant port cities—that they still had not relinquished by the time of Washington's speech. John E. Bodnar writes that a flourishing black community in the 1890s in Steelton had three churches, its own newspaper, and several blacks in the police force, and would soon have a member on the town council. A significant percentage of black workers had moved up the job ladder at the steel mill, as well.

But within months of Washington's speech in 1895, a large wave of Italians, Serbs, Croats, Slovenes, and Bulgarians broke over Steelton, and this was followed by one wave after another until World War I. Bodnar found that the immigration had a "devastating impact upon the town's black working force." Black workers stopped progressing up the job ladder, they lost semi-skilled occupations to the Slavs and Italians, and many were forced to leave town in search of work. The black population declined.[15]

Job displacement was occurring in all cities. In 1870, of all black men in Cleveland, 32 percent had skilled jobs; by 1910, only 11 percent were in skilled trades. "It did not take Jim Crow laws to drive blacks out of such jobs in the North, which could draw on a huge pool of immigrant labor flowing into the cities," says Lawrence Fuchs of Brandeis University.[16]

History has repeated itself at the end of the twentieth century, as a new wave of immigration has driven black Americans out of the North once again. Just as new civil rights laws of the 1960s seemed to be opening great new opportunities for black people, the high flow of foreign workers into the highest-wage cities in the North and West tended to block many black Americans from taking advantage of those new opportunities. For a half century under low immigration, the blackpopulation had been shifting from low-wage southern centers to the North and West. But then in the 1970s, northern and western black residents began moving back to the South. Demographer William Frey of the University of Michigan's Population Studies Center discovered in the early 1990s that tens of thousands of native-born Americans were being pushed out of centers of upward mobility by immigrants. Black and white Americans with low skills were the most likely to leave the high-wage centers and to move to states with lower wages.[17]

If members of Congress and successive presidents since 1965 had been more familiar with the black side of our immigration tradition, they might not have been so apathetic about the ever-increasing flow of foreign workers. Anybody concerned about fulfilling the spirit of the civil rights era would have been given pause by a look back a century ago at what happened in interior industrial centers such as Pittsburgh, McKeesport, Wilkes-Barre, and Johnstown in Pennsylvania; Lorain in Ohio; and Buffalo in New York. In tight-labor conditions immediately after the Civil War, those cities had needed the migration of black labor. They witnessed black growth that was modest in numbers but almost explosive in terms of percentages. With the biggest surge of immigration after 1899, however, black growth in those cities essentially stopped or populations actually declined.

High immigration to the nation's cities had assured that the black worker "would have to start his economic climb over again—from the bottom," Bodnar says.[18]

In hindsight, it is easy to regard the immigration policies during Reconstruction and the Gilded Age a century ago as an incredible, national racist conspiracy against the freed slaves and their descendants. That is painting with too broad a brush, however. The majority of white citizens never asked for the surges in immigration and never approved of them when they occurred. As we saw in Chapter 2, the white majority repeatedly elected members of Congress who overwhelmingly tried to stop the Great Wave. But the political power of the immigrant-controlled cities and the cheap-labor industrialists was just enough to keep the foreign labor supply flowing.

* * *

The captains of industry had great assistance from the unions in setting up a system that denied full economic freedom to black Americans.

Immigrant leaders used the further influx of foreign workers to increase their domination of unions. The ethnic-immigrant control of unions effectively blocked black Americans from reasonable access to the better-paid union jobs until well after the passage of the Civil Rights Acts of 1964 and 1965, according to Herbert Hill.[19]

Roy Wilkins, head of the National Association for the Advancement of Colored People (NAACP), brought the immigrant union problem to the fore during the battle to pass the civil rights laws in the 1960s. While the unions tended to support laws precluding businesses from discriminating against blacks, most unions successfully had fought legal requirements that they also have non-discriminatory practices. As in pre–Civil War New York, about the only way many businesses could hire black people for skilled jobs in any numbers was as strikebreakers and scab labor. The NAACP's aggressive challenge to the unions almost split the coalition that eventually was successful in pushing through the 1960s civil rights laws, but Wilkins made clear that black Americans no longer would be junior partners with liberal whites whose institutions often were in conflict with the best interests of the black community.

Wilkins denounced the discriminatory practices throughout AFL-CIO unions, but heaped special condemnation on the International Ladies Garment Workers Union (ILGWU). The union began in 1900, heavily influenced by the socialist traditions of the Russian and Polish Jews who were flooding New York City at the time. Like other immigrant nationalities before them, they quickly organized in ways that shut out black workers. Hill's study concluded that the garment union's six-decade discrimination against black Americans resulted not from a conscious racist ideology but from intense ethnic protectiveness that tried to ensure all benefits and power for immigrant members. After Congress greatly reduced immigration in 1924, for example, the garment unions found they needed black workers; but they still kept them out of the more skilled, better-paying trades, and barred them from union leadership through a series of restrictive procedures finally highlighted in the 1960s by the New York State Commission for Human Rights and the U.S. House Committee on Education and Labor.

There have always been those who looked at the poor economic condition of a disproportionately large segment of black Americans and said it proves the inferiority of their innate intelligence or their culture or their character; they point out that one immigrant group after another has arrived in the United States poor or destitute and has overcome hostile barriers, moving solidly into the middle class. Blaming slavery for current black problems is said to be a cop-out; after all, the Civil War ended nearly 150 years ago. What the critics of black Americans fail to realize is that black workers from the Civil War of the 1860s to the Civil Rights Acts of the 1960s, and even to the present, have been systematically blocked from the economic base that made possible the celebrated achievements of immigrant communities. And often, it has been the immigrants themselves who blocked the black Americans.[20]

The filling of the trade unions with European immigrants decades ago, and the barring of most black workers from membership, continues to have repercussions throughout the U.S. economy. Although they make up about 12 percent of the U.S. population, for example, black Americans contribute less than 5 percent of the nation's 1.28 million carpenters.

In many ways, the situation for black Americans is getting worse, according to the *Chicago Tribune*. Chicago's population is nearly 40 percent black, but in September 1994 only about 11 percent of the skilled trades hours on the huge new main post office were worked by black tradesmen. While black workers have yet to break the stranglehold of earlier waves of European immigrants on Chicago's trade unions, they are losing ground as new immigrants move in ahead of them. There has been a huge surge in Latin American immigration into the Chicago region. Black residents still outnumber Latinos by nearly 2 to 1 in the population, but there now are just as many Latino as black painters in the region. And Latinos outnumber black carpenters by a 3 to 2 margin.[21]

It seems that little has changed from a hundred years ago. The unions and employers continue to prefer new immigrants over the descendants of slavery. In carpentry, the largest skilled trade, Latinos have been allowed entrance in almost exactly the same proportion as their presence in the Chicago population—20 percent. But nearly 150 years after the Civil War, black workers aren't even close to a fair representation—about 15 percent of carpenters and 40 percent of the population.

A review of the record suggests that black Americans after the Civil War "did everything they possibly could to neutralize racism and advance their economic fortunes," Ena Farley concludes. "They failed, not because of any fault in their own strategies, but because the racial barriers set up by the dominant group were too unyielding."[22] One of the most important tools in building barriers black Americans could not surmount was the federal policy of mass immigration.

From Frederick Douglass to Booker T. Washington to W. E. B. Du Bois to hundreds of other leaders, African Americans did not suffer the insults of immigration silently. Until the Great Wave was stopped in 1924, African-American newspapers, preachers, politicians, and scholars throughout the country vehemently denounced the importation of European, Mexican, Chinese, and Japanese workers. The descendants of slavery learned from what they saw and experienced in the labor marketplace, and turned it into a militant anthem of insistence that the government stop using immigration to displace black Americans from their jobs, housing, health care, and other services.

It is not unusual in the 1990s to hear white commentators give impassioned pleas to keep the immigration gates opened wide, because to do less would dishonor their parents or grandparents who got into the United States through similarly open gates.

But they never seem to imagine the dishonor and deep historical insult their advocacy brings to today's black Americans. The ancestors of the "failed black third" repeatedly were displaced, intimidated, and overwhelmed by the European-immigrant ancestors of many of those who advocate today for a level of immigration that continues to disadvantage African Americans.

The white appeals to continue immigration on the basis of tradition are like saying to black Americans, "Because our ancestors delayed your ancestors' economic development, it is only right to bring in more immigrants today to delay *your* progress." Or, to paraphrase Frederick Douglass's expression of cruel irony, it is like saying, "Because our ancestors cut off your ancestors' ears, we now have the right to pluck out your eyes."

9

On the Backs
of Black Americans:
The Present

The log cabin where Frederick Douglass was born is gone—as is the plantation house. But many of the descendants of the slaves who once worked the region's fertile soil remain in the area. And so does an economic system that sometimes seems stacked against a black worker ever getting ahead.

"The economic situation isn't too good for blacks around here," says a white neighbor across the road from the former plantation. He notes that local black residents now face the additional challenge of job competition from immigrants. What has happened to black workers near Douglass's birthplace is symptomatic of the negative effects of recent immigration on lower-skilled black Americans throughout the country.

At the corner of the plantation, two black residents fishing from the bank of Tuckahoe Creek are well acquainted with the local job market and the increasing influence of foreign workers. One man is a cook. The other, Robert, works at a poultry-processing plant. After ten years there, he earns a wage that keeps him just a step ahead of poverty. "I think the company must get something out of bringing in immigrants," Robert says. "They put a lot of effort in recruiting."

As it turns out, the road from where Douglass lived in slavery runs directly to one of America's fastest-growing low-wage industries. Just two miles down the blacktop to the west is Cordova, Maryland—a small town with a big poultry-processing plant.

One would think that the popularity of poultry these days and the great profitability of the industry would pave a road to improved wages and working conditions for the industry's workers. One of every sixteen new industrial jobs in America in recent years has been in poultry processing. Employment is booming in the "poultry crescent" that extends from Maryland, down through Georgia and Alabama, and swinging back up to northern Arkansas and Texas. While employment has declined by one-third in the slaughterhouses for beef, pork, and lamb, it has doubled over the last 15 years to more than 150,000 jobs in poultry plants.[1]

America's growing appetite for white meat, however, has not been translated into improvements for black workers, who predominate in the poultry plants that traditionally have been located in southern rural areas with large black populations. Despite tightened rural labor markets around the plants and increasing demand for the products, real wages (adjusted for inflation) have been falling at the Cordova plant and throughout the industry.

Rather than improve wages, the poultry industry is turning to foreign workers. Robert says the major changes he has seen during his ten years at the Cordova plant have been the hiring of foreign workers and the speeding up of the line, and the two are not unrelated. Ten years ago, "I don't think there were more than maybe ten immigrants in the whole plant." Now, almost half the five hundred workers are foreign, he says. "Parts of the plant are entirely Spanish-speaking. Many of the line leaders speak Spanish."

A spokeswoman for the Cordova plant later confirms that about half the employees are immigrants and that nearly all the native workers are black.

It isn't that the area around the Cordova plant doesn't have people who could fill those jobs. A lot of local residents are without jobs or have just part-time jobs, says the cook as he casts again into Tuckahoe Creek. So why is the company bringing in foreign workers? Robert and the cook answer in unison, "Because they'll work cheaper." The cook used to work at the poultry plant, "but I got out of it." He wanted to work where he didn't have competition from the immigrants, and they as yet haven't moved into the restaurant jobs of this largely rural county.

As has been true ever since Frederick Douglass escaped from slavery and since the Civil War ended it nationally, a renewal of high immigration has once again blocked the road to middle-class security for many black workers, and has detoured them back into a morass of low wages and dismal expectations.

* * *

The anthropology team at East Carolina University has turned up some disturbing evidence from the bottom of the economic pecking order. It appears that Congress through its immigration policies has provided poultry companies with the means not only to avoid improving wages but also to begin replacing their black American workers.

The team, led by anthropologist David Griffith, studied poultry plants throughout the "poultry crescent." Team members discovered that managers often were explicit in their desire to hire immigrants to replace their "sorry black workers."

"The white and black work ethic is sinking," one plant manager said, explaining why he prefers to hire Latin American and Asian immigrants. "Koreans have an excellent work ethic," another manager said. "We have problems with blacks—30 to 40 percent do not care if they work or not." Repeatedly, the team members heard managers berate their "lazy" black workers and extol immigrant workers. An excellent work ethic would imply that a worker is dependable and would stick with a job. But the immigrants often don't last a year on the job. Many employers don't seem to hold that against them because there always is a fresh supply of compliant foreign workers to take their place at the same wages and working conditions, or lower.

Immigrant networking can change a workplace almost overnight. Each new foreign worker sends the word out to friends and relatives that a foothold has been gained in a plant. In just six months at one plant, blacks in the workforce dropped from 65 to 49 percent, while Hispanics and Asians doubled from 20 to 40 percent.

"If anyone quits, they won't get their jobs back," said Madge, a forty-two-year-old black worker. Black and white American workers long have moved in and out of poultry plant jobs, in part to recuperate from the stressful and physically demanding conditions. Poultry processing has the third worst record for cumulative trauma injuries such as carpal tunnel syndrome. But the hiring of immigrants is undermining the native workers' job strategies. Madge has had friends who quit, but when they came back to start again, Mexicans had their jobs.

Many plant managers are eager to replace white Americans, too, but black workers bear the biggest displacement burden. Not only do blacks lose their jobs, but the immigrants are more likely to move into their neighborhoods and displace them in their social and cultural spaces.

Because they know the company has replacements in waiting, American workers are less likely to complain about working conditions. So market pressures that otherwise would be brought to bear to force improved working conditions are artificially suppressed. As a result, injuries are so pervasive in the poultry plants that the anthropology team found that "nearly all workers we interviewed mentioned swollen hands, cuts, slips and the high incidence of carpal tunnel syndrome. . . ."

John, a black nineteen-year-old, said he believed the influx of immigrants into his plant is keeping his wages down. But that is sort of the American way, he said, fairly accurately summarizing U.S. immigration history.

The parallels between the last thirty years and the thirty years after the Civil War are uncanny. Both the Civil War's great black emancipation in the 1860s and the Civil Rights Act's great black enfranchisement in the 1960s raised high expectations among black citizens for improved economic possibilities. But in both centuries, immigration was allowed to run at such a high level in the eighties and nineties that black progress was stopped and many black Americans saw their economic situation deteriorate.

It isn't that Congress has not been warned of what it is doing to American blacks with its immigration policy.

On 13 March 1990, for example, Frank Morris went to the U.S. House of Representatives as something of a latter-day Booker T. Washington. He used no "cast down yourbucket" oratory, but his message was the same. Morris, the dean of graduate studies at Morgan State University and a former executive director of the Congressional Black Caucus Foundation, beseeched Congress to look at what immigration already had done to the black population:

> It is clear that America's black population is bearing a disproportionate share of immigrants' competition for jobs, housing and social services. . . . There is little basis for repeated assurances that African Americans have not been harmed by heavy immigration of the less-skilled during the past two decades. Many of the immigrants compete directly with blacks in the same labor markets and occupations and have become substitutes for black workers more often than they have become com-

plements. Studies claiming to show insignificant change in rates of African-American unemployment or labor force participation fail to take into account employment opportunities closed to black Americans who might otherwise migrate to metropolitan labor markets increasingly impacted by immigration. The pervasive effects of ethnic-network recruiting and the spread of non-English languages in the workplace have, in effect, locked many blacks out of occupations where they once predominated.[2]

Morris urged the members of Congress to "resist impulses" to use immigrants to "impede or delay the working of natural labor market forces" which, without immigrants, would stir employers to offer black citizens, earlier immigrants, and handicapped Americans "a rare opportunity to gain training, improve their bargaining power, and better their wages, conditions and employment prospects."

Congress responded by passing the 1990 Immigration Act, which greatly *increased* immigration over a level that already was larger than during the Great Wave.

Five years later, in May 1995, Morris tried again on the Senate side. He said studies are clear that African Americans always do best during times of tight-labor markets. Any federal program that loosens labor markets is a program against the interests of blacks. "Immigration is not the cause of all of the problems, but it has made the situation much worse . . . and places us at a great disadvantage," he maintained.[3]

Congressional leaders this time are proposing cuts, but only back to the high 1965–90 level that had led to all the damage Morris decried in his 1990 testimony.

A glance around the country suggests that these levels of immigration are harming the "failed black third" and, to a lesser extent, other African Americans in four broad ways:

· Lengthening the hiring line and moving blacks to the back.
· Limiting hiring to immigrants' contacts through ethnic networking.
· Allowing employers to substitute immigrants for black Americans in affirmative action programs.
· Eroding African Americans' special relationship as the historic minority population in a predominantly bi-racial nation.

CUTTING IN LINE

In California during the 1980s, the employment of African Americans as bank tellers fell 39 percent while foreign-born tellers increased by 56 percent.

The extraordinary influx of foreign workers affected blacks throughout California's economy. The number of black hotel maids and housemen in California dropped 30 percent during the 1980s while the number of immigrants with those jobs rose 166 percent. The 1990 Census also found that immigrants replaced native-born Americans in the occupations of garment sewers, restaurant waiters, and busboys, hospital nursing assistants and orderlies. Blacks "have been squeezed into a smaller segment of the economy," says Roger Waldinger, a UCLA sociologist.[4]

Such results appear to occur for two primary reasons. First, *immigrants often can outcompete black citizens—and other Americans—in the job market because of their lower Third World expectations.* They often can live on lower wages because their living costs are so much less than for native-born Americans who have developed an intolerance for crowded, multifamily households with few amenities and recreation. Carter G. Woodson remarked on that trait in his exploration of the effect of Mexican immigration in earlier decades. Blacks then complained that the Mexicans took their jobs by offering to work for lower pay while living with their families, "boarded up in Fords like so many cattle en route to the cotton fields."[5]

Second, *American employers in general always have put blacks at the back of the hiring line, preferring virtually all other nationalities and ethnicities.* Harvard's Ronald F. Ferguson addressed this phenomenon for the National Academy of Sciences: "If employers hire from the front of the queue and if blacks are disproportionately at the back—behind immigrants and native-born members of other racial groups—then blacks will suffer the greatest deterioration in employment when the number of immigrants grows."[6] Antonio McDaniel of the University of Pennsylvania said blacks may be forced to the back of the line because their race is considered the most different from that of the American majority. He noted strong support among sociologists for the proposition that all humans have natural proclivities for attachments to their own race.[7]

When the hiring line is short—and especially if it is shorter than the number of jobs to be filled—the racial proclivity of the white majority is less harmful to black Americans. By bringing in additional immigrants, Congress lengthens the hiring line and almost assuredly moves blacks farther from the front. Professor Ferguson indicated that the propensity for blacks since 1973 to occupy less lucrative occupations and to work in industries that offered lower pay is at least partly due to Congress filling the front of the hiring line with so many new immigrants.

That certainly could be seen in the janitorial industry in Los Angeles in the 1980s. Some commentators, both white and black, have taken somewhat of a "let them eat cake" attitude about these types of jobs, suggesting that it is okay for blacks to lose lower-skilled jobs because that means they can aspire to higher-level work. But those jobs play an important entry-level, "foot-in-the-door" function, providing experience to new workers so they can move on up the ladder. These first stepping-stone jobs are especially important to the young black men who in recent years have been substantially unemployed. Unfortunately, in industry after industry, such jobs have been denied the young black workers. As the immigrant gets the stepping-stone advantage, the American remains unemployed.

Janitorial work by the early 1980s was far more than a stepping stone, however. It had become a great middle-class occupation in many cities. Since World War II, the janitors for downtown Los Angeles office buildings had won excellent wages and working conditions through their union, according to a U.S. General Accounting Office study. The ability to deliver credible threats to strike had played an important role in that success.[8]

But the federal program that brought hundreds of thousands of foreign workers into the country each year changed that. Congress inadvertently had provided some aggressive non-union janitorial firms the opportunity to disrupt or ruin the economic lives of the downtown janitors, about half of whom were black. The non-union firms hired immigrants at half the wages and fairly quickly underbid the unionized firms, taking over the office building contracts. Real wages have dropped further since then.

From an estimated 2,500 black janitors earning wages equivalent to around $18 an hour (1995 value), only 600 were left in their jobs by 1985, with just 100 of them still earning union wages.

Having helped drive the black Americans out of those good jobs, the immigrants soon found that it was hard to raise families on the pitifully low wages they had accepted. In October 1991, for example,

Jose Domingo Diaz stood on Rodeo Drive holding a large sign: "Janitors are Down & Out in Beverly Hills." He and other non-union janitors, complaining about having no medical or health care, carried out a protest march in which they approached store clerks and asked what they could afford in the stores on $4.25-an-hour wages.

At one time, blacks commonly could be found as waiters throughout the hotels of Washington, D.C. But *The Washington Post* noticed in 1993 that the nicer the restaurant, the slighter the chance that the waiter would be black, the positions having been filled mostly by immigrants. In Washington, long a majority black city, it has become increasingly difficult to find a native-born black worker on construction sites, in the parking garages, in janitorial firms, or in the taxi cabs. Congress has filled the nation's capital with foreign workers, while conditions of unemployment for low-skilled young black men have helped spawn one of the most violent cultures in the nation.

Anthropologist Katherine S. Newman of Columbia University led a research team in a study of the inner-city labor market of New York City. What they found among native black residents was a desperate search for jobs at any level and any price—a search that belied many negative stereotypes that prevail against them. In the fast-food industry with jobs offered at $4.25 an hour, there were fourteen times more people looking for jobs as there were job openings during the five-month study period. When the university researchers contacted the rejected job seekers a year later, 73 percent of them still did not have a job, even though they had "continued to pound the pavement. There simply were not enough jobs to go around." Of the black residents who got jobs at the fast-food restaurants, 58 percent had a high school diploma, and most of the rest were still enrolled in school.[9]

Top New York City officials continue to defend bringing more foreign workers to add to the competition in such a brutal job market. But it isn't even a level playing field, Professor Newman discovered. New York employers *prefer* immigrants over natives. During the study period, Newman found that even in Harlem, which is overwhelmingly populated by black residents, low-wage employers hired 38 percent of Latino and Asian applicants but only 13.6 percent of African-American applicants.

ETHNIC NETWORKING

Much of the power of immigration streams comes from "ethnic net-working," in which immigrants after obtaining a job use word of mouth to bring relatives and other acquaintances from their country into the same workplace. Immigrants today act like the immigrants early this century, who took whole occupations and turned them into their own preserve, quickly shutting native-born Americans—especially blacks—out of a workplace.

The changeover has occurred quickly in the seafood industry in North Carolina, Virginia, and Maryland. In 1989, the workers were predominantly African-American women, as had been the case for decades. That changed completely due to the actions of one woman whose family owned four plants in Virginia and was having trouble attracting workers through the usual wages and recruitment. The Virginia Employment Commission told her how to secure foreign workers. With the help of the state government, the woman went to Mexico and gained the services of a labor contractor. Another labor contractor, who had dinner with the Virginia woman and was excited to learn of the possibility of gaining a foothold in that market, began to contact seafood plants up and down the Atlantic Coast, offering the services of Mexican girls.[10]

Within five years, the workforce of seafood plants in North Carolina, Virginia, and Maryland had changed from being predominantly African-American to mainly teenage girls and young women from Mexico!

A study for the West Virginia state government in 1994 found the same phenomenon at worksites all over the country where foreign workers had gotten a foothold. Partly because immigrants are less likely to complain than natives, employers are happy to depend on the immigrants to recruit further employees. Businesses cease to advertise jobs. Natives don't hear about openings as they are announced through word of mouth of the foreign workers in their local community and also across the country and even into other countries.[11]

This process is even stronger in firms owned by immigrants. Take Korean firms, for example. Although 25 percent of New York's population is black, only 5 percent of the employees at Korean-owned stores are black, according to studies by Pyong Gap Min, a sociologist at Queen's College who is Korean-American. Even in black neighborhoods, he found, Korean stores hire more Hispanics than blacks. The majority of owners don't believe blacks are as intelligent or honest as others, Min says. "They haven't met middle-class blacks, so it is easy to generalize."[12]

Researchers at UCLA discovered that only 2 percent of Korean businesses hire blacks in Los Angeles—which has a 17 percent black population. But 17 percent of them hire Hispanics.

Jonathan Kaufman's report in the *Wall Street Journal* described how there is a kind of "unwritten law" that immigrant businesses don't hire blacks. He found young black men who sought jobs at dozens of immigrant businesses without success. Even black immigrants don't like to hire black Americans, the Harvard sociologist Mary Waters learned.

The difficulty black urbanites have in obtaining jobs fuels the image of them as lazy and not wanting to work when actually they are competing fiercely to get any kind of job. At a single McDonald's in Harlem, some three hundred people a month—most of them black—seek jobs at $4.25 an hour.

Black job seekers find more and more frustration as a larger percentage of the jobs are controlled by immigrants, either as owners, managers, or shift chiefs. An estimated one of every four low-wage jobs in New York City and Los Angeles is in an immigrant firm.

Thanks to ethnic hiring networks and the growing numbers of immigrant-owned small businesses, "there are tens of thousands of jobs in New York City for which the native-born are not candidates," writes Elizabeth Bogan in her book, *Immigration in New York*.[13]

Plathel Benjamin, a black columnist for the *New York Daily News*, got firsthand experience in the power of ethnic networking during seven years trying to work at construction sites around the city. On one project after another, he found that very few black Americans could get on the payroll because most of the jobs were filled by immigrants. Even though most of the projects were huge, multiyear efforts involving large sums of public money, immigrants clearly had priority over black New Yorkers. He managed to get into one public painting project, which he discovered had been converted through ethnic networking to be used almost exclusively to hire Russian Jews as they arrived into the country. A lot of them weren't painters and had to be trained, but when the work slowed down a little, they were kept on and the few blacks on the job were laid off. On another large project, there were only two black workers—Benjamin and a black immigrant. Most of the other painters were white Portuguese immigrants who helped the contractor meet his affirmative action requirements. When he went to the hiring office for a project at a public hospital, Benjamin couldn't find anybody who spoke English. After looking into the operation further, he found that the man who had won the paint contract had gone back to his home village in Greece and hired his whole crew there.

In his final year in the construction business, Benjamin landed a lucrative job as a laborer on a project that he expected to last two or three years. A lot of public money was involved, and promises had been made to hire construction workers from the community. Benjamin arrived at work and found that his Irish-American foreman had filled most of his crew with Irish immigrants "right off the boat. I was the only black American and there were two or three West Indians. The Irish kept making comments that the only reason I was on the job was because they had to have some blacks. I was there about a month and they replaced me with an Irish guy." That was the last straw. Benjamin became a regular contributor to *The Village Voice, The Times* (London), and other publications as he moved full time into a new career in writing—a career largely protected from the competition of non-English-speaking ethnic networks.

Black Americans are underrepresented by more than half in Southern California's rapidly growing electronics industry, which has a large number of immigrant firms. Hispanics, on the other hand, are hired at about their proportion of the population, and Asians are hired at twice their proportion. David Sun, a Chinese immigrant, told the *Wall Street Journal*'s Jonathan Kaufman that his technology firm had only a handful of blacks among its 370 employees. Charles Woo, owner of a Los Angeles wholesale toy business, said blacks have a negative image and don't mix well with workers of other backgrounds.

Supposedly, it is illegal to limit hiring to one ethnic group, especially when it bars African Americans. When blacks are shut out of businesses by white workers, they have easy recourse to the courts. But redress is far more difficult when foreign workers are involved. A Korean-owned janitorial company in Chicago kept blacks from employment by hiring only Koreans. The federal Equal Employment Opportunity Commission took the company to court but lost in the federal Court of Appeals. According to the ruling, it isn't discrimination if blacks are blocked from jobsbecause of word-of-mouth advertising through immigrant networks.[14]

UCLA sociologist Roger Waldinger studied the hotel and restaurant industries in Los Angeles and hotels in New York and Philadelphia. Employers complained about native blacks' high expectations of benefits and working conditions and said they preferred to hire immigrants. Once a crew becomes comprised primarily of immigrants, it is likely to stay that way, with blacks effectively barred from those jobs. In such cases, blacks don't get much help from federal anti-discrimination programs, says George La Noue, the director of the policy sciences program at the University of Maryland Graduate School: "Enforcement agencies are more likely to take on an all-white workforce than an all-Hispanic one. It's a matter of political will."[15]

AFFIRMATIVE ACTION

Frederick Douglass would have no trouble in the 1990s finding the phenomenon of blacks being "elbowed out of employment by some newly arrived immigrant." What surely would amaze him, however, is the way that today's immigrants, in a legal sense, are portrayed as blacks in order to help them cut into the hiring line ahead of the descendants of slavery.

Ironically, programs of affirmative action—meant to compensate for centuries of legalized discrimination against blacks—now are being used by employers to avoid hiring blacks. This can happen because an immigrant who first set foot in the United States yesterday is considered to have exactly the same claim for redress as the descendants of slavery.

A former director of an employment agency for Cambodian refugees in Chicago, for example, said he was surprised how often companies would tell him directly, "We want to phase out our blacks and bring in Asians. It keeps us clear in EEO [the federal Equal Employment Opportunity Commission] and gets us better workers."[16]

Affirmative action has been turned on its head by immigration so that it sometimes hurts the very people it was designed to help. The policy was begun under the Johnson administration in the 1960s to improve black participation in some of the more desirable areas of the economy where black Americans previously had trouble entering. It was never intended for immigrants. Its impetus was not concern for something called "ethnic minorities;" its impetus was concern for black Americans. If it were not for the nation's regret for the legacy to black Americans of two hundred years of slavery and one hundred more years of racial caste segregation, there never would have been anything like affirmative action policy in this country.

But President Nixon's Labor Department significantly watered down affirmative action as a tool to redress the lingering effects of slavery, racial apartheid laws in the South, and immigrant unions' closed hiring halls. In his study, *Affirmative Action for Immigrants: The Entitlement Nobody Wanted,* James S. Robb noted that Nixon's Labor Department "in effect created several new minority groups out of whole cloth. Persons who formerly might have thought of themselves as Mexican-American, Cuban-American, or Brazilian-American, now discovered they belonged to a single minority, 'Hispanics.'" Now, Hispanics and Asian-Americans could benefit from the program that had been intended for the descendants of slavery.[17]

The benefit of affirmative action for blacks became less and less as it was expanded to include a larger and larger percentage of people living in America. Cincinnati businessman William A. Cargile went to court based on the belief that, as Robb expressed it, "every place made at the affirmative action table for a new group must necessarily result in less room for all the others." At issue for Cargile was a state program that reserved 5 percent of construction projects and 15 percent of goods and services contracts for minority-owned businesses. As a black owner of a business, Cargile had benefitted from the program but found it more difficult to win contracts as more ethnic groups were added to the preferential program. When Ohio governor George V. Voinovich opened up minority set-aside contracts to Asian-Indians, Cargile decided inclusiveness had broadened to a ridiculous degree. Of all ethnic groups in the United States, Asian-Indians ranked second highest in terms of income and education (whites ranked sixth, and blacks ranked tenth). Cargile couldn't figure out what historic racial grievances these recently arrived immigrants could make.

Cargile filed suit, saying Indian immigrants were getting contracts that should have gone to black Americans. State attorney general Lee Fisher ruled that the inclusion of Asian-Indians was improper and ordered sixty-four Asian-Indian companies decertified for the minority contracts. But Judge Tommy L. Thompson ruled the Asian-Indians had to be given all privileges of blacks under affirmative action because they are "Orientals," one of four minority groups recognized by the state.

In Washington, D.C., during the late 1980s, a construction company owned by a Portuguese immigrant was the biggest beneficiary of minority set-aside contracts. Thus, millions of dollars intended primarily to give a boost to native black-owned businesses went to a white European. In South Florida, a couple of white Cuban brothers worth around $500 million have routinely won contracts that were set aside for minority firms.

Jews from Mexico can be considered Hispanic, and English trans-
plants to Hong Kong can pass themselves off as Asian/Pacific Islander.
Some Arab-American activists have been lobbying for minority status
since they don't qualify under the black, Oriental, Hispanic, or Native
American categories.

Compensatory actions for black slavery benefit a wide spectrum of
people. Ed Fernandez, an official at the Census Bureau, said his white
European-American sons are open to advantages in college by identifying themselves (as is legally allowed) as Hispanic, even though his own
ancestors came from Spain and his wife is a Spanish immigrant.

Colleges and universities with poor track records in admitting native-born black Americans have been notorious in disguising such records by packing their "minority" enrollment figures with foreign-born
students who then are labeled black, Asian-American, or Hispanic.

The same distortion can be found in colleges' claims about the
hiring of "minorities" for faculty positions. The University of Michigan, for example, boasted that it had made great progress in boosting
its minority faculty numbers. But the faculty senate discovered that
18.8 percent of the "black" faculty weren't American minorities;
rather, they were foreign-born. And 23.3 percent of the "Hispanics"
and 56.1 percent of the "Asian-Americans" were not U.S. citizens,
either.

In 1993, some leaders at Stanford University grew uneasy with the
charade that is so common at American universities. They had a program that was intended to boost the faculty presence of blacks, Mexican-Americans, and Native Americans, who were seriously underrepresented. The administration felt native minority students of those three
backgrounds might perform better if they had more role models on the
faculty. As an incentive, the administration promised that for every two
"minority" teachers hired, a department would be given the money
for an extra faculty member. By 1993, however, the administration
realized that more than half of the "minority" teachers who had been
hired weren't American minorities at all; they were foreign-born, primarily from Asia. "Foreign-born and foreign-educated faculty members may not be as effective as role models for minority undergradu-
ates," an internal report stated. The Stanford administration decided
to exclude non-citizens from their affirmative action program. The
outcry from immigration advocacy groups was so loud, however, that
the plan was dropped. So Stanford continues to provide subsidies to
departments for hiring foreign teachers instead of Americans.

As the faculties of universities increasingly are filled with foreign-
born teachers, the already substantial preference for foreign graduate

students increases. A 1990 survey by the National Research Council estimated that black Americans had to finance 63 percent of their doctoral studies from their own money, while foreign students had to come up with only 14 percent. The biggest reason for the difference was that the universities provided more than twice as much financial assistance to each foreign student as to each black American.

Behind most schools' records of minority enrollment lies a revealing story. Of all the "blacks" who received science doctorates in 1993, for example, the majority were foreign-born. The same was true of "Hispanics." And ten times more doctorates were awarded to non-citizen Asians than to actual Asian-Americans!

Throughout the American economy, affirmative action has become a tool "that greases the displacement of blacks by immigrants," according to Jonathan Tilove. Immigration is reversing affirmative action's underlying mission to help black people, Tilove wrote for the Newhouse Newspapers chain.

In a landmark series of articles in late 1993, Tilove revealed how employers are able to use immigrants to subvert the purpose of Johnson's executive order on affirmative action in 1965. Legally, they are not supposed to do it, but many employers meet their minority hiring targets by employing immigrants instead of black Americans.

A pharmaceutical company which had shown a very favorable increase in minority hiring did so primarily by hiring Pakistani, Indian, and Vietnamese workers. William Kilberg, a former Labor Department solicitor, commented: "A lot of these people are easy to hire. They're trained, they're educated, they're hardworking, and you get a bonus. Not only are they people who you would have hired anyway, but they are characterized as minorities." By filling minority slots, the business lessens pressures to hire black Americans.

The use of immigrants to shed blacks from the workforce or to avoid hiring them does not just occur in a few isolated incidents. Tilove said expert analysis suggests that "employers might be laying off blacks while retaining or hiring other minorities to meet their affirmative action goals."[18] That was made rather clear in 1993 when a major study by the *Wall Street Journal* analyzed federal EEOC records during the 1990–91 recession. Reporter Rochelle Sharpe discovered something astounding: At all the nation's companies that have to report to the EEOC, there was no net loss of employment during the recession for Hispanics and Asians.

But there were plenty of losses for the descendants of slavery. While Asians during the recession *gained* a net of 55,104 jobs at those firms reporting to the EEOC and Hispanics *gained* a net of 60,040 jobs, blacks *lost* a net of 59,479 jobs. Mid-size and big businesses increased their employment of Asians in thirty-nine states while they cut their employment of blacks in thirty-six states. Blacks suffered their worst losses in the states with the highest immigration: Florida, Illinois, New York, California. Only in Alabama, Arkansas, and Louisiana, where immigration is minimal, did the employment of blacks increase significantly.[19]

Some leaders of various ethnic groups have made the claim that they are as deserving as blacks for affirmative action because they have their own histories of discrimination in this country. Their arguments fail on at least two counts. First, very small percentages of those ethnic populations can trace their American roots back before the Civil Rights Acts of the 1960s, let alone to the time of the most egregious of stated slights, such as actions against the Chinese in the last century and the U.S. conquest of the Southwest in 1848. More importantly, only one American ethnic group has endured anything like the breadth and longevity of state-endorsed mistreatment of black Americans. As the National Academy of Sciences put it, "the case of black Americans is unique—in its history of slavery and of extreme segregation, exclusion and discrimination."

The only other group that can lay claim for redress similar to that of black Americans is the descendants of the indigenous peoples of the land. Not only did the invasion of European settlers in the seventeenth and eighteenth centuries kill large numbers of Indians, primarily through disease, but it drove the eastern tribes off their land. Native Americans, like blacks, have a long history of coming out on the losing end during periods of mass immigration. After the Civil War, nearly all U.S. civilian and military officials operated under the assumption that the perhaps quarter of a million population remaining in the West would have to "surrender most of their land and cease to be Indians," according to Eric Foner.[20] The massive importation of European settlers was an important tool in achieving those goals. Without them, the settling of the West would have been much slower, giving Native Americans more time to adjust and perhaps even to persuade the American people to honor earlier treaties. Mass immigration has harmed Native Americans in the job market much as it has blacks. J. F. Moser reported that in 1899, for example, Indians who worked in the fish canneries of Alaska tried to use the lack of labor in the area to gain better wages and conditions. Managers responded by importing Chinese workers to replace them.[21]

BI-RACIAL VS.
MULTICULTURAL SOCIETY

While many black leaders have touted the benefits of immigration in building a larger non-European population through which blacks can have more electoral power, others have worried that blacks are losing a special status as America's chief minority.

It may be helpful to look at this phenomenon through the eyes of another special minority in another country.

In the two islands of New Zealand, the Maori have been the historic minority since the land was colonized by the British and established as a country in 1840. Their situation today is not greatly unlike that of blacks in the United States. The Maori share a long history with the European majority in their country and have enjoyed a certain special place in society because of obligations incurred during that history. That is changing rapidly because the New Zealand business community persuaded the government to increase immigration considerably as a way to promote economic growth and provide laborers.

The Maori people, with unemployment as high as 50 percent in some communities, oppose the new immigration, according to Ranginui J. Walker, a professor at the University of Auckland: "The government needs to demonstrate that it is capable of educating, training and providing employment for the present population, before entertaining doubling its problems by increasing the population through immigration."

Walker says the Maori people view the new immigration policy as a covert strategy to suppress Maori efforts to gain their full rights. By swamping the country with thousands of immigrants from many different Asian nationalities, the Maori are becoming just one of many minorities, and one of the smaller populations if the program continues, he explains.

Leaders from academia, business, and government have promoted the virtues of multiculturalism for New Zealand. They have said that a kind of rainbow coalition of immigrants and Maori will help the Maori better fit into society as an equal social group, rather than being one small minority amidst a huge European majority.

But the Maori have resisted the multiculturalist ideology, insisting that New Zealand is a bi-racial nation. Even though the Maori have suffered great discrimination and hardship at the hands of their British colonizers, they much prefer to share New Zealand with only those

European settlers, Walker says. The Maori have historic claims that they can make on the European majority, claims that have no power over immigrant peoples who come from other continents.[22]

Similarly in the United States, the prospects for national attention to black needs were much stronger thirty years ago when the country still was a substantially bi-racial culture. When a policy of mass immigration was begun in 1965, 75 percent of all minorities in America were blacks. Today, the population of other minorities is larger than that of the descendants of slavery.

Not only have African Americans become just one of many minorities, but they are losing the white majority upon whom any historic claim of specialness or affirmative action rests. Many African Americans, for example, are not soothed by the fact that whites soon will be a minority of the population in California. The Latino population is much larger than the number of blacks, and the Asian community already is about the same size. Whatever happens demographically in California over the next few years is expected to occur for the nation as a whole by the middle of the next century—if Congress does not change the immigration flow.

Unlike many native-born white Americans, immigrant groups feel no responsibility to blacks because of past slavery and racial apartheid practices. Individuals in those immigrant groups correctly point out that not only did none of their ancestors own American slaves but none of their ancestors even knew a slave. Consequently, immigrants are not reluctant to use affirmative action laws in California to try to increase their employment in government institutions by reducing the number of black Americans in those jobs.

When California had a population that was overwhelmingly white, African Americans achieved a presence in government jobs higher than their presence in the general population. Now, immigrants are trying to change that in many of the major immigrant centers. Amaryllis Gutierrez, the associate director of the pharmacy at Martin Luther King Jr./Drew Medical Center in Watts, sued the hospital, claiming that it discriminated against her in favor of blacks. Her attorney told Jonathan Tilove that when blacks claim they have some special status because there was slavery in Alabama, that is "bull. . . ."[23]

Whites already are a minority in Los Angeles County. That has not elevated the status of blacks. Between the Watts riots of 1965 and the Los Angeles riots in 1992, the Latino share of the population soared from 10 percent to nearly 40 percent. Then there are the increases in Asians, Middle Easterners, and so on.

As the Maori fear will happen to them in New Zealand, blacks already have lost nearly all special minority status in Los Angeles. Unfortunately for blacks, immigrants are far more likely than white Americans to hold negative attitudes about African Americans. A 1994 survey asked people their reaction to the statement: "Even if given a chance, [blacks] aren't capable of getting ahead." Only 12 percent of whites agreed. But the pejorative stereotype was held by double the Asians and triple the Latinos.[24]

When nearly nine of every ten Americans were white, it was much easier to ask them to give a little preference to the one of ten Americans who was black. Whatever the personal cost of affirmative action to individual whites, it was far smaller in the 1960s than it is today because a smaller and smaller portion of the population that is white must carry the costs for a larger and larger portion of people who are being treated legally as if they are black. Thus, it is no surprise that the drive to eliminate affirmative action programs would start in California, where the per capita potential for inconvenience to whites is so much greater. After all, how could it be feasible to expect a minority white population to give preferential treatment in jobs and schooling to a population of "minorities" that outnumbers them? Affirmative action would appear to be workable only if there is a majority population, and probably only if there is a population that is a substantial majority. So affirmative action programs for the descendants of slavery are now threatened even though blacks form about the same small portion of the population they did in the 1960s.

All of the above raises questions for American blacks that the New Zealand Maori are asking: Is it better to be one of many minorities in a multicultural society, or the special historicminority in a bi-racial one? It is a question that still matters because many parts of the United States retain the old bi-racial culture. Orlando Patterson, professor of sociology at Harvard, comments: "The demands of Hispanics, Italian Americans, Polish Americans, Native Americans and others diluted and eventually trivialized the very special claims of blacks for national attention. . . . By the end of the '80s, the multicultural emphasis on the equality of all subcultures and de-emphasis on the common culture had the same consequence for African Americans as the traditional racist emphasis on the supremacy of WASPS: It belittled the extraordinary contribution of African Americans to the overarching national culture."[25]

African Americans are not unaware of their shifting place in American society. Unlike the beginning of the century, though, they now have little in the way of political leadership to guide their seething anger; rage occasionally spills out in destructive expressions.

Deborah Sontag reported in *The New York Times* on the growing incidence of such rage, including the example of a Salvadoran dishwasher who was assaulted and robbed by a group of black natives who told him: "You steal our jobs, we steal your money."[26] After the 1992 riots in Los Angeles, roving gangs of black residents intimidated contractors who were attempting to rebuild with immigrant labor.

In a long cover story for the *Atlantic Monthly* in October 1992, Jack Miles delivered a ground-breaking analysis of the L.A. riots. The court acquittal of white policemen on the charge of beating a black motorist was only the spark for the nation's worst riot, Miles argued. The deep reservoirs of rage that fueled the riots were created from the economic, social, and political frustration of a black population that has been under siege for thirty years from the competition of a massive influx of foreign workers into their neighborhoods, he suggested.[27]

An editorial in the Mexican-American *La Prensa San Diego* spoke directly about the matter: "Faced with nearly a million and a half Latinos taking over the inner city, blacks revolted, rioted and looted. Whatever measure of power and influence they had pried loose from the white power structure, they now see as being in danger of being transferred to the Latino community. Not only are they losing influence, public offices and control of the major civil rights mechanisms, they now see themselves being replaced in the pecking order by the Asian community, in this case the Koreans. . . ."[28]

Prospects are not particularly bright for domestic tranquility under the current set of ethnic tensions and immigrant flows, according to John Higham, long regarded by many as America's authoritative historian of immigration and as generally a friend of immigration. He looks at the results of three decades of mass immigration and says, "The brute fact of tension, of conflict, of susceptibility to riots and so on, has to be regarded as a really serious problem." As author of the classic *Strangers in the Land: Patterns of American Nativism 1860–1925,* Higham knows well the ugly exchanges and violence surrounding immigration early this century. But he believes the concentration of foreign workers and their families in the United States today is more dangerous.[29]

The National Academy of Sciences' massive study on black Americans concluded in 1989: "We cannot exclude the possibility of confrontation and violence. The ingredients are there: large populations of jobless youths, an extensive sense of relative deprivation and injustice, distrust of the legal system, frequently abrasive police-community relations, highly visible inequalities, extreme concentrations of poverty, and great racial awareness. Such conditions sometimes produce apathy when disadvantaged persons feel that their situation is hopeless. But the surface calm can disappear very quickly."[30]

Miami, for example, has erupted at least three times in the last fifteen years, and there is no indication that the underlying tensions between native blacks and the immigrant populations have dissipated. Not least among the incendiary factors is the widespread belief among black residents that the immigrants who flooded their city and neighborhoods were given economic assistance not afforded to black residents. The anthropologist Alex Stepick of Florida International University studied the minority economic development programs that grew out of the 1960s civil rights movement to help black Americans. What he found was that the blacks in Miami didn't get much help from them; once again, most of the financial aid went to immigrants.[31]

* * *

Amidst all the dreary recitations of the seemingly intractable problems of the "failed black third," perhaps the greatest hope for immediate improvement can be discovered in an exhibition of fifty-five-year-old art that has been touring the country in recent years.

The Migration Series by Jacob Lawrence portrays the event that did more than any other—outside of the Civil War's emancipation—to raise the economic and social status of black Americans. That event was the Great Migration of southern blacks—during World War I and during and after World War II—into the high-wage industrial cities of the North and the West, an epic captured by Lawrence on sixty panels.

Lawrence wastes no time in his series of paintings in stating explicitly why that transforming event, the Great Migration, occurred: Foreign immigration was reduced—not modestly but drastically.

His caption under Panel No. 2 declares that southern black labor suddenly became valuable during World War I because immigration of foreign workers almost stopped and many young white workers went to Europe for the war. Faced with a labor shortage, northern industrialists finally made their jobs available to the horribly underemployed descendants of slavery in the South. Black Americans could resume their march of economic progress that had been so tragically stymied when the Great Wave of immigration was allowed to begin in 1880.

The immigration reduction from 1915 through 1919 due to the war was something of a trial run, and Lawrence was born in the midst of it in 1917 while his parents were en route from the South to New

York City. A return of mass immigration after the war interrupted the black migration.

Fortune magazine catapulted the twenty-three-year-old Lawrence into fame by publishing all sixty paintings in its November 1941 issue. The editorial introduction explained that the continuing black migration in the 1940s was made possible by the decisive congressional action in 1924 that cut foreign immigration back to a lower, more traditional level—an average of below 200,000 a year through 1965.

The hope for the 1990s is not in repeating the black migration of midcentury but in repeating the tight-labor conditions that made black Americans more economically valuable. To an optimistic viewer, Lawrence's series evokes the possibility that the abysmal conditions of the "failed black third" today do not have to continue. The work suggests that although there likely is no quick fix to all the problems, there is a quick action—a dramatic cutback in immigration—that might turn the tide.

Panel No. 4 portrays a solitary black man driving a spike. The caption reads: "All other sources of labor having been exhausted, the migrants [southern blacks] were the last resource." Only when the hiring line shortened did industrialists take Booker T. Washington's advice and "cast down their buckets" for the black workers at the end of the line.

The wonderful quality of a labor shortage is captured in Lawrence's painting of northern employers flooding the South with labor agents. The economist Gavin Wright of Stanford says they offered the southern blacks free transportation and assurances of jobs. Black Americans were faced with economic opportunities in the North that were too powerful to resist, concluded a group of scholars in the *Research in Economic History* journal.[32]

To capture the thrill, one must imagine what it would be like today if employers actually needed the labor of young black men and women and set up recruiting and training stations smack in the middle of the inner cities. It probably is too much to hope that cutting immigration flows once again to below 200,000 would tighten the labor market immediately. But it would remove an enormous barrier that has blocked the ability of many pro-active efforts that have been under way to bring success to the "failed black third." Certainly, the farther below 200,000 immigration can be cut, the better for creating those all-important tight-labor conditions.

Reynolds Farley of the University of Michigan endorses a labor shortage as something of an all-purpose medicine. He says many factors since 1965 ought to have worked in favor of the blacks and would suggest that blacks should have done much better than they did during the time of national economic expansion in the 1980s. Among the positive factors were "the civil rights changes of the 1960s and the apparent removal of the many barriers which once kept blacks in the back of the bus, out of schools, confined to menial jobs, and away from the polling booths in southern states." In addition, the large gaps between black and white school enrollments in 1960 "have just about disappeared."

All those positive factors for blacks—despite the economic stagnation and regression that blacks found in the 1980s—still can build toward a positive future if the country can once again tighten its labor market, Farley maintains.[33]

Nicolas Lemann in *The Promised Land* advises against fatalism and bitterness when considering the seemingly insuperable condition of the black slums in big cities, saying, "it is encouraging to remember how often in the past a hopeless situation, which appeared to be completely impervious to change, finally did change for the better. . . . In this century legal segregation looked like an unfortunate given, impossible to eliminate, until well after the end of World War II. That black America could become predominantly middle class, non-Southern, and nonagrarian would have seemed inconceivable until a bare two generations ago."[34]

Dare we imagine that the foundational act—restricting immigration—that freed the descendants of slavery from the southern plantations might also allow those now trapped in the slums to find vitality in life? Considerable scholarship even suggests that the 1924 immigration restriction—because it enabled the black migration—was the foundational act for the ending of segregation, as well. "The outmigration of blacks from the South after 1940 was the greatest single economic step forward in black history, and a major advance toward the integration of blacks into the mainstream of American life," says Gavin Wright.[35]

Between 1940 and the 1960s, the South lost most of its surplus labor. Once again, the fortunes of poor southern whites and blacks were tied. What few people realize is that the size of the white migration to the North after the reduction in immigration actually was larger than that of the great black migration. Under tight-labor conditions, the South finally had to mechanize and improve education, working conditions, and wages for the black and white workers who remained.

In 1940, state governments in the South were largely organized around protecting white supremacy. But thirty years later, they were primarily concerned with development on the part of a national economy. To the extent that segregation policies retarded industrial development and outside investment, business leaders were susceptible to appeals to break down racial barriers. "This change in the fundamentals of southern society ultimately made possible the success of the civil rights revolution of the 1950s and 1960s," says Gavin Wright.[36]

Sociologists Piven and Cloward have concluded that "economic modernization had made the South susceptible to political modernization." A complete domination of blacks based on terror no longer was essential to the ruling class.[37] Meanwhile, the growing black population outside the South and outside the feudal controls there began to organize politically. Not only did black northerners protest their own conditions but they applied the key pressure on northern lawmakers to cease support for the southern system of racial apartheid.

When black Americans finally got federal protection for voting rights in 1965, they had already enjoyed twenty-five years of rapidly rising wages. On average, their incomes still remained well below those of white Americans. But over that twenty-five-year period leading up to the new civil rights laws, black workers' real wages rose almost twice as fast as the rapidly rising wages of white workers.

The general long-term improvements deriving from immigration reductions between 1924 and 1965 and from the great black migration, however, cannot hide a great deal of suffering along the way.

Later panels in Lawrence's *Migration Series* portray how life in the new northern tenements often was better only by degrees from what the black southerners had fled. For the North, the black migrants had much the same effect as large flows of immigrants from Europe had. When they arrived in smaller numbers, they did quite well. But as the volume increased and continued, the social and economic structures sagged beneath the burden.

Piven and Cloward say that "the circumstances of urban blacks worsened precisely because their numbers increased." As is the case with today's immigrants, it may not have been the fault of the individual newcomers; but their increasing numbers nonetheless became harmful to the earlier black migrants, and to the northern natives, who suffered as they had from other large waves of immigrants from foreign lands. Among the consequences of this "migratory upheaval" was the beginning of the erosion of the black family structure that helps drag down the "failed black third" today.

The difficulty in incorporating the huge new black populations contributed to simmering northern and western ghettoes, which exploded in terrifying insurrection in the 1960s. Cities that had more rapid recent in-migration of black southerners were the most likely to suffer serious riots.

Ironically, the civil rights successes in the South probably contributed to the riots in the North and West by breeding impatience with the lack of political and social progress there. Black residents of the North and West, despite decades of economic improvement, engaged in desperate and destructive acts as they concluded that the whites of their regions were not ending the discrimination of the union hiring halls or the hostility of police departments, according to the historian Harvard Sitkoff.[38]

The renewal of mass immigration in 1965 certainly did not by itself bring about the end of black progress in the early 1970s. There were many factors. The war in Vietnam sapped federal resources and created a divisiveness throughout society that eliminated the sense of national purpose most conducive to racial improvements. New civil rights laws stirred a strong backlash among a minority of racist whites. And changes in the structure of the U.S. economy and in federal policies on foreign competition destroyed jobs in the industries and regions where blacks disproportionately had found work at good wages.

Although massive annual flows of foreign workers did not cause those problems, it made no sense to unleash mass immigration while the problems were unresolved. Because of their status in the economy, black Americans are more vulnerable than others to changes in public policy and the national economy, according to the nearly one hundred scholars who studied the subject for the National Academy of Sciences. Pouring foreign workers into black communities could only exacerbate the social disintegration already taking place and deepen the economic trauma they were suffering from industrial restructuring.

But the majority of white Americans weren't paying a lot of attention in the 1970s to whether policies hurt blacks. Sympathetic whites, whose support was essential, had lost enthusiasm for the cause in the late 1960s as black integration leaders waned in their influence over African Americans. As white supporters and more moderate, longtime black civil rights leaders were pushed out of the limelight, the most publicized black leaders preached against integration and interracial harmony. The outbreak of riots focused Americans' attention on issues of order and safety. Like many white abolitionists after the Civil War, most white liberals acquiesced to the desire of conservative economic interests to avoid the black workforce by turning to cheap foreign workers during the seventies and eighties. Unlike the last century, however, there was no expanding manufacturing base or open western frontier to help absorb the immigrants.

Once again, beginning in the 1970s, the federal government was filling the labor pool with immigrants, loosening labor markets, and standing by as black Americans were forced to the back of the hiring line. Two-thirds of black Americans have held on to middle-class status nevertheless. Most had gained it during the decades when Washington restrained the entry of foreign workers and allowed black Americans for a long and shining moment to flourish in tight-labor markets.

* * *

Is it possible that America could rekindle its commitment to help the impoverished descendants of slavery?

Nicolas Lemann believes that, despite "an undeniable strain of racial prejudice in its character," the United States also has a conscience that will respond to the horror of the urban ghettoes which now are among the world's worst places to live. He mentions two conditions which he says traditionally have helped the ghettoes and which don't require much in the way of government programs or money:

1. "For most of our history, the issue of race has been linked to the issue of nationhood. During periods of fragmentation—periods when a multiplicity of local, ethnic and economic interests held sway—racial problems have been put on the shelf. It is during the times when there has been a strong sense of national community that the problems have been addressed."
2. "The ghettos partake in the fluidity of American society . . . their condition improves in tight labor markets and worsens in more competitive ones."[39]

Both of Lemann's preconditions for helping the black ghettoes would be enhanced considerably by the simple act of cutting immigration back to the average annual flows of below 200,000 that existed from 1924 to 1965.

To Lindsey Grant, a former deputy assistant secretary of state, the moral obligation to do that is clear:

The nation a generation ago, in rare unity, launched perhaps its greatest moral crusade: to eliminate racism and to bring blacks into the economic mainstream. Since then . . . we have inadvertently done the one thing that could most effectively sabotage that crusade. We have allowed the almost unfettered entry of competition for entry-level jobs, at which the blacks could be starting their entry into the economy. . . . It is not enough to argue that the immigrant—hungry and fearful of deportation—will work harder. One must also answer the question: The blacks are Americans; how do we bring the increasingly alienated, restless and isolated ghetto blacks into the system?[40]

On the night of 11 March 1993, listeners of the liberal alternative radio station WBAI in New York City heard Vernon Briggs of Cornell University make a similar plea. He said African Americans in the northern and western cities are "losing the struggle" because of the massive wave of immigration: "The treatment of the African-American population is a national blemish of the highest order, and every policy ought to be judged on the following criteria: that it does no harm to the African-American population."

Briggs acknowledged that there are a lot of different opinions about what the government should *do* to help the "failed black third." But everybody should be agreed on what the government should *not do:* Washington should not do anything that harms black Americans, "and that's what our immigration policy is doing."[41]

Later that year, in December, Eugene McCarthy addressed a crowded Senate hearing room on the subject of immigration. The former senator and Democratic presidential candidate had been one of the chief co-sponsors of the 1965 revision that led to mass immigration. The elder statesmen explained that the increase in immigration had been entirely unintended. He said the increases have been immensely harmful to the country and should be rolled back.

A reporter queried McCarthy about how the country could live up to its moral obligations if it cut immigration drastically.

McCarthy didn't hesitate in his response. The moral priority for the United States, he said, remains that of addressing the descendants of two centuries of slavery and another century of racial apartheid who remain in the underclass. To the extent that large-scale immigration interferes with meeting black Americans' needs, he stressed, the immigrant must wait.

10

The High Cost of Cheap Labor

Finally, it is the local community as a whole that is forced to assume the costs of immigration. While many of the owners of business and capital may view immigrants—whether low-skilled or high-skilled—primarily as a source of cheaper labor, those workers can be quite expensive to the rest of the members of a community. And while some private organizations may promote immigration as a way for them to express charitable feelings, all the other members of a community end up paying most of the costs.

In myriad ways, a community subsidizes those who benefit from high immigration.

Some of the subsidy is monetary: social services to foreign workers who do not earn enough money to rise above poverty; issuance of new school bonds to educate the foreign workers' children; additional infrastructure to handle an expanding population that cannot pay enough taxes to cover the costs; social services to American workers who lose jobs or drop into poverty wages because of the foreign job competition.

Other costs to a community are less tangible but probably more disconcerting to the American people. They involve changes—many of which are considered *losses* by natives—in the quality of life in a community. High immigration tends to lengthen the time it takes people to travel to work; it tends to increase air pollution, to add pressures on already vulnerable environmental resources, and to lower the quality of the schools; and it tends to add transience to a community while diminishing social cohesiveness, decreasing public safety, and generally changing its ambiance and lifestyle.

A tale of two prairie towns in 1972 featured in *Fortune* magazine vividly illustrates some of those high costs of cheap foreign labor. A picture of the citizens of Spencer, Iowa, filled the magazine cover. Inside, the article on small towns also saluted Garden City, Kansas. Both places were said to be prospering economically while continuing to offer their residents the "uniquely American lifestyle" of a small town. The article extolled small towns' low crime and taxes, an idyllic environment for children, friendliness, the absence of an underclass, and a strong sense of community unity.[1]

Much has changed since then. Garden City has become home to thousands of immigrants; Spencer has not. Spencer has retained most of the attributes that so impressed the *Fortune* writer; Garden City has not.

Congress has made the decision that the nation should move in a Garden City–like direction. And it is Garden City that provides a glimpse of the future for all American communities and the price they may be forced to pay for Washington's immigration policies—if they aren't paying them already.

* * *

In some ways, immigrant-enlarged Garden City looks to be the more successful of the prairie towns. The two were about the same size in 1972. Since then, Spencer has barely grown to 11,000, but Garden City now is more than twice that size. Spencer quickly faded from national attention; Garden City received continuing national recognition through the 1980s and 1990s as a meat-processing boom town and a home of increasing cultural diversity.

Garden City measures up well under a "bigger is better" standard. Not only has its population surged, but it has many more jobs—a 55 percent increase between 1980 and 1988 alone. By 1991, *Kansas Business Review* could boast that the town had added seventeen more eating and drinking establishments and thirty-nine new retail stores, including a new shopping center anchored by J. C. Penney and Wal-Mart.

But below those obvious signs of growth lies a much grimmer picture of the costs to Garden City natives of having industries that rely heavily on immigrants.

Increasingly, Garden City's conditions have moved toward Third World standards. In 1987, for example, the county had the second highest birth rate in Kansas and was the only county in which less than 50 percent of the mothers received adequate prenatal care. In the first five years of recruiting immigrant workers into Garden City, confirmed cases of child abuse and neglect tripled.

Garden City taxpayers now have a much heavier load of impoverished residents to support. Even as the number of jobs was expanding, the unemployment rate rose 50 percent between 1979 and 1986, partly because of the number of immigrants who were injured on the job or who found they weren't willing to put up with the conditions at the meatpacking plants.

Economic growth based on low-wage immigrant labor "had the effect of reducing relative income levels," said the *Kansas Business Review*. Per capita income for the county, in comparison to the rest of Kansas, dropped throughout Garden City's "booming" 1980s.

Because of the low wages and the high number of children, many of the immigrant families couldn't make ends meet on their incomes. The taxpayers had to supplement the workers' food, medical care, and other basic needs. The taxpayer-supported psychiatric hospital experienced sustained admissions, as did treatment centers for alcoholism. The availability of health care in the county deteriorated as the doctor to resident ratio dwindled by about a third.

According to a team of scholars writing in the *Aspen Institute Quarterly*, Garden City has been typical of the way taxpayers subsidize most industries that expand in midwestern cities while using immigrant labor. The Mid-Nebraska Community Services, for example, experienced a huge increase in the demand for social services after the introduction of immigrant labor into its region. Use of the food pantry rose 405 percent, and programs for the homeless experienced a 1,000 percent jump in activity, after the first year. Lexington, Nebraska, the site of a major immigrant worker center, saw its crime rate rise to the highest in the state, twice the state average.

The Aspen Institute scholars noted that a "local community assumes it will benefit from a growing payroll and improved purchasing power. However, the case of Lexington demonstrates that the economic expansion may not be sufficient to support new-worker households at the living standards of older residents. The unexpected result is a net gain in poverty and expanded demands for understaffed and underfinanced health and social services. Less visible costs are reflected in the need for new education programs and expanded police protection." In part because governments give industries tax incentives to expand their immigrant-reliant operations, the tax receipts do not expand sufficiently to meet the additional needs of the immigrant workers. The native taxpayers have to pay a subsidy to the industries in the form of higher taxes and deteriorated services.

In Garden City—which once typified the very term "heartland"—residents watched as their crime rate rose steadily and violent crimes nearly doubled in the county, while crime in the rest of Kansas was dropping.

In 1990, the superintendent of Garden City schools had to acknowledge the highest dropout rate in Kansas. Trying to provide a good climate for education proved increasingly difficult with a growing student body—a 37 percent increase over one six-year period—and immigrant students who often seemed just to be passing through, thanks to chronic absenteeism and turnover of almost one-third of the students each year. Minority enrollment—mostly Southeast Asian, Mexican, and Central American—had hit 36 percent by 1989. While the school system struggled to find teachers who could speak Vietnamese and Spanish, the racial imbalance among the elementary schools grew so stark that the school board proposed busing, only to cancel it after vigorous protest from the natives. Taxpayers consented three times to major bond issues to build new schools for the immigrant children. But according to Professors Michael Broadway and Donald D. Stull, who did in-depth studies of the town, "the struggle to provide a sufficient education for all of Garden City's children is being lost."[2]

A sense of unity and egalitarianism has been lost amidst all the transience. A longitudinal analysis of families enrolling their children in the Garden City school district for the first time found that 40 percent of them had left within a year. Another 20 percent were gone at the end of the second year.

Some Garden City people approve of the immigrant influx. They occupy the same professional sector as those who seem to speak favorably about immigration in most local communities: educators, clergy, and other people who provide government or private relief services to the immigrants. Those residents are proud that Garden City is now more "cosmopolitan," with bi-lingual education, ethnic festivals, and social service challenges like the big cities. They like the national attention they have received about their cultural diversity. For the overwhelming majority of residents, however, high immigration has brought few benefits and many costs, not the least of which is an irreparably changed style of living.

* * *

Spencer may look a little staid in comparison to Garden City, but that is all right with its citizens. It doesn't have ethnic festivals; the number of retail stores has expanded, but it can't boast of two McDonald's restaurants as does Garden City; its economy is solid but not robustly growing. It had a major setback just a few years after the 1972 *Fortune* article, which had noted that Spencer Foods Inc. was ranked 328th in the magazine's annual directory of the 500 largest U.S. industrial corporations. Because of the construction of competing plants such as those in Garden City, Kansas, which relied on immigrants to work at much lower wages, Spencer Foods left the meatpacking business. The Spencer plant eventually closed down, erasing around one thousand high-wage, high-benefit jobs from Spencer's economy.

Nonetheless, the town slowly diversified and bounced back. Most residents are very happy with their quality of life, says Michael L. Zenor, the county's district attorney: "This is a wonderful place to live."

Spencer citizens on 27 March 1995 overwhelmingly endorsed the notion that they are content with the status quo when—largely out of fear of an influx of immigrants—they rejected a company's bid to reestablish meatpacking in Spencer. They had no desire to get a chance to become more like Garden City.

Just as *Fortune* described in 1972, Spencer's children still have "big yards—almost endless spreads of grass—to play in," and the schools are free of most big-city problems. The majestic neoclassical courthouse still anchors the town, and a large park and public campground line the Little Sioux River which winds through. Crime is low. So is unemployment, at between 3 and 4 percent. There are no huge disparities of income and living conditions between significant groups in town.

The biggest problem Spencer faces may be in finding ways for its young adults to come back after they finish college, says Bob Rose, a business leader. "They want to return because they realize the benefits of living five minutes from the office; being able to get on the golf course at any time of day; fishing in the nearby lakes; being able to turn the kids loose."

And in Spencer, the citizens don't have to subsidize any local industries that are cutting corners by taking advantage of cheap foreign labor.

As the tale of two prairie cities illustrates, cheap foreign labor comes at a high cost for local communities, regardless of their size. Let's take a look at six of the most significant costs.

INFRASTRUCTURE

Immigrants—through their arrival from other countries and through their fertility rates, which are much higher than natives'—are the chief cause of U.S. population growth today. The majority of population growth in most cities is due either directly to immigration or to the arrival of native-born Americans fleeing high-immigration centers. In many cities, immigrants account for all the population growth.

In the heavily populated United States of the 1990s, residents who are added to a community seldom pay enough taxes to cover the extra costs they pose for the local infrastructure. The result is a combination of more monetary costs for natives and deterioration in a community's overall infrastructure.

Boulder, Colorado, found that it is cheaper to stop expansion than to accommodate it. It discovered that it could take undeveloped land in and around the city and maintain it for $75 an acre, while the public cost of maintaining it as developed land for an expanding population was between $2,500 and $3,200 per acre.[3]

A simple look at bridges helps illustrate the extraordinary costs of population growth. The Woodrow Wilson Bridge was opened in 1961 south of the Washington, D.C., metropolitan area to carry an Interstate highway across the Potomac River. But as a prime immigrant destination center, Washington's population has exploded and spread far past the bridge. Designed to carry 75,000 cars and trucks a day, the Wilson Bridge now carries nearly 175,000 vehicles a day. It is not expected to survive another ten years without at least $52 million in renovations and the building of a twin bridge. Some estimates suggest it will take nearly $1 billion to handle the additional traffic. As expensive as it will be to try to improve and expand the transportation infrastructure to handle the present population, that is just a beginning. Regional planners are predicting a 70 percent increase in traffic over the next twenty-five years and the likelihood of eighteen-hour-a-day congestion if the population continues to grow as expected.[4]

All across America, the growing population has not been able to generate enough taxes to pay for the extra wear and tear on infrastructure while at the same time paying to expand the infrastructure to accommodate the additional residents. It is difficult to see how the infrastructure can be expanded to meet the needs of a constantly growing population while federal politicians are competing to see who can most cut taxes and spending.

More than 40 percent of the country's highway bridges are considered structurally deficient or functionally obsolete. According to a horror story about crumbling concrete in the *Atlantic Monthly,* water mains are in such disrepair that most major cities suffer regular breaks, with some losing as much as 30 percent of their daily water supply that way.[5]

A U.S. Transportation Department study estimates that it would cost about $50 *billion* to take care of the national bridge problem and $315 *billion* to maintain existing highways through the year 2000 in their 1983 condition. It would cost $3.3 *trillion* over a nineteen-year period to repair all of the public infrastructure for the current population, according to the Associated General Contractors of America.[6]

The United States is not even close to meeting the maintenance needs for the infrastructure of its own population of 265 million. Yet it runs a massive immigration program that is projected to add another 110 million people to the country over the next five decades (in addition to the growth of some 20 million people among Americans whose families have been here since before 1970). Those 110 million additional immigrants and their descendants are not likely to create or gain the kind of jobs that will provide sufficient taxes in the future to cover the price of the infrastructure they will need. Every job requires capital investment of some kind, and the type of jobs that can continue America's recent standard of living require lots of capital. Total private business investment in the United States is more than $100,000 per worker, to say nothing of the gigantic investment in housing and governmental infrastructure. Unless each new immigrant is backed by an additional investment of $100,000 to $200,000 million, the average U.S. standard of living and the U.S. infrastructure will continue to deteriorate.[7]

Immigration advocates who suggest that the solution to our problems is to bring in more immigrants, because they will generate the necessary answers and the money, obviously have not noticed the crumbling of our infrastructure during the last thirty years of high immigration.

EDUCATION

Between 1992 and 2003, school enrollment nationwide is projected by the U.S. Census Bureau to increase by nearly 9 million students. The vast majority of them will be immigrants or the children of immigrants.[8]

America is faced with the daunting challenge of building enough classrooms to accommodate all the children immigration policies have added and are on course to add in the future. Texas needs to complete two schools every *week*—indefinitely—to keep up. The pace is even tougher in California, which needs to build an entire school every *day*, seven days a week, fifty-two weeks a year.[9]

Who is going to pay for all the classrooms for the 9 million additional students? Probably not the immigrants, according to a major study by the RAND Corporation of the school districts where most immigrants settle, which points out: "The one common characteristic of most immigrant children is poverty."[10]

It is highly unlikely that immigrants will pay the approximately $15,000 per child it costs to build new schools, says physics professor Albert Bartlett of the University of Colorado. And that doesn't count the actual annual cost of educating the child. So native-born Americans are paying higher taxes to pick up some of the cost, but not nearly enough. The prospect of raising even higher taxes is not good. The National League of Cities has reported a falling approval rate for new bonds. American citizens increasingly are reluctant to pay the extra educational costs for immigrant students they regard not as their children but as the federal government's.

The shortfall means that education is deteriorating in communities with high immigration.

In most communities, construction does not keep pace with population growth, and students attend increasingly crowded schools. The *Dallas Morning News* reported on one young Hispanic student, Mari Galindo, as she graduated from high school in an immigrant-congested section of the city. She had never known anything but crowding. In elementary school, she was taught cello in a storage closet and had her gym class in a portable building. Her middle school added portable buildings the day she arrived. In high school, she had to share desks with other students, to practice cheerleading in foyers, and to eat in shifts in overcrowded lunch rooms.[11]

The worst crowding in Dallas is in neighborhoods where immigrants settle. Not only do they have more children per family, but more families live in each house or apartment. Dallas taxpayers have approved one bond proposal after another to provide for the immigrant children. "How many bond programs does it take to get rid of overcrowded schools? Dallas hasn't found the answer yet," Larry Bleiberg and Christopher Lee wrote in April 1995. "Across the city, parents, teachers and school officials are discovering that the school district's biggest construction program on record won't guarantee every child an uncrowded classroom."[12]

The RAND study sought to uncover what all the crowding has meant for educational quality in the districts across the country where immigrants have added significantly to enrollments. All of the school districts studied were found to be suffering major cutbacks in per capita spending. Every one was cutting out activities the school board once had considered essential for a quality education. All were reducing extracurricular activities and supportive after-school services.

"The districts are profoundly troubled and are finding it difficult to provide sound educational experiences to any of their students," the RAND researchers concluded.

It is not just the numbers of immigrants that harm the educational efforts. Their erratic attendance is immensely disruptive, not just to themselves but to native students and to teachers. Immigrant students—even after being in the country several years—arrive at different times throughout the school year. Most schools in the RAND study had an overall turnover rate of more than 50 percent during the year; in some schools, the rate was near 100 percent. Teachers and administrators could not plan for what the mix of languages would be. Immigrant parents often take their children out of school for weeks or months at a time. The ones from the western hemisphere commonly remove students before Christmas, send them to their home country, and don't return them to school until March or April.

"School officials, from superintendents and school board members down to teachers and aides, are trying hard, at least in most cases, but they are not able to give immigrant children all they need to become full participants in American life," the RAND study concluded.

While the big-city school systems are failing the immigrant children, they are not doing much better with the American natives, the researchers said. Where immigrants settle heavily, the schools "are failing virtually all their students," including native blacks, native Hispanics, native whites, and even middle-income children.

It is difficult to give the standard educational attention to native-born American children while contending with immigrants who often are illiterate in their native language and arrive at school without even the most rudimentary of skills, such as using a pencil or eraser.

When looking at the crumbling big-city school systems of the country, Congress should ask: Which would make it easier to improve the educational quality there? (1) A continuation of present immigrant flows; or (2) a virtual cutoff of new immigrants. The answer seems so obvious that one must assume members of Congress have never considered the question, else they already would have cut the foreign flow.

Our U.S. representatives and senators, however, seem oblivious to the results of their legislative handiwork. They work in a city where half of all children live in poverty! Yet every year, they accede to federal policies that pour new immigrant children into the failing schools that are about the only hope most Washington, D.C., kids have of ever being able to escape their dire circumstances. The Census Bureau projects that if Congress does not change its policies, it will add another 112,000 immigrants to the District of Columbia by the year 2020.[13]

In one stressed urban school district after another, U.S. immigration policy appears designed to inflict damage. The U.S. Commission on Immigration Reform heard testimony in 1994 that referred to the Chicago school system's near failure to open the previous autumn because of a $300 million budget shortfall. That same budget contained spending for $450 million for educating recent immigrants, the commission was told. Congress has sent more than a quarter million immigrants (not counting the children they bear after they arrive) into Chicago over the past decade; why would it send still more when the city is struggling to even open the schools?

Higher taxes to build new schools. Higher costs per student to provide bi-lingual instruction. Lower abilities for the students who are turned out into the community as products of a deficient education. All of these are costs the communities pay for the cheap foreign labor used by the industrialists and other employers.

WELFARE

For years, public officials have talked about, debated, legislated, and administered plans for moving Americans out of welfare dependency and into the self-sufficiency of full-time jobs. Such efforts have accelerated in the mid-1990s, with major proposals aimed at pushing 2.5 million adults from welfare into jobs.

The problem as always is the jobs. The government can train, motivate, cajole, and coerce the welfare mothers, but it can't succeed unless there are jobs for the moms to take.

Federal officials can blame themselves. In one of the most glaring instances of working at cross purposes, they have imported millions of workers—a large percentage of whom compete against the welfare mothers for entry-level jobs—while berating the women for not finding a job.

Vanderbilt University anthropologist Virginia Abernethy says the federal arithmetic is a mess: In 1992, for example, the U.S. economy improved considerably over previous years and created nearly 2 million net new jobs. About 900,000 more Americans entered the workforce that year than retired and otherwise left it. The equation offered great hope in whittling away at the millions of Americans who entered the year unemployed or underemployed. But federal officials made certain the American people could not receive that benefit. That year they issued 1.3 million work authorizations to foreign workers; and another 300,000 new aliens were allowed by a Swiss cheese immigration enforcement system to enter the U.S. workforce illegally, according to government estimates.[14]

Frances Piven and Richard Cloward—in the 1993 revision of their classic *Regulating the Poor: The Functions of Public Welfare*—pointed out that with the labor market "flooded with immigrants from Asia, from Mexico and other Central and South American countries . . . there was no evidence, in short, that business required the labor of AFDC mothers."[15] The Urban Institute reported in the summer of 1994 that the economy might be able to come up with the 2 to 3 million jobs needed for the mothers that Congress and the president were discussing kicking off welfare, but that "two decades of stagnant or falling wages among low or unskilled workers will make it difficult, if not impossible, for welfare recipients to find jobs that pay enough to lift them out of poverty."[16]

More than twenty years of wage depression, due in part to high immigration, is making welfare reform very difficult. The evidence is widespread.

The Center on Budget and Policy Priorities in 1990 looked back over studies of welfare work programs. It found that only a tiny percentage of welfare recipients secured "a stable source of employment that provides enough income for a decent standard of living (at least above the poverty line) and job-related benefits that adequately cover medical needs."[17] That same year, the Brookings Institution could not find any welfare work program that raised the income of welfare mothers more than $2,000 above public assistance levels.[18]

In *Forgotten Americans,* John E. Schwartz and Thomas J. Volgy note: "No matter how much we may wish it otherwise, workfare cannot be an effective solution. Among the most important reasons for this is the absence of enough steady, decent-paying, full-time jobs to go around" because "low-wage employment riddles the economy."[19] Women do not turn to welfare primarily because they are "pathologically dependent on hand-outs or unusually reluctant to work," argue Christopher Jencks and Kathryn Edin. "They do so because they cannot get jobs that pay better than welfare."[20]

There are other experts, however, who wonder if the talk about jobs is the wrong focus. The key factors in welfare dependency—and in poverty in general—may be divorce and illegitimacy. Almost everybody who receives welfare is connected to one of those two factors. A study by Mary Jo Bane and David Ellwood of the U.S. Department of Health and Human Services found that more women got off welfare by marrying than by finding a job. The most important indicator of long-term welfare dependency is "marital status," they said.[21]

But that raises a number of questions about why more men are not marrying these mothers, and also why so many of these women have gotten rid of their men. There surely is something to the claim of David Blankenhorn, author of *Fatherless America,* that the answer lies partly in "the shift toward expressive individualism, the idea that your basic responsibility is to yourself, which means that your obligation to others becomes weaker."[22] But the decreasing ability of lower-skilled men to earn a "family wage," and the fact that their earnings have fallen much faster than those of women, also help explain the tragic rise in the percentage of children being raised in impoverished single-parent households.

In *Dollars and Dreams,* Frank Levy noted W. E. B. Du Bois's observation that when a man cannot bring much income into a marriage, "many women would rather raise their children alone than keep the man as a husband." And many men who might otherwise marry the women they have impregnated don't even consider the possibility because they can't see any way they could financially support the family.[23]

The role of immigration in this pessimistic web is seen daily by Jesse Peterson. He is the national leader of the Brotherhood Organization of a New Destiny (BOND), which he says tries to "rebuild the black community by rebuilding the black man." He especially targets low-income black men who have not taken responsibility for emotionally and financially supporting their children and their children's mothers. Peterson complains:

Once we deal with the emotional problems of young men, we have a program where we try to place them on jobs. But due to immigration, it is virtually impossible to get the jobs. Blacks finally have an opportunity to enter the middle class, but now we have to deal with immigration. It affects blacks more than anybody else competing at the entry level. We tell them that they have to start somewhere and they should be willing to start at the bottom and then work up. We work with them until they realize that. But employers won't hire them because they would have to pay full benefits and they have so many immigrants they can pay under the table without benefits.

Chalk up at least a portion of the Americans trapped in welfare dependency as part of the very human cost of Washington's decision to add a million or more foreign workers to the economy each year. And include the monetary cost of the taxpayer having to continue to support those people on welfare.

"Welfare reform presents new challenges as thousands of Americans now receiving public assistance will be required to enter the labor market," says Susan Martin, executive director of the bi-partisan U.S. Commission on Immigration Reform. "The commission believes that it is not in the national interest that they should face additional competition from unskilled foreign workers."[24] Unfortunately, the commission recommended eliminating only the small category through which immigrants could be imported specifically for unskilled labor. Its recommendations would continue to allow hundreds of thousands of unskilled immigrants to enter through other (mostly family preference) categories.

Something close to a total pause in unskilled immigration "would let welfare reform proceed smoothly," says Virginia Abernethy, author of *Population Politics*. "The market could absorb the unemployed, reengage the discouraged worker and relieve the welfare burden."[25]

DOMESTIC TRANQUILITY

Americans are substantially agreed that immigration has not made their communities calmer, more peaceful places to live. One of the most insidious costs of federal high-immigration policies is the increase in social tensions and crime.

In 1992, a *BusinessWeek* poll found that 59 percent of Americans said immigration had worsened race relations in the cities. And 55 percent of respondents told Gallup pollsters in 1993 that the diversity of cultures brought in by immigrants "mostly threaten" American culture.[26]

To say that the imposition of a foreign culture into an American community is disruptive is not necessarily to say there is anything negative about that foreign culture itself. The point is that differing cultures often tend to clash. And no matter how admirable the traits of a foreign culture, it can produce less than admirable results when introduced too rapidly and in too large a dose into the middle of a community. Most people anywhere in the world feel a strong right to surround themselves with whatever local culture they prefer. Americans have not been happy when the influx of immigrants has seemed to threaten their local way of life. The higher the volume of immigration, the higher has been the sense of threat and resulting tensions.

That proved to be true in Wausau, Wisconsin, during the 1980s. On the main street into Wausau from the highway, an "All American City" sign is a symbol of another era. It reminds residents that, no farther back than 1984, they treated their new Southeast Asian immigrants so kindly, and the newcomers felt so welcome, that a panel of national judges deemed Wausau's generosity worthy of honor. Some people in the city had set out in 1979 to show their compassion toward people of other countries who wanted to move to the United States, and they had succeeded.

But much has changed since 1984. The number of Southeast Asians burgeoned, and the city's ability to welcome, nurture, accommodate, and assimilate the larger numbers shrank. Most immigrants were unable to enter the mainstream of the economy. Residents resented the social costs of caring for many more newcomers than anybody had been led to believe would arrive. The high-fertility rate of the immigrants quickly helped fill one of every four classroom seats with a Southeast Asian child. Young immigrants complained of disrespectful treatment by native youths. Economically and socially frustrated immigrant youth and young adults were particularly susceptible to recruitment by organized crime syndicates. Inter-ethnic violence and other tensions proliferated in the schools and in the parks and streets of a town that formerly had been virtually free of social tensions and violence. The peaceful townspeople were shocked to see local TV newscasts of immigrant youth gangs attacking native individuals with baseball bats and iron pipes and footage of the aftermath of a drive-by shooting involving the cars of immigrant groups of different Asian nationalities. A homecoming dance had to be canceled after an ambulance was called to mop up a fight between immigrant and native girls.

"At first, most saw the new residents as novel and neat; people felt good about it," said Fred Prehn, a dentist and father. "Now, we're beginning to see gang violence and guns in the schools. Immigration has inspired racism here that I never thought we had. You see things that weren't even an issue before, like walking down the halls of high schools and the junior high and seeing all the pregnancies. It has put a burden on the property tax rolls. It has brought interesting diversity. But it is detrimental when there is no way to stop it."

Prehn was a member of the school board when interviewed. He later was swept out of office in an election recall of everybody on the board who had voted to institute busing to alleviate problems in several schools where English was becoming a foreign language. The turmoil over busing and the recall election has left deep divisions in the society.

On my visit to Wausau, I found some anger. But the overwhelming emotion seemed to be sadness about a social revolution that the community as a whole had never requested or evendiscussed. While most residents spoke well of the foreign residents as individuals, they thought that the volume of immigration had crossed some kind of social and economic threshold. Many sensed that their way of life was slipping away, overwhelmed by outside forces they were helpless to stop.

The experience of community breakdown and tension is a basic pattern for most communities that receive a significant influx of immigrants. Worthington, Minnesota, for example, went from a culture of almost no crime to one of drive-by shootings, gang activity, drug dealing, and assaults. While some residents say their city of 10,000 has been revitalized by all the immigrants from Laos, Sudan, Vietnam, Ethiopia, and Mexico, most native residents apparently feel as though their farming hamlet lifestyle has been taken from them and their home turned into a rural ghetto. The local newspaper in 1993 asked residents for their view of the new immigrants: out of almost 250 responses, nearly all were negative.[27]

The problems that U.S. communities encounter when large numbers of immigrants enter from other countries is not unique to Americans, according to a 1995 study by the National Center for Policy Analysis. Immigration can create a type of cultural diversity, which anthropologists identify as a universal source of social conflict and often as a barrier to personal freedom and economic progress. The role of culture in a society is to standardize human contact so that people can make reasonably confident assumptions about the reactions of other people. "Multiculturalism sounds fine in theory," said Gerald R. Scully, the author of the study, "but we find that where there are multiple cultures there's almost always conflict. Most homogeneous cultures have more civil and political freedom, while culturally heterogeneous ones have less." The study by the free-market-oriented think tank found that increasing the number of languages and cultures in a country actually harmed economic progress: "Even if different groups live together peacefully, the lack of a common language and common norms reduces cooperation and increases the cost of transacting."[28]

Criticism of cultural diversity tends to grate on the ears of Americans, who think of their country as a great respecter and appreciator of diversity. That sense of national identity is so ingrained in many altruistic Americans that immigration trumps all other issues: the belief is that the more diversity the better, no matter what the cost. Much of the confusion may arise from the fact that few people alive have experienced American diversity—until recent years—under conditions other than the low immigration flows following 1924. Many have falsely assumed that because the diversity of the 1950s and 1960s was good for society, more diversity would be even better. But the diversity of national origins was a delightful spice during that period because it was in small enough proportions that the minority cultures could achieve common bonds with the majority culture. One of the leaders of the early Southeast Asian community in Wausau understood that concept when she thanked the city leaders for the town's great hospitality to her people, but warned them that it probably would not be a good idea to allow the immigrant population to grow above perhaps 5 percent of the total population. A larger proportion might create problems and lead to enmities that would cause the hospitality toward her people to turn into resentment, she said. As continued migration more than doubled that percentage, her warnings were borne out. By insisting on more and more immigrants, the multicultural enthusiasts kill the very thing they supposedly seek: a healthy diversity in which all Americans respect the cultural variations of each other.

The truism that too much immigration will kill healthy multiculturalism seems to apply everywhere, despite claims in a number of national newsmagazines and newspapers that New York City is an exception. "Civil war in Los Angeles, but civil in New York," read a headline for an article in *USA Today* that said, "in New York City, people and politicians are not upset about immigration. . . ." The statement was half-right: A group of politicians *has* made aggressive pro-immigration statements. "Without question, we believe here that New York is a city of immigrants; we are all aware of the cultures and traditions and we love it," said ex-mayor Ed Koch.[29]

In fact, though, New York City is an important model for what is wrong with the nation's immigration policies. New York residents know that—and they don't "love it." They disagree with their local officials about immigration and are not at all happy that some 30 percent of the population is foreign-born. An Empire State Survey in 1993, for example, found that New York City residents by a 2 to 1 margin said that immigration was making the city a worse place to live. Even the majority of the immigrants there said immigration was harming the city.[30]

While immigration advocates point to a few neighborhoods they say have been revitalized by immigrants, much of the city reels under the competing ethnic forces of immigration. In Upper Manhattan, the recent flood of immigrants has strained city services, and the newcomers live six or more to a two-bedroom apartment. The *Christian Science Monitor* reported that the immigrants have transformed the Washington Heights section into a miasma of ethnic commerce, drug dealing, and murder. Besides drug-related killings, there are the constant slayings of store owners in robbery attempts—fifty-one in one twelve-month period.[31]

The treatment of children in the New York City schools almost ensures that the area will become more dangerous in the future, say some city officials. In the thirty-three overcrowded high schools of Queens, teachers must deal with sixty languages. And the immigrant flows change so rapidly, says the superintendent, that "the languages we need this September will be different than the languages we'll need the next September."[32] Immigration has so overwhelmed the schools in Washington Heights, Manhattan, that teaching is done in shifts. Rapid immigration has left the neighborhood crammed with twice as many children under twelve as lived there before the boom in immigration that began twenty years ago. Some 25,000 children share two school playgrounds because portable classrooms have covered all the rest. "There are thousands of children trapped inside crowded apartments with nowhere to play because of the drug trade and the violence on the streets outside," wrote Malcolm Gladwell of *The Washington Post*. High school dropout rates exceed 50 percent.[33]

But Congress keeps sending more immigrants, and New York City's mayors keep saying, "Thank you."

The social fabric has so torn in New York City that bushes are being ripped out and walls pulled down to open up secluded public places where residents once could feel like they were getting away from the bustle and the grime of the city. The new rules for urban design caused Sigurd Grava, a Columbia University urban planner, to comment: "We are no longer in the Renaissance. We are back in the Dark Ages, where you had to assume that everyone was evil."[34]

New York City was not always this way. During the decades of low immigration this century, it was "a city that enjoyed tranquility and civility to an extent quite unimaginable today," in the words of essayist Jonathan Yardley. New York City during that time was "a model and an ideal" for the rest of the nation, says David Gelernter.[35] U.S. Senator Daniel Patrick Moynihan points out that New York City today "is immeasurably worse in nearly every aspect of urban life: violent streets, disintegrating families and crumbling infrastructure." The city once had "the most admired urban school system in the world, the finest housing, the best subways and in many ways the best-behaved citizens."[36] New York City always has been an immigration center, but during its golden years the flow was modest and nourishing instead of torrential and eroding.

"The evidence of our senses is that areas with a high concentration of immigrants tend also to be areas of ethnic conflict," says John O'-Sullivan, editor of *National Review*. "That is not to say that immigrants are responsible for such violence; very often they are the victims of it. But it tends to confirm that immigration fosters conditions in which ethnic cultures thrive, the sense of national solidarity is weakened, and the rules and conventions that order our lives (i.e., the common culture) fall into disuse."[37]

Let me conclude this section with a quick sampling of recent newspaper clippings and other reports from across the nation:

- In Miami, black and white residents overwhelmingly want to halt flotillas of Cuban immigrants into their city. When President Clinton blocks the flotillas, Miami's immigrant community snarls traffic in four days of protests that lead to scuffles and shouting matches between Latin Americans and native blacks and whites. "We gringos don't appreciate the traffic slowdowns," says Robert Campbell, an equipment salesman.[38]
- A Hispanic school official in Los Angeles County proposes non-citizen voting in school board elections. The black community erupts in protest, charging the immigrants are trying to dilute hard-won black influence.[39]

- A similar proposal in Sacramento stirs charges of disrespect toward black Americans. "We worked for years for the right to vote; people died for that right," says black leader Madi Greer. "It seems like just a little too much to just hand it over to somebody." She storms out of a meeting when a supporter of noncitizen voting makes his argument in Spanish. "He speaks English," she says, "I know it."[40]
- In Washington, D.C., Hispanic leaders denounce a popular black radio host for expressing concern that immigrants are taking over black neighborhoods and diminishing the quality of life for black residents.[41]
- Fights break out between Cambodian and Latin-American students in Stockton, California.[42]
- Rising ethnic tensions follow the arrival of nearly a half-million immigrants in northern Georgia. Some communities are overwhelmed in a cacophony of languages and the clashing of cultures. Immigrants complain that the businesses want them for their cheap labor but the communities get upset when they take their culture into the streets during their leisure time. Natives complain that it no longer feels like Georgia in many areas. In Cross Keys High School in Atlanta, for example, students speak fifty-two languages. An observer notes that a walk in the halls finds nobody speaking English except the principal.[43]
- Latino groups blast middle-class black residents in Los Angeles County as being racist for seeking an ordinance to prohibit the congregating of immigrant day laborers in their community. The black residents say the immigrants were trespassing, making lewd comments, littering, and generally eroding their quality of life.[44]
- In Dubuque, Iowa, a meatpacking plant shuts down, due in part to competition from immigrant workers in other plants in other towns. The town's national image is marred by black and white racial friction. One cause, says Iowa historian Ken Cox, is that "low-skill laborers have been pitted against each other for less and less desirable jobs."[45]
- Latinos in Compton, California, accuse black elected officials of oppression for keeping almost all political control in the hands of black leaders. Compton leaders charge back that Latinos don't appreciate the long black struggle for power.[46]
- A federal grant of $1 million to turn a Washington, D.C., school into a special bi-lingual program splits the teachers and parents into hostile camps. Of the 434 students, 269 are immigrants;

most of the rest are black natives. "Many black parents are struggling as it is to teach their kids good English," protested Katherine Warner, a black math teacher. "Why are they suddenly going to start teaching them 80 percent in Spanish?" Many black parents organize to fight the changes. They resent their community school having to change to accommodate newcomers from other countries. Immigrant students, parents, and teachers accuse their black opponents of being guilty of racial prejudice, immigrant bashing, and deception. "I never thought we had racism in this school, but now I know it exists and it hurts," says Isabel Martinez, an English-as-second-language teacher.[47]

Many commentators fear that heavy immigration is "Balkanizing" the United States—that is, breaking the country down into competing ethnic groups and nationalities that may even resort to warfare as has long been the history among the Balkan nations in Southeast Europe. Peter Brimelow argues that it is almost impossible for multi-ethnic societies—such as the one immigration is creating in the United States—to survive. In *Alien Nation,* he cites the recent examples of Ethiopia before Eritrea split off, Czechoslovakia before division, Soviet Union before collapse, Yugoslavia before collapse, Lebanon before partition, Cyprus before partition, Pakistan before Bangladesh split off, and Malaysia before Singapore split off. Then there are the protracted separatist revolts continuing in India, Sri Lanka, Turkey, Iraq, Iran, Sudan, Chad, and Nigeria; and the heated political disputes of the multi-ethnic societies of Canada, Belgium, and Brazil. Only Switzerland—which has a highly regimented way of life; German, French, and Italian ethnic groups far more similar to each other than the ones in America; and no large influx of new ethnic populations—has seemed to escape harm.

Viewing that record and the incredible and unprecedented flow of cultures from all over the world into the United States today, some observers warn that communities are losing their core culture and that the communities and even the United States may be in danger of losing their very identity. Others believe immigration is leading to a less dramatic fate. Richard Bernstein in his *Dictatorship of Virtue* says: "My own sense is that we are more likely to end up in a simmering sort of mutual dislike on the level of everyday unpleasantness than we are in full-scale Balkan warfare. But that is bad enough."[48]

Michael Lind of the *New Republic* also doubts that continued high immigration and a policy of multiculturalism will fragment the country along racial and ethnic lines. But he does think they will further fragment the country along class lines: "The real threat is not the Balkanization but the Brazilianization of America." By that, he means that the richest Americans—whom he calls the "white overclass"—increasingly will use their wealth to separate themselves from the spreading squalor and social disintegration of society, conditions accelerated by the high immigration which also enhances the wealth of the overclass. As is normal in Brazil, and becoming more and more common in large U.S. immigration centers such as Los Angeles, the wealthy live barricaded from the rest of the nation in a world of private neighborhoods, police, health care, and even roads, Lind says. "Like a Latin American oligarchy, the rich and well-connected members of the overclass can flourish in a decadent America with third-world levels of inequality and crime."[49]

The proliferation of so-called gated communities may be the clearest and most disturbing sign that "the problems of the city will continue to get worse, and someday there may be no 'city' left," says Roger K. Lewis, professor of architecture at the University of Maryland. Americans buying walled-off homes in both the city and the suburb are not just seeking to escape the problems of the city: "They are abandoning the whole *idea* of city—its culture, its physical form, its intellectual and commercial vitality, its complexity and unique capacity for accommodating disparate individuals within a shared environment."[50]

The drive of so many Americans for protection, exclusion, and separation in gated communities is fueled by immigration, a growing underclass, and a restructured economy, according to Edward J. Blakely, professor of planning and development at the University of Southern California. He and Mary Gail Snyder of the University of California–Berkeley studied the gated communities and found them to be most popular in the states of California, Texas, Florida, and in or around the cities of New York City, Chicago, and Phoenix. All these areas except Phoenix have the highest U.S. concentrations of immigrants—and Phoenix is filling up with native-born urban refugees who have been traumatized by the social breakdown in California.[51]

In the midst of the growing crime, deteriorating schools, and multicultural tensions that accompany high immigration, residents of every economic status are being drawn to walled-off communities. They seek a sense of safety, of more control over their surroundings, and of a homogeneity in which they can take comfort in being surrounded by people who think as they do. Immigration has forced such rapid change and increased diversity that it is causing Americans to shun even their previous lower level of diversity.

"Welcome to the new Middle Ages," says Professor Lewis. "We are building a kind of medieval landscape in which defensible, walled and gated towns dot the countryside." The members of Congress and the presidents who have supported high immigration during the last two decades may some day in the not-too-distant future be seen as the ones who—more than any other—killed the American cities.

In the late 1980s the Ford Foundation, which has provided the principal funding to immigrant organizations that successfully have lobbied Congress to continue and increase high immigration, initiated a sweeping study of community tensions in areas of high immigration. Its authors in the end denied that immigration is causing a truly "fragmented" society. But they said the main reason there is not more violence among immigrant groups, and between them and the native population, is that "newcomers and established residents co-exist primarily by maintaining their distance from each other." Researchers learned that even in communities in Houston where immigrants and natives live near each other, there still is separation and no large-scale interaction. The researchers heard citizens of Garden City, Kansas, say that "people get along because the different ethnic groups don't mix."[52]

When there is mixing, the cultural misunderstandings can result in tragedy—as occurred with the first murder in the history of Hawarden, Iowa, on 14 January 1994. Richard and Vicki Youne blame the death of their son Justin in part on federal immigration policies that began to push foreign workers into their town of around 2,700 in the early 1990s. "Not in anybody's wildest imagination would somebody around here go for a knife in a fight," Richard says. "I'm not saying there weren't fights. But you'd duke it out and go on. It's a different culture that goes for a knife."

Police chief Jim Landau blamed cultural misunderstanding. He said Justin Youne—a nineteen-year-old white native and a Dean's List sophomore at the University of South Dakota—was attending a large house party that included alcohol and a few young men from Mexico. Landau told the *Sioux City Journal* that the native boys "were showing off wrestling moves. They were having an OK time. The Hispanic guys were getting into it; they had never done anything like that before." When an argument broke out between two of the white men, the immigrants tried to jump in to help out the one who was their friend. Justin, a black belt in karate, blocked them to keep the fight fair. The immigrants ran to the kitchen, grabbed knives, and stabbed Justin to death while injuring the boy who was fighting with their friend. "What it boils down to is kids around here think fighting is a normal way of life," the police chief said. "If they felt like fighting, they did and then they got it over with and went home. In this case, somebody was playing by a different set of rules."

Justin's mother said she'd had fears that the introduction of such a different culture intoHawarden was dangerous: "We've had drug busts, domestic abuse, different things like that," since the immigrants arrived. "We used to not lock our doors and leave keys in cars. I used to walk around town, but I couldn't do that anymore. The general feeling of safety is gone. I always told Justin and my other two boys, 'These people don't handle things the way we do; one of these days, they are going to pull a knife on you.' My boys kept saying, 'Mom, you aren't right; they're cool.' "[53]

Immigrant residents of Hawarden, while not justifying the murder, can point to their own reasons for fear. A couple of years earlier, eleven native residents were arrested for beating three immigrant men. Two of the attackers were charged under Iowa's hate crimes law.

Cultural differences, mutual mistrust, and the feeling that they need to band together for protection against "others" in a community is what led to a phenomenon that has spread across the country, according to Los Angeles police: youth gangs formed as a vigilante type of ethnic group protection. Police say the Mexican Mafia of hardened criminals played a major role in starting the gangs in the 1950s and in influencing them today. Fueled by thirty years of relentless immigration from all over the globe, the types and numbers of youth gangs have multiplied in Los Angeles. Police there estimate upward of 1,000 gangs, with perhaps 150,000 members.[54]

During the last decade of explosive immigration the rate of violent youth crime has soared. Youth arrests for major violent crimes rose from 83,400 arrests in 1983 to 129,600 in 1992, a Justice Department study shows. And the rate is even higher in urban areas of high immigration. Attorney General Janet Reno has warned that over the next decade, the United States may face violent crime that will "far exceed what we have experienced."

Immigration can play a key role in fostering a gang culture. In the Virginia suburbs of Washington, D.C., for example, police list eighty-seven law-violating youth gangs, around fifteen of them hard-core. Area police attribute their formation and proliferation to the massive influx of many nationalities into the area since 1980. Immigrant groups felt they needed to protect themselves from each other. In the process, continual friction and occasional violence erupted between the immigrant groups and the native black population, as well. The immigrant youths' tendency toward gangs is explained by some police as being a response to intense frustration: They often come from a peasant culture without a tradition of education; their parents don't value education or aren't able to help them; they can't keep up in school; they feel constantly harassed by police for actions such as drinking and urinating in public parks which they consider culturally permissible; they see little chance of obtaining jobs for much more than the minimum wage; and they live impoverished, overcrowded lives in the midst of communities with some of the highest average incomes in the country.[55]

"Mob assaults" have become a major problem in the northern Virginia schools, with most of the perpetrators immigrants. Nationwide, school violence is skyrocketing, according to a survey by the National League of Cities. Although there has been a slight decline in major crimes by all ages in recent years, the national crime rate remains far above what it was before the 1965 change in the immigration law. The murder rate, for instance, still is double what it was in 1960.

All of this disintegration of the social fabric almost seems predictable. It has accompanied every other surge in immigration, according to crime historian Ted Robert Gurr of the University of Maryland. Most immigrants, of course, do not come to America to steal their way to the American dream. But a sizable minority for various reasons—perhaps disenchantment with an economy that doesn't need or reward large numbers of low-skill foreign workers—turns to crime once here. More than 25 percent of the felons in federal prisons are immigrants.

Then there is the matter of organized crime. Some immigrants move to America expressly for the purpose of criminal activity. The FBI and the Immigration and Naturalization Service have warned that international crime organizations are actively establishing and expanding operations here, using the new streams of immigrants.[56]

When a large population moves from another country into the United States, it becomes much easier for that country's crime organizations to transport their operations through many of those immigrants. It happened with European ethnic groups during previous immigration waves, and it is happening now. Federal officials who thought they were close to conquering the Italian Mafia are faced with dozens of new foreign syndicates operating in many languages. "One reason the Mafia has no role in drug dealing anymore is that they are at a huge disadvantage," Harvard's Mark A. R. Kleiman has commented. "The FBI has plenty of Italian agents. But just try finding agents who speak Chinese dialects. It's a nightmare." In the Washington, D.C., area, police have been overwhelmed by the growth of Thai, Chinese, Dominican, and Pakistani drug organizations.[57]

An international investigation by *Newsweek* revealed that the new crime lords "are far more sophisticated, more international and just plain more dangerous than either the Sicilians or the Medillin cartel ever were." Senator John Kerry of Massachusetts has called the new immigrant syndicates "the new communism, the new monolithic threat" to the United States.[58]

Waves of immigration from Russia have brought in what may be the most cunning of new crime bosses. But they are getting stiff competition from other immigrants working for organized crime syndicates headquartered in China, Japan, Hong Kong, Jamaica, Cuba, Israel, and Nigeria.

Foreign crime organizations actually have an interest in ethnic conflict breaking out in American cities, according to a major study by Richard H. Shultz and William J. Olson of the National Strategy Information Center. The syndicates exploit the conflict to create cover for their own operations; they also gain extra help from non-criminal immigrant groups who seek contact with the criminal syndicates for their own protection from the conflict with other ethnic groups.

Shultz and Olson said the foreign crime syndicates increasingly are linked to immigrant gangs of youth in U.S. cities, who help them with their drug trafficking, smuggling, theft, murder, extortion, credit card fraud, prostitution, and illegal gambling. The result is that some U.S. urban communities have become "combat zones in which law-abiding citizens are prisoners to violent gangs around them."[59]

Our federal immigration policies clearly are working against domestic tranquility for the citizens of this country. Among the six reasons our nation's founders gave for creating this system of federal government was to "ensure domestic tranquility." It was not an afterthought or something that would be nice to have if it didn't interfere with the pursuit of profits; in the Preamble to the U.S. Constitution, domestic tranquility ranks right there alongside establishing justice and providing for the common defense among the top priorities of government.

Through their recent immigration policies, the president and the Congress have violated their social contract with the American people. Part of that contract is spelled out in Article IV, section 4 of the Constitution, which states that the federal government is obligated to "protect each state against invasion" and "against domestic violence." Today's federal immigration program does exactly the opposite.

ENVIRONMENT

"What does it mean to be an American? What makes America great? Who are we as a people?" The National Parks and Conservation Association suggests that Americans are able to find answers to those questions in their National Parks, "the crown jewels of a nation without royalty." It is a reminder that this country is not simply a set of principles, or a constitution, or a type of economic system, but a nation of particular people living on a particular chunk of land.

And what a chunk it is! Ask an American what elements of this country are essential to his or her concept of America and the list likely will include the natural wonders: the Mississippi, the Everglades, the Grand Canyon, Yellowstone, the Great Lakes, the Rockies, the Smokies, plus whatever the individual's own local region offers in the way of rivers, creeks, bogs, lakes, forests, mountains, and meadows, and including the birds, the trees, the frogs, the bugs, and the animals whose sightings and sounds provide the essential backdrop and musical score to that person's particular life in America. Would it still feel like America without access to all of this?

For tens of millions of Americans, their quality of life would be diminished if not destroyed if they couldn't fish, hunt, hike, birdwatch, backpack, camp, or canoe in what is left of America's natural open spaces. Asked the essential ingredients of his quality of life, a man in Ashland, Alabama, included being able to leave work and to be hunting in the woods within fifteen minutes. A man in Wausau, Wisconsin, said that within fifteen minutes of leaving work he needed to be seated on a frozen lake, fishing through a hole in the ice. For others—such as residents of Simi Valley, California, and Phoenix—it is simply the ability to view nearby desert mountains without their slopes being marred by development.

Such close proximity to the natural world no longer is possible for most Americans, almost half of whom now live in metropolitan areas of more than 1 million people. Increasingly, as immigration swells the U.S. population, Americans are being cut off from the natural heritage of their country in several ways:

- Growing congestion in their cities and on the highways creates longer and longer travel times for reaching open spaces.
- The natural areas themselves are too congested with visitors to afford a top-quality experience. Many National Parks are so crowded that their natural health is deteriorating, and some now require reservations.
- The expanding population is filling in, cutting down, paving over, and building up many of the rural areas.
- The animal and plant inhabitants of the natural areas are threatened or in decline because of the pollution and other damage from the growing population.

Consider the Chesapeake Bay, which members of Congress can reach within an hour. The reasons for its precarious condition and why efforts to restore it are falling short resemble the circumstances of natural areas all over the country.

Since Captain John Smith's time, the Chesapeake has been an incredible cornucopia of oysters, blue crabs, and varieties of fish, in addition to serving as the recreational jewel for the region's human population. Estuaries like the bay are nature's premier biodiversity factories. The Chesapeake is the largest of some 850 estuaries in the United States and plays an essential role in fostering the important part of the nation's food supply that is harvested up and down the Atlantic Coast.

But the Chesapeake Bay—195 miles long and from 4 to 30 miles wide—appears to be dying from human abuse.

The oyster beds—until recently the bay's chief food product and its chief filtering device to keep the water clear—have crashed. Only a decade ago, watermen still could harvest 2 million bushels a season; the yield now is only around 300,000 and may fall further. Total oyster beds throughout the bay are estimated at only about 1 percent their size before the Civil War.

Excess nutrients from sewage plants, farm and lawn runoff, and from air pollution, plus sedimentation from development in the watershed, are killing off the underwater grass meadows that work in tandem with the oysters to filter the bay. Just as importantly, the human pollution is depleting the water of oxygen. In one recent summer, more than one-fourth of all the water in the bay either had so little oxygen that all aquatic life in the "bad water" was severely stressed, or it had no oxygen at all—a watery desert. The amount of oxygen-low "bad water" was found to have increased fifteen-fold between 1950 and 1980. There is no evidence of improvement since then, despite the gargantuan sums of money going into cleaner autos, industries, and sewage treatment, according to the Chesapeake Bay Foundation.

After years of study, it appears that the single greatest problem for the Chesapeake Bay may be population growth in the bay's watershed, according to Christopher D'Elia, provost of the University of Maryland Biotechnology Institute. And the single greatest cause of population growth in the Washington, D.C.,–Baltimore metropolitan area in the watershed is immigrants and their children.

"Make no mistake, most of the problems with the Chesapeake Bay are the cumulative impact of every one of the nearly 15 million people who live in its watershed," writes Tom Horton in his authoritative book on the bay, *Turning the Tide.*[60]

Until the 1960s and the 1970s, additional people could move into the bay's 64,000-square-mile watershed without posing grave risk because the total size of the population had not yet exceeded the bay's carrying capacity. But eventually the bay no longer could process the population's wastes and still function as a healthy, living ecosystem.

Governments, industries, and individuals have spent billions of dollars since 1970 to reduce air pollution and water pollution to save the bay. But the federal government has undercut all those efforts by forcing—through immigration—continued intense population growth in the watershed. At the same time that Herculean efforts were slashing the average impact on the bay of each watershed resident, congressional immigration policies were adding hundreds of thousands of new automobile-using and toilet-flushing residents.

Not every immigrant, of course, drives a car immediately upon arrival. But most eventually do, adding pollutants to air that already receives more noxious emissions than it can handle. Air pollution may be as much of a threat to the bay as water pollution. Rain washes the auto exhaust and industrial emissions directly from the sky into the bay and its tributaries. An Environmental Protection Agency study suggests air pollution may be responsible for as much as 25 percent of the excess nitrogen that depletes the water of oxygen and is so harmful to the underwater grass prairies.

And immigrants and their descendants eventually are drawn to the same recreational qualities of the bay that entice native residents. By now, tens of thousands of boaters hit the bay every weekend, so that some areas are too crowded for a boater to enjoy an experience that is safe, relaxing, and without tension from other boaters.

The experts have known for years that the bay cannot handle more population growth. At the end of a major conference on saving the bay in 1977, J. L. McHugh of the Marine Sciences Research Center of the State University of New York spoke forcefully: "One theme has run like a thread through all the papers and discussions in this conference, as it does in all discussion of environmental management. It is an issue that is almost always evaded, and certainly never addressed seriously. Yet this is the root problem of the environment, the basic cause of all the other problems—the human population explosion. . . . If we cannot cope with it, maybe everything else will be in vain."[61]

If the federal government had a true commitment to the food supply provided by the Chesapeake Bay—or to its human recreational opportunities, or its biodiversity and ecosystems—it, at the least, would not do anything to encourage the addition of inhabitants to the watershed that extends from Cooperstown, New York, and Scranton, Pennsylvania; from West Virginia; and which includes much of Virginia, Maryland, and Delaware. As Tom Horton says: "Every drop of rain that runs off these lands flows toward the bay. So does the discharge from every sewage pipe, industrial outfall and uncontained oil spill, every styrofoam coffee cup casually tossed into a drainageway. When soil erodes from farmland, or from a forest bulldozed for development, the sediment can head only in one direction—bayward."[62]

But the federal government's immigration program for thirty years has brought so many millions of new people to the country that it was inevitable that large numbers would settle in cities like Washington, D.C., which already had sizable numbers of immigrant families to act as magnets. In that sense, the federal government *forced* population growth on a gigantic scale throughout the watershed—in the process further wounding the bay and contributing to deteriorating schools, wages, infrastructure, public services, and public safety.

The outline of this story of the Chesapeake Bay could be used for scores of polluted, sick, or threatened natural resources across the country. Just substitute the name of another natural habitat and its surrounding cities and the plot line will work the same: (Act 1) Population grows until the natural resource cannot stay healthy. (Act 2) Lots of money is spent to reduce per capita environmental impact to save the natural resource. (Act 3) Immigration-fueled population growth undermines enough of the improvements to keep the resource threatened.

These environmental cases offer a clear illustration of the logical error of immigration advocates who insist that the United States ought to be able to handle present immigrant admissions because they account for a lower percentage of the total population than in the past. Lester Brown of Worldwatch Institute explains: "As populations grow, the effect of population growth changes. Demographers and economists often focus on the rate of current and projected growth of population. If they are concerned about population growth and see that the rate of growth is declining, they are likely to feel satisfied. Biologists, however, distinguish between rate of growth and absolute size. They are concerned with the relationship between the demand of a given population and its support systems. Once the local demand for water rises above the rate of aquifer recharge, for example, any further growth—however slow—will deplete the aquifer, leading to severe water shortages."[63]

In other words, as long as the Chesapeake Bay is not in sustainably good health, no immigration of any proportion or any size can occur in the watershed without further weakening a sick ecosystem.

If the federal government prohibited immigration into any watershed of a lake, river, estuary, or wetland that fails to meet clean water standards or where water is being withdrawn from an underground aquifer faster than it is replenished—and if immigration was forbidden into any air basin that fails to meet clean air standards—there would be very few places in which an immigrant could settle in the United States.

Such a proposal might seem harsh for potential immigrants. But to import people from other countries into environmentally threatened areas of the United States is terribly harsh to the natural resources, and to the nation's descendants who may be denied them in the future because of our mistreatment of the resources today.

A usual rejoinder to such talk of population limits is that the government should force the people already living in a threatened watershed to further restrict their waste, their mobility, their consumption, or some other aspect of their standard of living so that there will be environmental "room" for more immigrants.

Such "room" indeed could be found if the people would consent to deep enough cuts. But until the people and their governments lower the per capita environmental impact far enough to restore health to a threatened ecosystem, there can be no environmentally valid reason for inviting foreign citizens to expand the population.

For now, there is no sign that the American people or their governments have the desire or the will to force simpler lifestyles in higher-density living arrangements that don't require the using up of any more natural habitats. A case in point: States in the Chesapeake water-

shed have pledged to protect the bay by restricting the filling of wetlands and the cutting of forests; wetlands and forests play essential
functions in filtering out urban waste and sedimentation for the bay.
But the U.S. Fish and Wildlife Service reported that government agencies in the bay area turned down less than 10 percent of applications for
filling or draining wetlands to make room for more development between 1991 and 1993. Virginia already has lost 42 percent of its wetlands, and 73 percent have been destroyed in Maryland.[64] As long as
the population grows, there is little in our nation's history to suggest
the legal or political ability to stop developers.

The constant march of population-driven development prohibits
us from savoring even our greatest environmental victories. When the
U.S. Fish and Wildlife Service recently declared that it was taking the
bald eagle off the endangered species list, people familiar with the
bird's habitat in the Chesapeake Bay region could only cheer the pros-
pect of perhaps another generation of safety. The Atlantic Coast eagles
simply are running out of places to live as the ever-growing populations of Washington, D.C., Baltimore, and Norfolk–Virginia Beach
gobble up waterfront real estate and eliminate the eagle's habitat.

Further bad news for the bay: Part of the reason the Chesapeake is
so sick is that the Potomac River remains polluted with millions of
gallons per month of untreated human waste that the Washington,
D.C.–area sewage treatment systems cannot handle when it rains. Pes-
ticides and toxics in Washington's other river, the Anacostia, are so
high that the government warns of danger in eating fish caught in the
waters, except certain species in small quantities. A study of all options
by the region's council of governments concluded that under the best
possible scenario—with funding, technological and mechanical improvements, and tight enforcement of environmental rules—the
Washington, D.C., area could *slow the growth* of pollution flowing into
the bay. But the council could not see a way to actually reduce the
pollution or even hold the line.

In one metropolitan area after another across the United States,
this type of gloomy scenario is being played out among planning agencies. An environmentally cautious federal policy would suggest doing
nothing to add to the population until somebody can come up with a
feasible program, enact it, and fund it fully to protect the environment
from the strain of the population we have right now.

Instead, the federal government makes every bad environmental
situation worse, year after year, by adding more people. Having already
destroyed about 50 percent of all wetlands in the United States, our

growing population eliminates another 300,000 acres of wetlands each year. Having logged 90 percent of the northwestern old-growth forests, our growing population is applying intense pressure to cut down the remainder. In thirty-five states, we withdraw groundwater faster than it can be replenished to provide us our food, baths, sewage systems, consumer products, and industrial jobs; every year, we add 3 million more water users. With 60,000 square miles of the country already covered by pavement, an additional 1.3 million acres are black-topped each year to meet the needs of our growing population.

Every once in a while a writer or politician—usually somebody who has spent too much time in a coastal city and has forgotten that cities are not self-sufficient—flies over the United States, looks out the airplane window, and declares that the country has vast expanses of land on which to add population.

Well, those vast open spaces through the Midwest are largely empty of people and urban development for a very good reason: they feed us. And most of the vast expanses of trees are under private or government management to meet the nation's wood and paper needs. For each American, it takes many acres of farm, range, forest, and other land to feed, clothe, house, and provide the materials (and space) for transportation, commerce, residence, recreation, and waste disposal. David Pimentel of Cornell University points out that virtually all U.S. land capable of sustained farming is currently being cultivated. There isn't much more to be gained. In Illinois, for example, the pressure to raise as much food as possible has resulted in the destruction of 91 percent of the 8.2 million acres of wetlands that existed in the state at the time it entered the Union. It now is very difficult to add population without destroying farmland necessary for the food supply or eliminating the last remnants of natural ecosystems.

As for the vast open spaces in the West, most of them are thinly populated for another good reason: They have little or no economic use and lack enough water to support agriculture, industry, or urban concentration. On the West's habitable coasts, immigration-driven population growth already has pushed California's natural environment to the brink of extinction: only 3 percent of its wetlands remain; only 300 of the previous 10,000 kilometers of salmon streams in the Great Valley remain; other fish populations have dropped precipitously; 110 animal species are endangered or threatened; more than 200 plants are endangered, threatened, or rare. California's overpopulation harms far more than California. Its insatiable need for electricity and water transfers pollution and other resource damage to states throughout the West where power plants and water diversion projects are located. Visitors to the Grand Canyon in Arizona routinely see evidence that California's population has far exceeded the environmental carrying capacity of that state: The haze that often obscures the full grandeur of the canyon is filled with pollutants that have overflowed from Southern California.

The Audubon Society conducted a study comparing biodiversity loss at sites in the United States with loss at sites in Brazil, Guatemala, Indonesia, Kenya, Mexico, Pakistan, Thailand, and Zimbabwe. It found the rate of loss tended to be greater in the United States.

One does not have to be a nature lover or hold religious convictions against eliminating parts of creation to be alarmed at the loss of biodiversity. The National Association of Physicians for the Environment, for example, emphasizes "the importance of the natural world (plants, microorganisms, etc.) regarding the derivation of drugs and other therapeutic products used in patient care," and calls for the protection of biological diversity because "human health is inseparable from the health of the natural world."[65] The National Institutes of Health estimate that about 40 percent of modern pharmaceuticals originated in nature.

"Population growth is probably the single most important factor in the ability to protect biological diversity and manage the environment," says Thomas Lovejoy, the internationally decorated conservation biologist.[66]

As he reviewed the continuing losing battle to protect endangered species, wetlands, woodland habitats, and biodiversity of all kinds in the United States, Undersecretary of State Tim Wirth commented in autumn 1994 at a meeting of the President's Council on Sustainable Development, "We shouldn't rob from future generations to meet the needs of this generation. Should we move toward population stabilization?" He went on to suggest that one way the federal government might help would be to set each year's immigration level based on the last year's birth rate, making sure immigration would be low enough not to create population growth.

Under that scenario, immigration numbers could be raised upward as the total fertility moves farther below the replacement rate. At the present fertility rate, however, even a net immigration level of zero for decades would not allow the U.S. population to fall back to its current 265 million.

Cutting off immigration would not resolve the nation's environmental problems, but it would make it much easier to effect improvements. For now, the blunt fact is that every immigrant above the level of zero who is allowed into this country worsens our environmental problems.

LIFESTYLE

At present immigration levels, Americans in just a few decades will be living in the same kind of population density as Europeans. Because Europe's population already has stabilized, it won't be long until Americans will be even more crowded than the Europeans. There are serious reasons to wonder if Americans will adjust well and readily, considering the history of so many Americans insisting on a high degree of personal freedom, personal space, and proximity to natural areas.

Those are not frivolous wants on the part of Americans but may well be deep psychological needs, says Debbie Biniores-Egger, an analytical psychologist. A native of Arkansas who now is a Swiss citizen, she believes most Americans might find it psychologically difficult to adjust to a European-type lifestyle of congestion: "I'm committed to the premise that what we create on the outside in our society has a relationship to the inner psyche of a population. Americans have a total sense of open boundaries. This is in essence the American culture." The Swiss have evolved a very different culture to preserve their privacy and to limit opportunities for personal conflict within greater population density. So they consent to and even encourage their government to force the protection of personal boundaries. Just a sampling of such methods would include: You don't change residence without registering with the government; stores must close after 6:00 P.M. and all day on Sunday; no baths are permitted between 10:00 P.M. and 6:00 A.M. To preserve the farms and the beauty of the countryside and to protect the environment, land use is strictly controlled by the government, forcing the price of housing so high that most Swiss never will own a home or even rent a single-family dwelling. Most Europeans have far less living space than Americans.

Managers of U.S. parks and wilderness areas can attest to Americans' deep need for space and solitude. The problem is that with 265 million Americans, the open spaces no longer are sufficient: Americans are loving nature to death. There isn't much wilderness left to set aside and open up to the public. In 1993, Congress opened up 353 square miles at South Colony Lakes in Colorado's Sangre de Cristo Mountains. Within two years, it was so crowded that rangers were contemplating limiting the number who could visit. While 5,000 visitors a year and 50 a day is considered the maximum use without damaging the land and eliminating any sense of solitude, the wilderness already was receiving 7,000 a year and up to 100 visitors a day. The average visitor encountered thirty other people while seeking solitude on the trails. In state and National Parks near population centers, limits on visitors are becoming more common as the national population grows by nearly 3 million a year. If immigration advocates insist on annual admissions above 200,000 a year, the resulting population growth will quickly move the country to the sad fate of Americans being allotted only so many National Park and wilderness visits per lifetime.[67]

One would hope that federal officials would carefully study whether Americans would want to live in Swiss-style density—as well as Swiss-style regimentation and regulation—before their immigration policies leave Americans only a choice between that lifestyle and eradicating much of the nation's natural heritage.

Unfortunately, no Congress or president since Richard Nixon and the legislators of 1969 has shown the least bit of interest in where large-scale immigration eventually might take the nation in terms of the total population and what that would mean for Americans' lifestyles.

Meanwhile, Congress runs its relentless population-growth program, and native-born Americans are fleeing the immigration centers by the tens of thousands, according to the demographer William H. Frey of the University of Michigan. It is not just the core cities that Americans are deserting but suburbs that have been surrounded by layer upon layer of new suburbs. "Phoenix sprawls into the desert at the rate of an acre an hour; greater New York City stretches clear into Pennsylvania; strip malls, traffic, fear of crime have wrecked the tranquil 'burbs of Ozzie and Harriet's time," warned the opening lines of a special *Newsweek* report. The endless urban sprawl is a fairly clear signal that millions of Americans are unhappy with the never-ending growth in population centers, and that they continue to try to establish themselves on or beyond the urban edges.

Like latter-day Daniel Boones, the urban refugees want more elbow room. They seek to get away from life in the city and move far enough out so they can see nature or get to it quickly. But as long as the United States grows by some 3 million a year, there always are more people moving in next door. As Frances Emma Barwood told *Newsweek* about a popular development on the edge of Phoenix: "The

people who bought houses in Phase One were told they'd be surrounded by beautiful lush deserts, but instead they're surrounded by
Phases Two and Three."[68]

In a fascinating chronicle of urbanites seeking breathing space at
the metropolitan edge, David Finkel of *The Washington Post* offered
this ironic tableau:

> DiFilippo moved to Milestone Manor Court, which backs
> up to Appenine Court, which is where the Wilson family found
> a house with a view of Sugarloaf Mountain out the back win-
> dows. So fast was Milestone growing, though, that in the six
> weeks it took them to close and move in, the view of Sugarloaf
> had become obscured. "In six weeks, three houses went up,"
> Denise Wilson says. "I was stunned. God, it's amazing how fast
> they go up." That was their first lesson about the frontier.

The Milestone development is twenty-five miles from Washington,
D.C., along the northern edge of the metropolitan area. Until World
War II, there was still "edge-type" living near the D.C. border in the
community of Somerset, which at the time was surrounded by open
fields and woodland. Finkel says Somerset now is a "close-in,
hemmed-in enclave," and urbanization has marched northward
twenty-five miles. It will never stop marching; not as long as immigration continues above traditional levels.[69]

A small percentage of the urban refugees are giving up on seeking
the "edge" around the immigration centers of the coasts and are moving to the interior. Their presence, plus the smaller movements of foreign migrants into the interior, is creating mini-sprawls and is changing cultures in a way not at all appreciated by the interior's residents. In
Phoenix, native-born Americans fleeing immigration-weary California
are fueling a rampaging sprawl. According to the *Arizona Republic,* on
the lips of seemingly every resident is the great fearful declaration: "We
don't want to become another Los Angeles." The newcomers immediately sing the same refrain, hoping that they will be the last to arrive.
But Congress continues to pour hundreds of thousands of foreign citizens into California and the natives there continue to flee.[70]

The net outflow from California is largest in the Los Angeles area,
where three Americans left for every one American who moved in.
Almost a quarter of departing Californians move to the South; about
half move to other western states. The flight is rapidly changing the
ambiance of the Mountain states. Eight of the ten fastest-growing

states are in the West, says the Census Bureau. They are Nevada, Arizona, Idaho, Utah, Colorado, New Mexico, Montana, and Oregon.[71]

Most of the residents of the previously sparsely populated Mountain states are unhappy with the influx from both the West and the East coasts. Housing prices are driven up, pollution increases, schools get crowded, the old views of beautiful mountains are filled with condos and tract homes. The *Arizona Republic* ran an exhaustive series entitled "An Acre an Hour: The Price of Sprawl" that was full of the creative, expensive, and desperate efforts of Phoenix residents to gain or maintain at least a glimpse of the desert or mountains which they say was a key reason for living in Arizona. "If the next 30 years are like the last 30 years, this won't be a place most of us will want to live," said Phoenix vice mayor Craig Tribken.[72]

The immigration-driven population explosion of California has created an image that is almost universally considered to be that of a disaster. "Don't Californicate Colorado," reads a bumper sticker. Colorado's state demographer told a *Washington Post* reporter, "Coloradans have the idea that we'd just as soon not have this many people here. They hike out to their favorite spot and there are 25 people there, when it used to be empty." Former governor Richard Lamm said, "When people have screwed up their own areas, then they come here." But the Californians keep coming because, as one television producer said, "We didn't want our kids to grow up in California. It's extremely crowded, extremely expensive. You don't have control of your child's schooling."[73]

That was almost exactly what a Southeast Asian immigrant leader told me was the reason his people moved from California to Wausau, Wisconsin. It seems that nobody in the rest of the United States wants to imitate California's last twenty years of population explosion, multicultural fragmentation, urban sprawl, environmental desecration, traffic congestion, crime, and riots. But the elected federal officials of this nation are running an immigration program that—after terrorizing California—eventually is sure to "Californicate" all the other states.

* * *

High on a mountain in the Ozarks region of northern Arkansas, Mary Louise Chittenden and her husband love nothing better than just looking out over the misty green scenery. They left California and his job at Hollywood and Vine in 1991. They settled in theirmountaintop home, a mile from the nearest neighbor, two and a half miles of dirt road from the nearest blacktop, nine and a half miles from Berryville, which has about three thousand people and which is a long way from anything that legitimately can be called a city. "It's been a long time since I saw a freeway," Chittenden says with satisfaction. California was beautiful when they moved to the "little rural town" of Thousand Oaks in 1963, two years before Congress opened the way to mass immigration. Thousand Oaks long ago was swallowed by the Los Angeles sprawl.

Escaping the congestion elsewhere in America is an old Ozarks tradition. The county was settled in the 1830s by people who had moved to Tennessee when North Carolina got too congested, and then moved to Arkansas when Tennessee began to fill up. In the Carroll County Courthouse, built in 1853 on the Berryville town square, a history book describes the poor soil of much of the area and the few economic rewards for settling there. That seemed to suit the residents just fine because it repelled more people from moving in. The Ozarks attracted few new residents over the decades; all the immigration waves of the past bypassed Berryville. "Any individual has been required to possess a deep desire to live within the region if that individual was to remain . . . in what was at best a harsh, hostile region," wrote historian Jim Lair.[74] The reward for their marginal economic existence always was to drink in the sparsely populated mountainous view and to be left alone, living apart from whatever frenzied behavior was sweeping the rest of the nation at any moment.

But there is trouble in paradise. The Ozarks seem to offer something that is more and more scarce in an increasingly overpopulated, culturally tense nation: serenity and simplicity. More urban refugees are arriving, seeking a lifestyle they once had somewhere else but which was destroyed by population growth. Some stars and big shots in the music and movie industries are building getaway homes in the region, too. The Chittendens are getting more neighbors. Shallow top soil, inferior transportation, isolation, and a low material standard of living no longer are enough to protect the lifestyles of the residents of this remote area. America is moving in—and so are citizens of other nations: The corporate headquarters of plants located in Berryville and in a lot of other little towns dotted through the Ozarks have begun importing foreign workers to take low-wage jobs, even though the natives of these hills are chronically underemployed. Bi-lingual education is hitting the schools, and interpreters are needed in court. Some signs of precursors of gangs are popping up. "Now we're getting the graffiti like we had in California," Chittenden says.

Berryville did not ask the federal government for these changes—but neither did the communities from which the urban refugees are fleeing. In the out-of-the-way, time-passed-by, Deep South small town of Ashville, Alabama, Mark Tucker frets over the possibility that a local business will start an immigration stream there. The high school history teacher blames a segment of greedy business people across the country for denying local communities the right to their own lifestyle: "There is a feeling in this country that it is okay to spoil where you live if it helps you make money, because you can use that money to move somewhere else in America where it isn't spoiled. I want all of America to know that this is a remote area. If even we are going to be overrun by immigration, then you can be sure that there won't be a place in the country that won't be touched by this."

In 1924, Congress halted the power of immigration to change the social landscape of communities or to obliterate lifestyles of the American people without their permission. Thoughtless federal policies since 1965 have removed that protection. There remain many communities and Americans whose lives are not yet forcibly transformed by the new immigration wave; but as long as Congress allows immigration above historic beneficial levels, no American in any community—no matter how remote—can feel beyond its reach. Every American has a stake in drastically cutting the level of immigration.

Conclusion:
Picking the Right Number

A century ago, Congress struggled to gain control over a two-decade surge of immigration. The influence of powerful industrialists and immigrant political machines thwarted restriction efforts.

Americans in the 1990s find themselves in very similar circumstances.

Immigration's negative impact on the nation today is remarkably like that of the 1890s: As we have seen in this book, the importation of foreign workers in both periods played a significant role in depressing real wages for workers, in increasing disparity between the rich and the poor, in disproportionately driving black Americans out of skilled trades and into poverty, and in fueling a wave of crime and social disintegration in the cities. The Great Wave of immigration rapidly transformed the quality of life in local communities throughout America against their residents' will. Today's Greater Wave is doing the same damage.

For the majority of Americans who want to stop immigration's destructive path through the nation today, a reminder of how the political process worked in the late 1890s is a sobering one. Although the popular disgust with the country's immigration policies almost succeeded in closing the floodgates in 1897 and 1898, the captains of industry were able to keep mass immigration flowing for nearly thirty additional years.

Nobody should underestimate the power of a small elite that feels its profits threatened to subvert the desires of the majority. Today that elite, representing a significant percentage of the country's industrial owners, is insisting that their very existence as U.S. entities would be endangered by reducing immigration merely back to the extraordinarily high level of the Great Wave. When legislation late in 1995 timidly proposed such a small cut, "powerful elements of the American business community . . . descended on Capitol Hill," reported *The Washington Post*. "If they can't get the [foreign] people they want, they will move overseas," the senior policy director of the National Association of Manufacturers threatened.

The fact that the overwhelming majority of today's Americans *wants* immigration substantially cut does not guarantee any more responsiveness from the federal government than the majority got a century ago. The enormous influence of the business elite's personal contacts with federal officials and financial contributions to their election campaigns is difficult to overstate. To counterbalance that influence, the people's majority must engage in concerted and persistent demand that their elected officials set immigration levels based on what is best for all Americans. Without such voter pressure on the members of Congress, there is no reason to believe that annual immigration of a half million or more will not continue for another thirty years.

There is no need to get bogged down in assessing the exact costs of past immigration policy. The most important question for Washington is whether a continuing stream of foreign workers and dependents into the country over the next few years will make it more or less difficult to achieve the economic, social, or environmental goals of the American people.

In other words, for the first time in decades Washington should consider basing its immigration policy on how many immigrants the nation actually *needs*. Officials should start the process at the zero level and add only the numbers that actually will help the majority of Americans.

Let's look at several national issues and groups, considering how many immigrants a year would be best for each.

WAGE EARNERS—
OPTIMUM IMMIGRATION: ZERO TO 5,000

No American wage earner benefits from having his or her elected officials import workers who may compete for the same jobs or help to depress wages. That is true whether the American worker is an unskilled lettuce picker, a slightly skilled chicken slaughterer, a skilled construction tradesman, or a college-educated engineer.

The Robber Barons a century ago were willing to inflict the traumas of mass immigration on American communities because of their insatiable desire for cheaper unskilled labor. Jerry J. Jasinowski, the current president of the National Association of Manufacturers, says responsible businesses no longer need the hundreds of thousands of unskilled workers that get into the country through family preference categories. "Waves of unskilled immigrants may be dragging down the pay levels of similarly unskilled Americans, but not at industry's behest," Jasinowski maintains.

What the titans of industry crave today is *skilled* foreign labor, Jasinowski says.[1] Business lobbyists argue that U.S. industries need at least 140,000 skilled workers from other countries each year to stay competitive in the global economy, and thus to protect the lower-skilled jobs for Americans. They indicate that there aren't enough smart and trained Americans to do those 140,000 jobs.

Their claim seems doubtful even for the short term, when one considers that the United States has thousands of unemployed engineers, scientists, computer programmers, and Ph.D. holders. And it certainly cannot be true that in the long term a nation of 265 million people is incapable of producing enough children with high enough intelligence to be trained for the highest skilled jobs in this country. The continuing arrival of skilled foreign workers "has coincided with rising unemployment rates among young scientists and engineers, and the forced retirement of some middle-aged American workers in these fields," says David North, former assistant to a Secretary of Labor.[2]

It is quite possible, however, that in the large pools of unemployed skilled American workers and professionals there are not people with the exact qualifications for some of the 140,000 positions each year that are said to need immigrants. But such a shortage need be only a very temporary one. As Secretary of Labor Robert Reich has suggested, businesses always can handle a worker shortage through a combination of raised wages, more aggressive recruiting, and improved training for American workers. Or, Reich says, businesses can choose what they usually see as the cheaper option of importing foreign workers.

That is what industrialists are lobbying Congress to allow them to continue to do—take the cheaper option of importing foreign workers instead of training and enticing Americans to fill the jobs. If there indeed is a real shortage today, industries could end it in no more than five years if they provided enough wage and workstyle incentives, and if they aggressively recruited college students to study for—or adult workers in other fields to retrain for—the jobs in question.

Denying industries the immigrant workers they desire should not be a punitive measure. It is in the best interest of all Americans that our industries succeed—and, for that matter, that entrepreneurs and the owners of capital earn generous profits as they create jobs for the rest of us. The government should provide the industries the means to meet short-term labor emergencies, as long as they do not impede efforts to train Americans to fill the needs later. Nearly all skilled-job vacancies for which an American cannot be found should be filled by foreign workers given only *temporary* work visas, not by immigrants allowed to enter the United States for permanent residence. Senator Alan Simpson, Representative Lamar Smith, and the bi-partisan Jordan Commission all made useful proposals for charging businesses high enough fees (thousands of dollars per imported worker) to discourage them from bypassing American workers. The visas for skilled workers should last only long enough—no more than three to five years—for U.S. college students or experienced professionals to be enticed to prepare for the job in question.

An allowance for five thousand brilliant professionals would more than handle the number of scientists, professors, computer whizzes, and so forth who possess extraordinary genius and whom U.S. industries and universities want to steal from other countries each year.

Any permanent admissions of skilled immigrants above 5,000 appears to be against the interests of American professionals. Joel B. Snyder, chairman of the Institute of Electrical and Electronics Engineers, says the threats on the part of industry to move overseas if they can't import foreign professionals should be understood as a kind of blackmail: "In our view, such employers are not seeking a technical workforce in the Third World. They want a high-tech workforce in the United States that will accept Third World wages and working conditions. That's no way to maintain and develop the U.S. workforce that we need to continue to grow and prosper in the twenty-first century."[3]

Edith Holleman of the AFL-CIO doubts industry truly needs even temporary skilled workers. "The United States has the most fluid labor market in the world," she says. If a company can't find a specific kind of engineer, for example, other types of engineers usually can adapt to the task. Or if no engineers are immediately available, a company can move lower tasks to engineering technicians while parceling out the higher tasks to professionals such as physicists and computer programmers. Companies have endless ways to be creative in getting their tasks done, and they would find a way to do so with Americans if Congress didn't insist on providing them with foreign workers.[4]

If the labor law of supply and demand is once again to work in favor of most Americans, Congress should try to cut the number of workers entering the country each year to as close to zero as possible.

THE BLACK UNDERCLASS— OPTIMUM IMMIGRATION: ZERO

One-third of all the descendants of the American system of slavery live in poverty. That is triple the poverty rate of all other Americans and represents a worsening of conditions since 1973 after mass immigration was renewed. Historically, black Americans have been pushed to the back of the hiring line by flows of immigrants. It is difficult to conceive how *any* immigration could benefit this segment of the population.

Poor black Americans—as well as the lower proportions of white, Hispanic, Asian, and indigenous Americans in poverty—need entry-level jobs. And they need a tight-labor market that drives the wages of those low-skill jobs high enough to support a family above the poverty level. A federal policy that allows any unskilled immigrants is by its very nature a compromise that sacrifices the needs of impoverished Americans, especially the black underclass. Such immigration also compromises any efforts to move people off welfare rolls.

Skilled immigrants may not have as direct an effect. But to the extent that they push higher-skilled Americans to take medium-skilled jobs, which pushes people qualified at that level to take lower-skilled positions, the skilled immigrants indirectly help block the impoverished citizens from grabbing onto and moving up the economic ladder. Skilled immigrants also reduce the incentive for corporations to aggressively motivate and recruit bright kids in our inner cities.

Until the number of black Americans in poverty drops significantly for several years, Congress should set the immigration level as close to zero as possible.

URBAN SPRAWL—
OPTIMUM IMMIGRATION: ZERO

The outlook is grim for curtailing the population growth—more than 30 million from immigrants and their descendants since 1970—that is driving millions of Americans in their near-futile flight to move out of its sprawling reach.

The Census Bureau offers one of the most dismal glimpses of the future in its projection of what would happen if Congress cut immigration back to a replacement level in which the number of immigrants coming into the country matched the number of Americans permanently leaving. That sounds like the kind of drastic action that might come close to stopping the urban sprawl that mars modern life. But it wouldn't. And that is a dismal revelation.

According to the Census projection: (1) if 195,000 Americans permanently leave the United States each year, as is estimated; (2) if 100 percent of illegal immigration is eliminated; (3) if tens of thousands of foreign citizens no longer obtain indefinite residency here by fraudulently asking for asylum; (4) if children of various kinds of foreign visitors no longer are granted U.S. citizenship; and (5) if Congress cuts annual immigration from nearly 1 million to 195,000, the population of the United States still will surge. In fact, U.S. population would sprawl by another 40 million or so over the next five decades!

Growing by 40 million is far better than the 130 million increase projected under current immigration numbers, but it nonetheless means we face about the same amount of new sprawl, congestion, and dislocation as has afflicted us between 1970 and today.

The reason we would suffer so much additional population expansion underreplacement-level immigration is that the three previous decades of high immigration, and the high fertility of the immigrants, create what demographers call a "population momentum" that will take a half century to level off.

Unless Americans and their governments restrict all future population growth to areas already urbanized, and unless they sharply curb Americans' freedom of mobility in their use of the automobile, Congress will need to set immigration as far below 195,000 and as close to zero as possible if it is to avoid rampant additional urban sprawl and congestion.

Under current American fertility rates, eliminating all immigration still would allow the population to rise for a while, but it would be back down around our current level by the year 2050. If the immigrants and their descendants who already are here would lower their fertility to that of native-born Americans, the United States could take some immigrants in the future without adding population, sprawl, and congestion.

ENVIRONMENT— OPTIMUM IMMIGRATION: ZERO

In a country where nearly half the lakes and rivers do not meet clean water standards and where 40 percent of the citizens live in cities that can't meet clean air standards, anything that adds to the total number of Americans flushing toilets, riding in vehicles, and consuming electricity is anti-environment.

Under current fertility and other demographic conditions, any immigration over zero will increase the size of the U.S. population, and thus further damage our environmental resources.

If Congress were to run its immigration policy according to what is best for the environment, it would not allow any newcomers (1) until the percentage of water and air failing to meet health standards is a lot closer to 5 percent than to 50 percent; (2) until a credible body such as the National Academy of Sciences certifies that the United States no longer is destroying ecosystems and biodiversity at a significant rate; and (3) until the underground aquifers—upon which much of our agriculture and industry are dependent—no longer are being drained to ever lower levels year after year. When those three conditions are met, we will know that Americans have sufficiently reduced their consumption and waste, tightened their environmental laws, and strengthened their enforcement to once again allow a traditional level of immigration (between 175,000 and 300,000).

FOREIGN-BORN AMERICANS— OPTIMUM IMMIGRATION: ZERO TO 500,000.

In most ways, immigrants have the same needs for zero immigration as do native-born Americans. A total cutoff of immigration might even help the immigrants more, since they are more vulnerable to job competition from new immigrants and are more likely to have their children in the schools where new foreign students settle.

But many immigrants also have a burning desire after they become citizens to go back to the home country, choose a wife or husband—who often already has children—and to bring them to the United States. Many also want to include their parents, brothers, and sisters. They bring in around 500,000 total family members under current policies.

The immigrants among us are torn. While many want to bring in their relatives, most also tell pollsters they want immigration cut. One suspects that while a lower number within the zero-to-500,000 range would disappoint many immigrants because it would deny them bringing in extended family, most would be somewhat relieved because their own personal financial and social situation would begin to improve.

EDUCATION— OPTIMUM IMMIGRATION: ZERO TO 5,000

The worst education results in the country tend to be found in the school districts where most immigrants settle. That isn't entirely the fault of immigration; many of the school districts were in bad shape before Congress began filling them with foreign students. But none of them has anything to gain by receiving another immigrant child. Congressional immigration policies may be at their most cruel in the way they diminish the chance that the children of some of America's poorest families will gain at their schools the education, the imagination, and the motivation to work for their share of the American dream.

To the extent that the immigrant children in those districts might receive a significant boost from the work of an especially talented foreign educator, those needs should easily be met under the five thousand slots previously mentioned to be set aside for professionals with extraordinary skills.

Cutting off the immigration flow would allow those over-challenged districts to concentrate on educating the native and immigrant students at hand, instead of expending so much energy and money each year trying to accommodate additional students in an ever-expanding array of languages and cultures.

Some worry that a cutoff of immigration would condemn the schools—and urban areas in general—to a bland homogeneity. They should remember that the country already is filled with more than 30 million post-1970 immigrants and their descendants; they won't be leaving. They would be able to provide more diversity than most Americans crave even if the country never accepted another immigrant for decades. Ethnic restaurants won't disappear.

Halting most permanent visas to skilled and professional workers, and to foreign students after they gain postgraduate degrees from U.S. universities, would open the way for many of America's brightest students to rise to their highest potential. That would create vacancies in the next-highest tiers of achievement for the people below them to grab. A positive ripple effect would move down through all echelons of skills and education. This would help even the least-skilled and least-educated Americans by lessening their competition from the brighter of the lowest skilled, who would be able to move up to the next-higher job level.

Until urban school districts no longer complain of being overcrowded or of having high dropout rates, any additional immigration is likely to be harmful.

DOMESTIC TRANQUILITY— OPTIMUM IMMIGRATION: ZERO

Until the current national crime wave is over and until federal law enforcement units gain control of all the new organized crime operations, Congress should not take the chance of nurturing the environment for the criminals by bringing in more of their countrymen whom they potentially may exploit for illegal purposes.

If anyone doubts that Americans' sense of security is threatened by the current immigration policies, a 1995 poll by the Chicago Council on Foreign Relations provides proof. Given several options, 72 percent of the respondents to the national poll said large immigrant and refugee flows were the worst foreign threat facing the United States.[5]

As was the case after the Great Wave of immigration that was stopped in 1924, the American communities now need decades of low immigration so that people of many different cultures can begin to learn how to work, live, and play in healthy diversity and overall cohesiveness.

* * *

In weighing those various groups and issues, it becomes fairly clear that America needs substantially less than 100,000 immigrants a year. And only by giving a disproportionate consideration to the needs of immigrants over the needs of native-born Americans would the level even be above 5,000.

That gives us a target, but not necessarily a practical number, for now.

Two other considerations—having to do with relatives and with refugees—seem likely to force us to compromise over what is best for wage earners, impoverished black Americans, others in poverty, America's children, our environment, and all Americans whose quality of life has been wounded by the loose labor market, environmental degradation, crime, and the intercultural tensions associated with high immigration.

Most Americans probably would agree that the United States should shoulder its fair share of the international burden of caring for refugees. As was shown in Chapter 3, nearly all of that work is most appropriately done in the refugee camps near the home countries and in helping the refugees to move back home. But there will continue to be some refugees who face truly life-threatening situations and who will have no reasonable possibility of returning safely home, or of settling in a neighboring country, for years to come. Those are the people who will form the pool from which the United States should accept permanent refugees. Based on recent years' experience, a maximum of 30,000 slots per year should handle our share of such "special needs" refugees and asylees. There may be citizens from nearby countries who find themselves in need of temporary refuge; the United States must create a system in which it can provide safe haven in a truly temporary manner, with the ability to send such people back to their home country as soon as the threat to life—not the threat to economic well-being —is over. Anybody who honestly needs refuge will be more than happy to accept the terms of a merely temporary stay in the United States. After all, the point of refugee policy is to save lives, not to provide a path to citizenship.

The other matter is more problematic because it involves so many more people. The United States has a long tradition of allowing its citizens to adopt orphans from other countries and to marry people in other countries and immediately bring them to America. That tradition is sure to be continued. If we were dealing only with native-born U.S. citizens, this would not add many thousands of immigrants. But because of the explosion of immigration in the last thirty years, America is filled with a huge pool of foreign-born citizens who have a much higher proclivity toward marrying overseas. Many of those foreign spouses have minor children of their own, which adds further to the number of immigrants who come in under the category of immediate relatives of citizens. There is no limit on how many immediate family members can come in any year. The number has been rising steadily.

Approximately 200,000 immigrants each year are now entering the United States under the provision for citizens to marry and adopt overseas. Even though that number violates many needs and interests of most Americans, not continuing our unlimited acceptance of these immigrants would violate some basic understandings of our personal freedoms and rights as citizens.

But the same does not need to be said about the brothers, sisters, adult children, and parents of immigrants, another 300,000 of whom currently are allowed to enter each year. It must be remembered that the immigrants (not including legitimate refugees) made the decision to separate from their families by coming here. Nobody forced them. If they have a passionate need to live near their relatives, they should move back. In this day of fast and relatively cheap transportation and telephones, most immigrants can communicate with their extended family about as often as many native-born Americans dispersed across the country communicate with their parents. Even among some of the poorest of immigrants, it is not unusual to return to the home country for one to three months each year. Not including parents in the permanent immigration program may seem overly restrictive, but generous visitor visas could allow for extended visits that would afford more time together than is the case for large numbers of native-born American citizens and their parents. Also, an immigrant always is free to move back home to care for a parent during a crisis; and brothers and sisters usually are available in the home country to care for the parents. If immigrants had lower birth rates, and if Congress had not allowed such unprecedented numbers to come to America during the last thirty years, we could be more open in some of these categories. But in order to minimize the damage to the overarching needs of most citizens, it now is necessary to draw the line very sharply on future immigration. Currently, around 60,000 immigrants a year come in under the parent provision.

The total number allowed is the most important issue. Remember, any immigration above 200,000 will force Americans to have to contend with more than 40 million additional residents over the next 50 years. Even limiting annual immigration to around 200,000 and growing by some 40 million would make it exceptionally difficult to achieve three of our top priorities: tighten the labor supply, take pressure off the schools, and minimize the addition of new polluters. That would be 40 million on top of the current U.S. population, which Americans overwhelmingly believe already is too large. Adding so many people to the labor market would work in numerous ways against conditions that best increase productivity and lead to rising incomes.

It appears that, based on these calculations, about the best we can do in cutting immigration toward the target that best meets Americans' needs is to continue unlimited immigration for spouses and minor children of citizens, and to set a cap of 50,000 to cover *all* other admissions—refugees, those seeking political asylum, persons with extraordinary skills, special-situation parents, and any other category that might arise.

For now, that would add up to around 250,000 immigrants a year—compared to around 1 million now. The number might go up even higher than 250,000 for a few years as the huge bulge of immigrants who have not yet become citizens do so and obtain the right to marry outside the country and bring their spouses back.

In adopting such a high number, we must continually remind ourselves that it represents a compromise and probably is at least 200,000 above what is best for the nation as a whole. Thus, it is essential to set the figure in such a way that it can decline automatically. The good news is that with the immediate cutoff of most other immigration, there eventually will be far fewer recent immigrants to use the immediate-family category, and the total immigration level probably would drop below 200,000, perhaps even moving toward 100,000 over time.

* * *

We cannot deny that while greatly improving prospects for most Americans, cutting immigration will hurt some citizens. Most immigration lawyers might lose their livelihood and have to enter other specialties. Not surprisingly, they and their organization, the American Immigration Lawyers Association, have been the most aggressive in fighting any reductions whatsoever. But they are intelligent, educated, and resourceful people, and should be able to find another way to earn a living; it would be ludicrous to sacrifice the needs of the rest of the nation just to keep the immigration lawyers in business. Also suffering from the change—at least temporarily—would be the businesses which the lawyers represent and which have decided to rely heavily on foreign labor. But the cuts would reward those businesses that have invested in the American workforce. And they would reward most people in the workforce by improving the opportunities for increases in productivity and income. A number of national church bureaucracies and other private refugee organizations might have to cut their staffs. On the other hand, the charitable organizations should be able to find plenty of humanitarian work to do overseas—where nearly all refugees are, anyway—as well as among the black underclass and other impoverished citizens here in America; the church groups don't need massive refugee resettlement to keep busy. Then there are the ethnic immigrant organizations that had counted on a continuing flow of their countrymen to boost the power of their budding political machines; they will have to learn from previous ethnic machines who lost their immigration support and had to broaden their appeal across ethnic lines to form majority coalitions.

Those few groups that stand to lose money, power, or prestige with a cut in immigration wield tremendous power on Capitol Hill. People representing the broad public interest will have to speak very loudly to be heard. The majority of members of Congress previously earned their living in self-employed occupations or as executives; they think like employers who love a labor surplus instead of like most Americans who depend on paychecks and benefit from tight-labor markets. Both employers and employees, however, should benefit from gains in productivity that tend to accompany slow labor-force growth.

While insisting on moving toward the optimum level of immigration, citizens should expect that Congress will have to be forced to reduce immigration two or three times before finally getting it right; the pressure from the lawyers, businesses, the national church bureaucrats, and the immigrant organizations likely will blunt any moves Congress makes in the right direction.

The will of the majority will prevail only if the citizens push their elected officials to keep cutting over the next several years. That is how it happened the last time the country had a sustained wave of immigration. Congress yielded to decades of public pressure and cut back the Great Wave in 1917. Citizens continued to press until Congress cut immigration further in 1921, and until it finally ended the Great Wave in 1924 by choosing a level low enough to earn the support of the people over the next four decades.

Immigration is so high now that the cuts proposed in Congress reduce the numbers only back to the level of the Great Wave. In fighting that slight reduction, the National Association of Manufacturers proclaimed the great myth about immigration: "Legal immigration strengthens and energizes America. Throughout America's history, legally admitted immigrants have been a source of strength and vitality to our nation. Our current legal immigration policies are specifically designed to reflect American values and serve national interests."[6]

Nothing could be further from the truth, if "national interest" is defined by what is good for the majority of the public. High immigration almost always has reflected the values and served the interests of a small elite at the *expense* of the national interest. Current policies may have been designed in 1965 to reflect the public's desire for low immigration, but they have been allowed to create results wildly at variance with the public will. The only time that the majority of Americans seemed to feel that immigration strengthened and energized the nation was between 1925 and 1965, when annual admissions averaged 178,000. By the end, that period proved to be the best one in U.S. history for building an American middle class. It also was the only period when black Americans enjoyed steady and significant economic progress. That is the numerical immigration tradition we should seek to emulate now.

That golden era of immigration was a time of quite low numbers. It was begun in 1924 with the drastic reduction of admissions. That was when the Democratic Party decided that the needs of American workers—both native-born and immigrant—were more important than bringing in new foreign workers to increase the size of ethnic political machines, and when the Republican Party made the American people at large a higher priority than big business.

The 1924 action to bring immigration down to a level that matched the needs of the American people came nearly thirty years after Congress began trying to do that. It now has been more than thirty years since Congress in 1965 tried to improve on the 1924 act by eliminating national-origin preferences that entailed racial discrimination in the selection process. By accident, the new act unleashed the largest and harshest wave of immigration in U.S. history.

The American people should not have to wait another year—let alone another thirty years—for Congress to correct the unintended mistakes of the 1965 act and to restore what *was* intended in 1965: an immigration system without discrimination on the basis of national origin and with a numerical level consistent with that of the golden age of immigration from 1924 to 1965. It was supposed to be an immigration program of high ideals and practical considerations for the needs of the American people. It is the immigration policy for which nearly everybody thought they were voting in 1965. But it is a policy that has yet to be experienced.

Notes

Chapter 1

In addition to the resources listed in the notes, the following sources were relied upon in this chapter:

U.S. Bureau of the Census, *Population Projections of the U.S. by Age, Sex, Race and Hispanic Origin: 1993 to 2050* (Washington, DC: U.S. Government Printing Office, September 1993); *Time* magazine poll (September 1993), Roper Poll (April 1992), *Newsweek* magazine poll (July 1993), CBS News poll (May 1994); Carrying Capacity Network, "Our Immigration Crisis," *Network Bulletin*, 5 (June–July 1995): 1–2; World Resources Institute, *The 1993 Information Please Environmental Almanac* (Washington, DC: World Resources Institute, 1993).

1. Total immigration-related population growth was calculated in a three-step process: (1) Demographer Leon Bouvier determined the 1995 population of 1970-stock Americans (those who were in the country in 1970, plus their descendants, minus all deaths of the two groups by 1995). (2) The U.S. Census Bureau estimated the total U.S. population in 1995. The total included both 1970-stock Americans and post-1970 immigrants and their descendants. (3) I merely subtracted the 1970-stock American population from the U.S. total population to determine the segment of total population that can be attributed to post-1970 legal and illegal immigrants, plus their descendants. See Roy Beck, "Immigration: No. 1 in U.S. Growth," *The Social Contract* (Winter 1991–92).
2. Council of Economic Advisors, *1993 Annual Report to the President* (4 February 1994).

3. United Nations Population Fund, *State of the World Population 1993* (New York: United Nations Population Fund, 1993).

4. Paul Krugman, *Peddling Prosperity: Economic Sense and Nonsense in the Age of Diminished Expectations* (New York: W. W. Norton & Co., 1994).

5. Paul Romer, "Crazy Explanations for the Productivity Slowdown," *Macroeconomics Annual* (Cambridge, MA: National Bureau of Economic Research, 1987), pp. 181–183.

6. Jeffrey Williamson, *Inequality, Poverty and History: The Kuznets Memorial Lectures* (Cambridge, MA: Blackwell, 1991).

7. Roberto Suro, "Immigrants Crowd Labor's Lowest Rung," *The Washington Post*, 13 September 1994.

8. David A. Jaeger, "Skill Differences and the Effect of Immigrants on the Wages of Natives," Bureau of Labor Statistics Working Paper No. 273 (U.S. Department of Labor, December 1995).

9. Timothy J. Hatton and Jeffrey G. Williamson, "International Migration 1850–1939: An Economic Survey," in *Migration and the International Labor Market 1850–1939*, Hatton and Williamson, eds. (New York: Routledge, 1994), p. 19.

10. Krugman, *Peddling Prosperity*, pp. 124, 137–138.

11. George J. Borjas, "Know the Flow," *National Review*, vol. XLVII (17 April 1995): 49.

12. Norman Ornstein, "Can America Afford $5.15 An Hour?" *The Washington Post*, 12 February 1995, p. C1.

13. Robert M. Hutchens, *A Path to Good Jobs? Unemployment and Low Wages: The Distribution of Opportunity for Young Unskilled Workers.* Public Policy Brief No. 11 (Annandale-on-Hudson, NY: The Jerome Levy Economics Institute, 1994).

14. James P. Smith and Finis R. Welch, "Black Economic Progress After Myrdal," *Journal of Economic Literature* (June 1989).

15. John J. Donohue III and James Heckman, "Continuous Versus Episodic Change: The Impact of Civil Rights Policy on the Economic Status of Blacks," *Journal of Economic Literature* (December 1991).

16. Ronald F. Ferguson, "Shifting Challenges: Fifty Years of Economic Change Toward Black-White Earnings Equality," *Dædalus: Journal of the American Academy of Arts and Sciences*, vol. 124 (Winter 1995): 52–53.

17. Vernon Briggs, Jr., *Mass Immigration and the National Interest* (New York: M. E. Sharpe, 1992), pp. 214–215.

18. Roger Wilkins, interviewed by Daniel Schorr, "Weekend Edition," National Public Radio, 14 October 1995 (transcribed in "Morality and the Message," *Washington Post*, 15 October 1995).

19. Ann Scott Tyson, "Ethnic, Economic Divisions of US Growing," *Christian Science Monitor*, 7 July 1994.

20. Jordan Bonfante, "The Endangered Dream," *Time* (18 November 1991).

21. Robert Bach, *Changing Relations: Newcomers and Established Residents in U.S. Communities* (New York: Ford Foundation, April 1993).

22. Lorraine M. McDonnell and Paul T. Hill, *Newcomers in American Schools: Meeting the Educational Needs of Immigrant Youth* (Santa Monica, CA: RAND Corporation, 1993).

23. Ted Robert Gurr, *Violence in America: The History of Crime* (Newbury Park, CA: Sage, 1989).

24. "Interview: Thomas Lovejoy," *FOCUS*, vol. 4, no. 2 (Washington, DC: Carrying Capacity Network, 1994), pp. 63–67.

25. George F. Kennan, *Around the Cragged Hill* (New York: W.W. Norton & Co., 1993), pp. 151–154.

CHAPTER 2

In addition to the resources listed in the notes, the following sources were relied upon in this chapter:

Vernon Briggs, Jr., *Mass Immigration and the National Interest* (New York: M. E. Sharpe, 1992); Claudia Goldin, *The Political Economy of Immigration Restriction in the United States, 1890 to 1921* (Cambridge, MA: National Bureau of Economic Research, April 1993); Lawrence H. Fuchs, "The Reactions of Black Americans to Immigration," in *Immigration Reconsidered: History, Sociology, and Politics,* Virginia Yans-McLaughlin, ed. (New York: Oxford University Press, 1990); U.S. Committee for Refugees, *1995 World Refugee Report* (Washington, DC: U.S. Committee for Refugees, 1995); Frances Fox Piven and Richard A. Cloward, "The Civil Rights Movement" in *Poor People's Movements: Why They Succeed, How They Fail* (New York: Vintage Books, 1979); Frederick Rose, "Muddled Masses: The Growing Backlash Against Immigration Includes Many Myths," *Wall Street Journal,* 26 April 1995.

1. "California Schemin': Stop Prop. 187 Now," *Chicago Sun-Times,* 25 November 1994.
2. John Higham, *Send These to Me: Jews and Other Immigrants in Urban America* (New York: Atheneum, 1975); John Higham, *Strangers in the Land* (2nd ed. New York: Atheneum, 1963).
3. Otis L. Graham, Jr., "Uses and Misuses of History," *The Public Historian,* vol. 8, no. 2 (1986).
4. "Immigrants, Not Aliens," *The Washington Times,* 10 May 1995.
5. David Bennett, *The Party of Fear: From Nativist Movements to the New Right in American History* (Chapel Hill, NC: University of North Carolina Press, 1988).
6. John Higham, professor emeritus of history, Johns Hopkins University, speech on 10 June 1988 in Washington, D.C.
7. Eric Foner, *Reconstruction: America's Unfinished Revolution, 1863–1877* (New York: Harper & Row, 1989), pp. 470, 490.
8. Joshua L. Rosenbloom, "Employer Recruitment and the Integration of Industrial Labor Markets, 1870–1914," *NBER Working Paper Series on Historical Factors in Long Run Growth* (Cambridge, MA: National Bureau of Economic Research, January 1994), p. 18.
9. Timothy J. Hatton and Jeffrey G. Williamson, "International Migration 1850–1939: An Economic Survey," in *Migration and the International Labor Market 1850–1939,* Hatton and Williamson, eds. (New York: Routledge, 1994), pp. 17, 20, 23.
10. Frederick Jackson Turner quoted in Richard White, "Frederick Jackson Turner and Buffalo Bill," *The Frontier in American Culture* (Berkley, CA: University of California Press, 1994), p. 46.
11. John Higham, letter to the editor of *The New York Times* (July 1984), quoted in Otis Graham, Jr., "Uses and Misuses of History in the Debate Over Immigration Reform," *The Social Contract,* vol. 1, no. 2 (Winter 1990–91): 54.

CHAPTER 3

In addition to the resources listed in the notes, the following sources were relied upon in this chapter:

Phyllis Oakley, "Consultation on Refugee and Humanitarian Admissions," Commission on Immigration Reform hearing, 25 April 1995; Virginia D. Abernethy, "To Reform Welfare, Reform Immigration," *Clearinghouse Bulletin,* vol. 5 (January–February 1995): 5; Don Barnett, "Neither Responsible Immigration Nor Refugee Resettlement: Subsidized Migration from the Former USSR Continues on Automatic Pilot," *The Social Contract* (Spring 1995); Commission on Immigration Reform, "Briefing Material for Consultation on Refugees and Humanitarian Admissions," Washington, DC (25 April 1995); Hal Kane, "What's Driving Migration?" *World Watch* (January–February 1995): 30; Terry Coopman, spokesman for United Nations High Commission for Refugees, phone interview (5 June 1995); Population Reference Bureau, *1994 World Population Data Sheet* (Washington, DC: Population Reference Bureau, 1994); Population-Environment Balance, *Know the Facts: The United States' Population and Environment* (Washington, DC: Population-Environment Balance, September 1993); David Pimentel, "Land, Energy and Water: The Constraints Governing Ideal U.S. Population Size," in *Elephants in the Volkswagen,* Lindsey Grant, ed. (New York: W. H. Freeman, 1992); David Pimentel, "The National Carrying Capacity Conference" (Arlington, VA: Carrying Capacity Network, 4–6 June 1993); Don Barnett, "Asylum Policy Is Mired in Confusion," *Newsday* (8 September 1995); Michael Hedges, "Vast Soviet Refugee Fraud Detailed," *The Washington Times,* 4 November 1995.

1. See Roy Beck, "Immigration: A Test of Clinton's Commitment to the National Interest," *Scope* (Winter 1993).
2. See Philip Shenon, "Throngs of Boat People to Be Sent Home to Vietnam Soon," *The New York Times,* 3 April 1995.
3. See Kristen Huckshorn, "Boat People Find You Can Go Home Again," *San Jose Mercury News,* 25 July 1995, pp. 1A, 7A.
4. George F. Kennan, *Around the Cragged Hill* (New York: W. W. Norton & Co., 1993), pp. 153–154.
5. Lester Brown, *State of the World 1994* (Washington, DC: World Resources Institute, 1994).
6. World Resources Institute, "Who Will Feed China?" *World Watch* (September–October 1994).
7. United Nations Population Fund, *State of the World Population 1993* (New York: United Nations Population Fund, 1993).
8. Quoted in Esther Schrader, "Exodus of Men Haunts Mexico," *San Jose Mercury News,* 15 August 1993.
9. Robert A. Hackenberg, David Griffith, Donald D. Stull, and Lourdes Gouveia, "Meat Processing and the Transformation of Rural America: The Emergence of a New Underclass?" *Aspen Institute Quarterly,* vol. 5 (Spring 1993), p. 9.
10. David Simcox, "The Caribbean Immigration Centrifuge: A Portent of Continued Immigration Growth," *NPG Footnotes* (Teaneck, NJ: Negative Population Growth, February 1995).
11. Garry Pierre-Pierre, "Turmoil in Haiti Dims Future of Its Students," *The New York Times,* 6 July 1994.
12. See Todd Robberson, "Migration Grows, Heads South as Well as North," *The Washington Post,* 18 September 1995, pp. A1, A14.
13. Dan Stein, "Blanket Acceptance of Cubans Is an Idea 3 Decades Out of Date," *Palm Beach Post,* 28 July 1991.
14. Nancy Nusser, "Young Cubans See No Reason to Strive for Political Change," *The Washington Times,* 25 September 1994.
15. Christian Blanchet and Bertrand Dard, *Statue of Liberty: The First Hundred Years* (Boston: Houghton Mifflin, 1986); Elizabeth Koed, "A Symbol Transformed," *The Social Contract* (Spring 1991).

16. Katharine Betts, "The Problem of Defining Borders in Western Democracies," presented at the Third Annual Outlook Conference sponsored by the Board of Immigration, Multiculturalism and Population Research at Adelaide, Australia (22–24 February 1995).

17. "Wisconsin Leads U.S. in Asian Child Poverty," *La Crosse Tribune,* 17 February 1994; "Wisconsin Enters the Third World?" *La Crosse Tribune,* 18 February 1994.

18. Avis Thomas-Lester and David Leonhardt, "Sudanese Student Working Toward American Dream Dies After Street Attack," *The Washington Post,* 11 June 1994.

19. Maria Puente, "Immigrants' Images of Their Lives in the U.S.A.," *USA Today,* 5 July 1995.

20. Lorraine M. McDonnell and Paul T. Hill, *Newcomers in American Schools: Meeting the Educational Needs of Immigrant Youth* (Santa Monica, CA: RAND Corporation, 1993), pp. 5–6, 61, 63.

21. Government Accounting Office, *Illegal Aliens: Influence of Illegal Workers on Wages and Working Conditions of Legal Workers* (Washington, DC: Government Accounting Office, 1988), pp. 38–39.

22. The Diversity Coalition for an Immigration Moratorium, "Minorities Back Moratorium on Legal Immigration," news release (12 October 1995).

23. Rodolfo de la Garza, *The Latino National Political Survey* (December 1992).

24. Hernandez quoted in Norman Matloff, "Immigration Hits Minorities Hardest," *San Diego Union-Tribune* 26 February 1995, p. G3.

25. See Norman Matloff, "American Minorities Try to Hold the Line," *Los Angeles Times,* 30 September 1994; Yeh Ling-Ling, "US Can't Handle Today's Tide of Immigrants," *Christian Science Monitor,* 23 March 1995, p. 19; and Randolph Ryan, "Asian Mob Torments Newcomers," *Boston Globe,* 12 February 1995.

26. Richard R. Valencia and Jorge Chapa, "Latino Population Growth, Demographic Characteristics, and Educational Stagnation: An Examination of Recent Trends," *Hispanic Journal of Behavioral Sciences* 15 (May 1993): 179–181.

CHAPTER 4

In addition to the resources listed in the notes, the following sources were relied upon in this chapter:

Center for Immigration Studies, "Three Decades of Mass Immigration: The Legacy of the 1965 Immigration Act," *Center for Immigration Studies Backgrounder* (September 1995); Ellis Cose, *A Nation of Strangers* (New York: William Morrow & Co., 1992); Eugene McCarthy, *A Colony of the World: The United States Today* (New York: Hippocrene Books, 1992).

1. John F. Kennedy, *A Nation of Immigrants* (New York: Harper & Row, 1986), p. 80.

2. "By JFK," *Newsweek* (12 October 1964): 124.

3. Kennedy, *A Nation of Immigrants,* pp. 80, 82.

4. See Vernon M. Briggs, Jr., *Mass Immigration and the National Interest* (New York: M. E. Sharpe, 1992), pp. 1–2.

5. Commission on Population Growth and the American Future, *Report of the Commission on Population Growth and the American Future* (Washington, DC: U.S. Government Printing Office, 1972).

6. Peter Brimelow, *Alien Nation* (New York: Random House, 1995), p. 262.

7. *Select Commission on Immigration Policy and the National Interest* (Washington, DC: U.S. Government Printing Office, 1981), p. 7.

8. "National Origins Should Be Kept in the Immigration Law," *Saturday Evening Post* (20 April 1957): 10.

CHAPTER 5

In addition to the resources listed in the notes, the following sources were relied upon in this chapter:

Robert M. Hutchens, *A Path to Good Jobs? Unemployment and Low Wages: The Distribution of Opportunity for Young Unskilled Workers.* Public Policy Brief No. 11 (Annandale-on-Hudson, NY: The Jerome Levy Economics Institute, 1994); Jeffrey Williamson, *Inequality, Poverty and History: The Kuznets Memorial Lectures* (Cambridge, MA: Blackwell, 1991); Jeffrey Williamson and Peter H. Lindert, *American Inequality: A Macroeconomic History* (New York: Academic Press, 1980), pp. 281–291.

1. Alex Stepick and Guillermo Grenier, "Brothers in Wood," in *Newcomers in the Workplace: Immigrants and the Restructuring of the U.S. Economy,* Louise Lamphere, Alex Stepick, and Guillermo Grenier, eds. (Philadelphia: Temple University Press, 1994), pp. 148–149, 161.

2. General Accounting Office, *Illegal Aliens: Influence of Illegal Workers on Wages and Working Conditions of Legal Workers* (Washington, DC: U.S. General Accounting Office, March 1988).

3. See Frances Fox Piven and Richard A. Cloward, *Regulating the Poor: The Functions of Public Welfare* (New York: Vintage Books, 1993), p. 352.

4. Quoted in Kevin Phillips, *Boiling Point: Republicans, Democrats, and the Decline of Middle-Class Prosperity* (New York: Random House, 1993), p. 25.

5. "Effects of Most Recent Recession Seen in Longer Job Searches, Lower Incomes, and Health Insurance Losses, Census Bureau Reports," *United States Department of Commerce News* (12 January 1995).

6. Piven and Cloward, *Regulating the Poor,* p. 362.

7. Quoted in Frank Levy, *Dollars and Dreams: The Changing American Income Distribution* (New York: W. W. Norton & Co., 1988), p. 13.

8. Roberto Suro, "Immigrants Crowd Labor's Lowest Rung," *The Washington Post,* 13 September 1994.

9. Wolff quoted in James K. Glassman, "The Income Gap: Where's the Problem?" *The Washington Post,* 25 April 1995, p. A17.

10. See Gregory Manki, *Macroeconomics* (New York: Worth Publishers, 1992).

11. Michael Lind, *The Next American Nation: The New Nationalism and the Fourth American Revolution* (New York: The Free Press, 1995), pp. 200–201.

12. See Steven Pearlstein, "U.S. Finds Productivity, But Not Pay, Is Rising," *The Washington Post,* 26 July 1995, p. A9.

13. See ibid.

14. Piven and Cloward, *Regulating the Poor,* pp. 352–353.

15. See Leon Bouvier and Scipio Garling, *A Tale of 10 Cities: Immigration's Effect on Urban Quality of Life* (Washington, DC: Federation for American Immigration Reform, 1995).

16. Quoted in ibid.

17. Paul Krugman, *Peddling Prosperity: Economic Sense and Nonsense in the Age of Diminished Expectations* (New York: W. W. Norton & Co., 1994), pp. 227–228, 9.

18. George J. Borjas, "Know the Flow," *National Review,* vol. 47 (17 April 1995).

19. Robert M. Dunn, Jr., "Higher Pay for Low-Wage Earners?" *The Washington Post,* 25 August 1992, p. A21.

20. Stephen Moore, "Do We Need More Immigration? Yes," *American Legion Magazine* (April 1995).

21. Robert Walker, Mark Ellis, and Richard Barff, "Linked Migration Systems: Immigration and Internal Labor Flows in the United States," *Journal of Economic Geography* (1993): 234–248.

22. Peter H. Lindert, *Fertility and Scarcity in America* (Princeton, NJ: Princeton University Press, 1977), p. 233.

23. Ibid., p. 234.

24. Harry To. Oshima, "The Growth of U.S. Factor Productivity: The Significance of New Technologies in the Early Decades of the Twentieth Century," *Journal of Economic History,* vol. 44 (March 1984).

25. Carlos F. Diaz-Alejandro, *Essays on the Economic History of the Argentine Republic* (New Haven, CT: New Haven Press, 1970), quoted in Alan M. Taylor, "External Dependence, Demographic Burdens, and Argentine Economic Decline After the Belle Epoque," *Journal of Economic History,* vol. 52, no. 4 (December 1992): 907.

26. Taylor, "External Dependence, Demographic Burdens, and Argentine Economic Decline After the Belle Epoque."

27. Timothy J. Hatton and Jeffrey G. Williamson, "International Migration 1850–1939: An Economic Survey," in *Migration and the International Labor Market 1850–1939,* Hatton and Williamson, eds. (New York: Routledge, 1994), p. 29.

28. Ibid., p. 31.

29. Krugman, *Peddling Prosperity,* pp. 146–148, 257–266.

30. Paul Krugman, "The Localization of the World Economy," *New Perspectives Quarterly,* vol. 12 (Winter 1995): 37.

31. Simons quoted in Melvin W. Reder, "The Economic Consequences of Increased Immigration," *Review of Economics and Statistics* (August 1963).

32. Reder, ibid.

33. David Griffith, *Jones's Minimal: Low-Wage Labor in the United States* (Albany, NY: State University of New York Press, 1993), pp. 30–31.

34. Molly Moore, "Factories of Children," *The Washington Post,* 21 May 1995, p. A1.

35. David Simcox, *Immigration, Population and Economic Growth in El Paso, Texas: The Making of an American Maquiladora* (Washington, DC: Center for Immigration Studies, September 1993).

36. Griffith, *Jones's Minimal,* pp. 232–233.

37. Piven and Cloward, *Regulating the Poor,* pp. 348–349.

38. Lindsey Grant, "Into the Wind: Unemployment and Welfare Reform," *The NPG Forum* (March 1994).

39. Phillips, *Boiling Point,* pp. 216–217.

40. Lind, *The Next American Nation,* p. 210.

41. Katharine Betts, *Ideology and Immigration: Australia 1976–1987* (Melbourne, Australia: Melbourne University Press, 1988).

42. Vernon Briggs, "The Playthel Benjamin Show," WBAI Radio in New York (11 March 1993).

43. Grant, "Into the Wind: Unemployment and Welfare Reform."

44. John Larner, *Culture and Society in Italy 1290–1420* (New York: Charles Scribner's Sons, 1971), pp. 122–123, 131–132.

45. Richard B. Freeman, "Employment and Earnings of Disadvantaged Young Men in a Labor Shortage Economy," in *The Urban Underclass,* Christopher Jencks and

Paul E. Peterson, eds. (Washington, DC: The Brookings Institution, 1991), pp. 110, 119.

46. "Labor Shortages," *Wall Street Journal*, 21 March 1995.
47. Adam Levy, "New Sign of the South: Help Wanted," *Arizona Republic*, 30 April 1995, p. D1.
48. See David Griffith, Monica L. Heppel, and Luis R. Torres, *Labor Certification and Employment Practices in Selected Low-Wage/Low-Skill Occupations: An Analysis from Worker and Employer Perspectives* (Washington, DC: Inter-American Institute on Migration and Labor, February 1994).
49. "Ranks of Disabled at Work Stagnant," *Arizona Republic*, 23 October 1994, p. A12.
50. Griffith, Heppel, and Torres, *Labor Certification and Employment Practices*, p. 1.

CHAPTER 6

In addition to the resources listed in the notes, the following sources were relied upon in this chapter:

Marshall Barry, Labor Research Center, Boston, phone interview (7 April 1995); Monica Heppel, anthropologist, The Inter-American Institute on Migration and Labor, Mount Vernon College, phone interview (1 April 1995); Donald Stull, Professor of Anthropology, University of Kansas, phone interview (20 February 1995); "The Following Progressive Businesses Welcome IBP to Storm Lake," *Storm Lake Pilot-Register* (17 April 1982); "Executive Summary," Commission on Agricultural Workers, *Report of the Commission on Agricultural Workers* (Washington, DC: U.S. Government Printing Office, November 1992); Roger Conner, phone interview (17 March 1995); Janet E. Benson, "The Effects of Packinghouse Work on Southeast Asian Refugee Families," in Louise Lamphere, Alex Stepick, and Guillermo Grenier, eds., *Newcomers in the Workplace: Immigrants and the Restructuring of the U.S. Economy* (Philadelphia: Temple University Press, 1994); Ken Cox, Professor of History, Hawkeye Community College in Waterloo and the University of Northerna Iowa, phone interview (20 May 1995); Herbert Hill, "Black Workers, Organized Labor, and Title VII of the 1964 Civil Rights Act: Legislative History and Litigation Record," in *Race in America*, Herbert Hill and James Jones, Jr., eds. (Madison, WI: University of Wisconsin Press, 1993).

1. Donald D. Stull and Michael J. Broadway, "The Effects of Restructuring on Beefpacking in Kansas," *Kansas Business Review*, vol. 14 (Fall 1990).
2. Robert A. Hackenberg, et al., "Meat Processing and the Transformation of Rural America: The Emergence of a New Underclass?" *Aspen Institute Quarterly*, vol. 5, no. 2 (Spring 1993), p. 6.
3. Glenn Garvin, "The Real-World Consequences of Closed Borders," *Reason* (April 1995): 19–26.
4. See Joe Davidson, "Nine Companies Fined for Hiring Illegal Workers," *Wall Street Journal*, 27 September 1995.
5. Robert Kuttner, "A Decent Minimum Wage," *The Washington Post*, 29 January 1995, p. C7.
6. Peter Brimelow, "Immigration Isn't a Necessity," *USA Today*, 18 April 1995, p. 11A.
7. Stull and Broadway, "The Effects of Restructuring on Beefpacking in Kansas."
8. Michael Broadway, "Beef Stew: Cattle, Immigrants and Established Residents in a Kansas Beefpacking Town," in *Newcomers in the Workplace: Immigrants and the*

Restructuring of the U.S. Economy, Louise Lamphere, Alex Stepick, and Guillermo Grenier, eds. (Philadelphia: Temple University Press, 1994), p. 29.

9. Hackenberg, et al., "Meat Processing and the Transformation of Rural America," p. 3.

10. Ed Clark, "Bedell Eyes Packer Problems," *The Times Weekender* (Spencer, Iowa), 11 November 1977; Andy Anderson, "Cattlemen, Bergland to Talk," *Spencer Daily Reporter,* 8 November 1977.

11. Charles T. Crumpley, "Agriculture Still Vital to KC But in a Different Way," *Kansas City Star,* 5 December 1988; "Kansas City Rebounds as a Livestock Center," *Kansas City Star,* 10 April 1960.

12. Hardy Green, *On Strike at Hormel: The Struggle for a Democratic Labor Movement* (Philadelphia: Temple University Press, 1990), p. 42.

13. Hackenberg, et al., "Meat Processing and the Transformation of Rural America," p. 4.

14. John Harwood, "Ties Between Meatpacking Firm, Gramm Point to Economic Choices GOP, Clinton Offer Voters," *Wall Street Journal,* 15 August 1995, p. A16.

15. David Griffith and Ed Kissam, *Working Poor: Farmworkers in the United States* (Philadelphia: Temple University Press, 1995), p. 270.

16. Quoted in David Griffith, *Jones's Minimal: Low-Wage Labor in the United States* (Albany, NY: State University of New York Press, 1993), p. 207.

17. Wayne Rasmussen, *A History of the Emergency Farm Labor Supply Program* (Washington, DC: USDA Bureau of Economics, 1951).

18. Roy Theriault, *How to Tell When You're Tired: A Brief Examination of Work* (New York: W. W. Norton & Co., 1995), pp. 20–28.

19. David Griffith and Ed Kissam, *Working Poor: Farmworkers in the United States* (Philadelphia: Temple University Press, 1995), p. 247.

20. General Accounting Office, *Illegal Aliens: Influence of Illegal Workers on Wages and Working Conditions of Legal Workers* (Washington, DC: U.S. General Accounting Office, March 1988), pp. 37–38.

21. Robert Lee Maril, *Poorest of Americans: The Mexican Americans of the Lower Rio Grande Valley of Texas* (Notre Dame, IN: University of Notre Dame Press, 1989), p. 71.

22. Griffith and Kissam, *Working Poor,* p. 8.

23. Nathan Glazer, "The Closing Door," *New Republic* (27 December 1993).

24. General Accounting Office, *Illegal Aliens,* pp. 13–14.

25. See Elizabeth Koed, "The Loss of Cheap Labor and Predictions of Economic Disasters: Two Case Studies," *The Social Contract* (Spring 1991): 133.

26. Frank Swoboda and Margaret Webb Pressler, "U.S. Targets 'Slave Labor' Sweat Shop," *The Washington Post,* 16 August 1995, p. A13.

27. Richard Lamm and Gary Imoff, *The Immigration Time Bomb* (New York: E. P. Dutton, 1985), p. 147.

CHAPTER 7

In addition to the resources listed in the notes, the following sources were relied upon in this chapter:

Carrying Capacity Network, "Immigration Contributes to Projected Social Security Insolvency," *Network Bulletin,* vol. 5 (June–July 1995): 3; Donald Huddle and David Simcox, *The Impact of Immigration on the Social Security System* (Washington, DC: Carrying Capacity Network, July 1993); Norman Matloff, University of California at

Davis, *Are Foreign Nationals Needed in the Computer Industry?* (Private paper, 1994; Lindsey Grant, ed., *Elephants in the Volkswagen* (New York: W. H. Freeman, 1992), pp. 147–154; Center for Immigration Studies, "Employment Based Immigration," *Immigration Review* (Spring 1994): 3; Center for Immigration Studies Press Conference, National Press Club (15 April 1994); Leon F. Bouvier and David Simcox, *Foreign Born Professionals in the United States* (Washington, DC: Center for Immigration Studies, April 1994); Vernon Briggs, Jr., *Mass Immigration and the National Interest* (New York: M. E. Sharpe, 1992); G. Pascal Zachary, *Showstopper!* (New York: The Free Press, 1995).

1. Donald Lambro, "Legal and Illegal Immigration Apart: Misguided Perceptions," *The Washington Times,* 7 September 1995, p. A19.
2. William Branigin, "White-Collar Visas: Importing Needed Skills or Cheap Labor?" *The Washington Post,* 21 October 1995, p. A1.
3. David C. Lewis, board of advisers, American Engineering Association, statement at press conference, Washington, DC, 29 November 1995.
4. Joel B. Snyder, chairman, Institute of Electrical and Electronics Engineers, statement at press conference, Washington, DC, 29 November 1995, Institute of Electrical and Electronics Engineers press release, "IEEE-USA Asks Members to Speak Out in Support of the Immigration Reform Act of 1995."
5. Norman Matloff, "Debugging Immigration," *National Review* (9 October 1995).
6. Larry Richards, executive director of Software Professionals' Political Action Committee, testimony before the Subcommittee on Immigration Senate Judiciary Committee, Washington, D.C., 28 September 1995.
7. Norman Matloff, "Foreign Nationals vs. U.S. Workers," *San Francisco Chronicle,* 28 March 1995, p. A17.
8. Matloff, "Debugging Immigration."
9. Eric Nalder and Paul Andrews, "Giving Jobs Away," *Seattle Times,* 20 June 1993, p. A1.
10. Branigin, "White-Collar Visas: Importing Needed Skills or Cheap Labor?" p. A16.
11. G. Pascal Zachary, "Skilled U.S. Workers' Objections Grow as More of Their Jobs Shift Overseas," *Wall Street Journal,* 9 October 1995; Margaret A. Jacobs, "U.S. Businesses Fight a Cutback of Green Cards," *Wall Street Journal,* 11 July 1995.
12. "Slamming the Door," *48 Hours* (CBS News, 11 May 1995).
13. Linda Kilcrease, statement at press conference, Washington, DC, 29 November 1995.
14. Ron Unz, "Value Added," *National Review* (7 November 1994): 57.
15. "Bipartisan Animosity," *Wall Street Journal,* 3 April 1995, p. A18.
16. "Immigration: New Law Allows the Admission of Workers with Needed Skills," *Kentucky Enquirer,* 5 August 1991.
17. "Global Mafia," *Newsweek* (13 December 1993).
18. Rosenberg quoted in Glenn Garvin, "No Fruits, No Shirts, No Service," *Reason* (April 1995).
19. Daniel S. Greenberg, "Surplus in Science," *The Washington Post,* 6 December 1995, p. A25.
20. See Malcolm W. Browne, "Job Outlook Gloomy for Some Ph.D's," *Dallas Morning News,* 30 July 1995, p. 1A.
21. David S. North, *Soothing the Establishment* (Lanham, MD: University Press of America, 1995).
22. Manuel P. Berriozabal, "Importing Brains Does Not Solve Shortage of Technical Personnel," *Vista* (3 February 1991).

23. Center for Immigration Studies Press Conference, National Press Club (15 April 1994).
24. David L. Goodstein, "After the Big Crunch," *Wilson Quarterly* (Summer 1995).
25. Ibid.
26. Leon Bouvier, Op-Ed column, *New York Newsday,* 22 August 1994.
27. Branigin, "White-Collar Visas: Importing Needed Skills or Cheap Labor?" p. A16.
28. Lindsey Grant, ed., *Elephants in the Volkswagen* (New York: W. H. Freeman, 1992), p. 150.
29. Warren E. Leary, "With Doctor Surplus, U.S. Is Urged to Cut Residency Training," *The New York Times,* 24 January 1996, p. A17.

CHAPTER 8

In addition to the resources listed in the notes, the following sources were relied upon in this chapter:

James P. Smith and Finis R. Welch, "Black Economic Progress After Myrdal," *Journal of Economic Literature* (June 1989): 519–564; Thomas A. Flowers, *Dorchester County, Maryland: A History for Young People* (Easton, MD: Economy Printing Company, 1983); W. E. Burghardt Du Bois, *The Philadelphia Negro, A Social Study* (Philadelphia: University of Pennsylvania, 1899); Booker T. Washington, "Education Before Equality: The Atlanta Exposition Address, 1895," from *Afro-American History: Primary Sources,* 2nd ed., Thomas R. Frazier, ed. (Chicago: Dorsey Press, 1988); Jeffrey Williamson and Peter Lindert, *American Inequality: A Macroeconomic History* (New York: Academic Press, 1980); Frederick Douglass, "Southern Barbarism" (April 1886—part of National Portrait Gallery Special Exhibit, 1995).

1. Williams quoted in Dorothy J. Daiter, "Diversity of Leaders Reflects the Changes in Black Community," *Wall Street Journal,* 6 May 1992.
2. Adrian Cook, *The Armies of the Streets: The New York City Draft Riots of 1863* (Lexington, KY: University Press of Kentucky, 1974), p. 205.
3. Frederick Douglass, *My Bondage and My Freedom* (New York: Dover Books, 1969), p. 454.
4. Iver Bernstein, *The New York City Draft Riots: Their Significance for American Society and Politics in the Age of the Civil War* (New York: Oxford University Press, 1990), pp. 142–143.
5. Ibid., p. 53.
6. Eric Foner, *Reconstruction: Unfinished Revolution, 1863–1877* (New York: Harper & Row, 1989), p. 16.
7. Michael Lind, *The Next American Nation: The New Nationalism and the Fourth American Revolution* (New York: The Free Press, 1995), p. 47.
8. Bernstein, *The New York City Draft Riots,* p. 143.
9. Ena L. Farley, *The Underside of Reconstruction New York: The Struggle Over the Issue of Black Equality* (New York: Garland Publishing, 1993), p. xi.
10. Page Smith, *The Rise of Industrial America: A People's History of the Post-Reconstruction Era.* Vol. 6 (New York: Viking/Penguin, 1984), p. xiii.
11. Gavin Wright, *Old South, New South: Revolutions in the Southern Economy Since the Civil War* (New York: Basic Books, 1986), p. 13.
12. Gavin Wright, "The Economic Revolution in the American South," *Economic Perspectives,* vol. 1. no. 1 (Summer 1987): 164.

13. Warren C. Whatley, "Getting a Foot in the Door: 'Learning' State Dependence, and the Racial Integration of Firms," *Journal of Economic History,* vol. 1, no. 1 (March 1990): 45.

14. Smith, *The Rise of Industrial America,* p. 640.

15. John E. Bodnar, "The Impact of the 'New Immigration' on the Black Worker: Steelton, Pennsylvania, 1880–1920," *Journal of Labor History* (Spring 1986): 228.

16. Lawrence H. Fuchs, "The Reactions of Black Americans to Immigration" in *Immigration Reconsidered: History, Sociology, and Politics,* Virginia Yans-McLaughlin, ed. (New York: Oxford University Press, 1990), p. 295.

17. William Frey, "Black College Grads, Those in Poverty Take Different Migration Paths," *Population Today* (February 1994).

18. Bodnar, "The Impact of the 'New Immigration' on the Black Worker," p. 229.

19. Herbert Hill, "Black Workers, Organized Labor . . . ," in *Race in America,* Herbert Hill and James Jones, Jr., eds. (Madison, WI: University of Wisconsin Press, 1993), pp. 268, 303.

20. Ibid.

21. J. Linn Allen and Jerry Thomas, "For Blacks, Trades Jobs Not on Level," *Chicago Tribune,* 4 September 1994.

22. Farley, *The Underside of Reconstruction New York,* p. 141.

Chapter 9

In addition to the resources listed in the notes, the following sources were relied upon in this chapter:

David Griffith, *Jones's Minimal: Low-Wage Labor in the United States* (Albany, NY: State University of New York Press, 1993); Plathel Benjamin, *New York Daily News* columnist, phone interview (4 November 1995); Jonathan Kaufman, "Help Unwanted: Immigrants' Businesses Often Refuse to Hire Blacks in Inner City," *Wall Street Journal,* 6 June 1995.

1. Robert A. Hackenberg, et al., "Meat Processing and the Transformation of Rural America: The Emergence of a New Underclass?" *Aspen Institute Quarterly,* vol. 5 (Spring 1993): 5.

2. Frank Morris, Testimony to the House Subcommittee Hearings on Immigration, Refugees and International Law (13 March 1990).

3. Frank Morris, Federation for American Immigration Reform Senate Staff Briefing (23 May 1995).

4. Stuart Silverstein, "Job Market a Flash Point for Natives, Newcomers," *Los Angeles Times,* 15 November 1993.

5. Arnold Shankman, *Ambivalent Friends: Afro-Americans View the Immigrant* (Westport, CT: Greenwood Press, 1982), p. 72.

6. Ronald F. Ferguson, "Shifting Challenges: Fifty Years of Economic Change Toward Black-White Earnings Equality," *Dædalus: Journal of the American Academy of Arts and Sciences,* vol. 124 (Winter 1995): 53.

7. Antonio McDaniel, "The Dynamic Racial Composition of the United States," *Dædalus: Journal of the American Academy of Arts and Sciences,* vol. 124 (Winter 1995): 108–181.

8. Government Accounting Office, *Illegal Aliens: Influence of Illegal Workers on Wages and Working Conditions of Legal Workers* (Washington, DC: U.S. Government Accounting Office, March 1988).

9. Katherine S. Newman, "Dead-End Jobs: A Way Out," *The Brookings Review* (Fall 1995): 24–27; Katherine S. Newman, "What Scholars Can Tell Politicians About the Poor," *Chronicle of Higher Education* (23 July 1995): B1–2.

10. David Griffith, Monica Heppel, and Luis Torres, *Current Practices in H-2B-Authorized Industries: An Analysis from Worker and Employer Perspectives* (Washington, DC: Inter-American Institute on Migration and Labor, March 1994), pp. 1–2.

11. David Griffith, Monica L. Heppel, and Luis R. Torres, *Labor Certification and Employment Practices in Selected Low-Wage/Low-Skill Occupations: An Analysis from Worker and Employer Perspectives* (Charleston, WV: West Virginia Bureau of Employment Programs, February 1994), pp. i–iii.

12. Jonathan Kaufman, "Help Unwanted: Immigrants' Businesses Often Refuse to Hire Blacks in Inner City," *Wall Street Journal,* 6 June 1995.

13. Elizabeth Bogan, *Immigration in New York* (New York: Frederick Praeger, 1987).

14. Jonathan Tilove, "Affirmative Action and Immigration: A Dangerous Dilemma," *Newhouse News Service* (20 December 1993).

15. Ibid.

16. Jonathan Tilove, "Native-Born Blacks Lose Out to Immigrants," *Portland Oregonian,* 20 December 1993.

17. James S. Robb, *Affirmative Action for Immigrants: The Entitlement Nobody Wanted* (Petoskey, MI: Social Contract Press, 1995), pp. 19–22.

18. Tilove, "Native-Born Blacks Lose Out to Immigrants."

19. Rochelle Sharpe, "Losing Ground: In Latest Recession, Only Blacks Suffered Net Employment Loss," *Wall Street Journal,* 14 September 1993, p. A1.

20. Eric Foner, "Reconstruction in of the North," in *Reconstruction: American's Unfinished Revolution, 1863–1877* (New York: Harper & Row, 1989), p. 462.

21. Griffith, Heppel, and Torres, *Labor Certification and Employment Practices in Selected Low-Wage/Low-Skill Occupations: An Analysis from Worker and Employer Perspectives* (Charleston, W.Va.: West Virginia Bureau of Employment Programs, February 1994), p. 79.

22. Ranginui J. Walker, "The Government's Economic Mantra of BIP Immigration," Seminar, Maori Studies Department, University of Auckland, Australia (30 September 1991).

23. Jonathan Tilove, "At a Hospital in Watts, It's Latino vs. Black," *Staten Island Sunday Advance,* 9 January 1994.

24. Lynne Duke, "Blacks, Asians, Latinos Cite Prejudice by Whites for Limited Opportunity," *The Washington Post,* 3 March 1994.

25. Orlando Patterson, "Black Like All of Us," *The Washington Post,* 7 February 1993.

26. Deborah Sontag, "Across the U.S., Immigrants Find the Land of Resentment," *New York Times,* 11 December 1992, p. A1.

27. Jack Miles, "Brown vs. Blacks," *Atlantic Monthly* (October 1992).

28. Editorial in *La Prensa* (San Diego), 15 May 1992.

29. Jonathan Tilove and Joe Hallinan, "U.S. Melting Pot Starts to Brew a Bitter Taste," *The Oregonian,* 9 August 1993.

30. Gerald David Jaynes and Robin M. Williams Jr., eds., *A Common Destiny: Blacks and American Society* (Washington, DC: National Academy Press, 1989).

31. Stepick cited in Gail DeGeorge, "Armageddon—Or Shining City of the Future," *BusinessWeek* (13 July 1992): 122.

32. Richard Vedder, Lowell Gallaway, Philip E. Graves, and Robert Sexton, "Demonstrating Their Freedom: The Post-Emancipation Migration of Black Americans," *Research in Economic History,* vol. 10 (1986), pp. 217–219, 227. See

also Gavin Wright, *Old South, New South: Revolutions in the Southern Economy Since the Civil War* (New York: Basic Books, 1986), p. 198.

33. Reynolds Farley, "The Common Destiny of Blacks and Whites: Observations About the Social and Economic Status of the Races," in *Race in America,* Herbert Hill and James Jones, Jr., eds. (Madison, WI: University of Wisconsin Press, 1993), pp. 197–233.

34. Nicolas Lemann, *The Promised Land* (New York: Vintage Books, 1992), p. 343.

35. Wright, *Old South, New South,* p. 237.

36. Ibid., p. 238.

37. Frances Fox Piven and Richard A. Cloward, "The Civil Rights Movement," in *Poor People's Movements: Why They Succeed, How They Fail* (New York: Vintage Books, 1979).

38. Harvard Sitkoff, *The Struggle for Black Equality 1954–1980* (New York: Hill & Wang, 1981), pp. 206–208.

39. Lemann, *The Promised Land,* pp. 353, 351–352, and 346.

40. Lindsey Grant, *Elephants in the Volkswagen* (New York: W. H. Freeman, 1992), p. 151.

41. Vernon Briggs, "The Playthel Benjamin Show," WBAI Radio in New York (11 March 1993).

CHAPTER 10

In addition to the resources listed in the notes, the following sources were relied upon in this chapter:

Spencer, Clay County, Community Quick Reference (Des Moines, IO: Iowa Department of Economic Development, June 1994); Michael Broadway, "Beef Stew: Cattle, Immigrants and Established Residents in a Kansas Beefpacking Town," *Newcomers in the Workplace: Immigrants and the Restructuring of the U.S. Economy,* in Louise Lamphere, Alex Stepick, and Guillermo Grenier, eds. (Philadelphia: Temple University Press, 1994); Robert A. Hackenberg, et al., "Meat Processing and the Transformation of Rural America: The Emergence of a New Underclass?" *Aspen Institute Quarterly,* vol. 5 (Spring 1993): 11–22; Jesse Peterson, interview (7 May 1995); Michael Zenor, interview (18 April 1995); Fred Prehn, interview (8 December 1993); Peter Brimelow, *Alien Nation* (New York: Random House, 1995); Richard H. Shultz and William J. Olson, *Ethnic and Religious Conflict: Emerging Threat to U.S. Security* (Washington, DC: National Strategy Information Center, 1994); Tom Horton and William M. Eichbaum, *Turning the Tide: Saving the Chesapeake Bay* (Washington, DC: Chesapeake Bay Foundation, 1991); World Resources Institute, *The 1993 Information Please Environmental Almanac* (Washington, DC: World Resources Institute, 1993); David Pimentel, "The National Carrying Capacity Conference" (Arlington, VA: Carrying Capacity Network, 4–6 June 1993); Debbie Biniores-Egger, interview (10 August 1994).

1. Rush Loving, Jr. "Small Town That Has Kept Its Vigor," *Fortune* (April 1972).
2. Michael J. Broadway and Donald D. Stull, "Rural Industrialization: The Example of Garden City, Kansas," *Kansas Business Review,* vol. 14 (Summer 1991).
3. Michael J. Kinsley and L. Hunter Lovins, *Paying for Growth, Prospering from Development* (Snowmass, CO: Rocky Mountain Institute, 1995).
4. Stephen C. Fehr, "Traffic Taking Toll on Wilson Bridge," *The Washington Post,* 2 September 1994, p. A1.

5. John Sedgwick, "Strong But Sensitive," *Atlantic Monthly,* vol. 267 (April 1991): 70–82.

6. Ibid.

7. *The 1994 Statistical Abstract of the United States* (Washington, DC: U.S. Department of Commerce, 1994), Tables 655 and 861.

8. Ibid.

9. California Department of Education, *California Schools Bursting at the Seams* (3 September 1991).

10. Lorraine M. McDonnell and Paul T. Hill, *Newcomers in American Schools: Meeting the Educational Needs of Immigrant Youth* (Santa Monica, CA: RAND Corporation, 1993).

11. Larry Blieberg, "School Construction Fails to Keep Pace, Data Show," *Dallas Morning News,* 30 April 1995; Christopher Lee, "Critics Say Quality Being Squeezed Out," *Dallas Morning News,* 30 April 1995.

12. Ibid.

13. D'Vera Cohn, "Immigrants Will Raise D.C. Population in 21st Century, City Predicts," *The Washington Post,* 11 March 1995.

14. Virginia D. Abernethy, "To Reform Welfare, Reform Immigration," *Clearinghouse Bulletin,* vol. 5 (January–February 1995).

15. Frances Fox Piven and Richard A. Cloward, *Regulating the Poor: The Functions of Public Welfare* (New York: Vintage Books, 1993), pp. 388–389.

16. Carrying Capacity Network, "Welfare, Immigration and the Low-Wage Labor Market," *Clearinghouse Bulletin* (January–February 1995): 3–5.

17. Kathryn H. Porter, *Making JOBS Work: What Research Says About Effective Employment Programs for AFDC Recipients* (Washington, DC: Center on Budget and Policy Priorities, March 1990).

18. Gary Burtless, *A Future of Lousy Jobs: The Changing Structure of U.S. Wages* (Washington, DC: The Brookings Institution, 1990).

19. John E. Schwartz and Thomas J. Volgy, *Forgotten Americans* (New York: W.W. Norton & Co., 1992), pp. 81, 106.

20. See Piven and Cloward, *Regulating the Poor,* pp. 390–391.

21. See Tracy Thompson, " 'Unhitched,' But Hardly Independent," *The Washington Post,* 13 May 1995, p. A1.

22. See William Raspberry, " . . . At the Root of the Problem: Fatherlessness," *The Washington Post,* 22 March 1995, p. A21.

23. Frank Levy, *Dollars and Dreams: The Changing American Income Distribution* (New York: W. W. Norton & Co., 1988, p. 115.

24. Susan Martin, "How Much Immigration We Need—And the Rules for Who Can Stay," *The Washington Times,* 27 June 1995.

25. Abernethy, "To Reform Welfare, Reform Immigration."

26. *Businessweek*/Harris Poll (June 1992); Gallup Poll (July 1993).

27. Jonathan Kaufman, "America's Heartland Turns to Hot Location for the Melting Pot," *Wall Street Journal,* 31 October 1995.

28. National Center for Policy Analysis, *Multiculturalism and Economic Growth* (Washington, DC: National Center for Policy Analysis, 1995).

29. Maria Puente, "Civil War in Los Angeles, But Civil in New York," *USA Today,* 3 July 1995.

30. Robert D. McFadden, "Immigration Hurting City, New Yorkers Say in Survey," *New York Times,* 18 October 1993.

31. David Rohde, "New Seekers of the American Dream," *Christian Science Monitor,* 24 October 1994, pp. 9–11.

32. Pam Belluck, "New School Would Serve Immigrants," *New York Times,* 20 March 1995.

33. Malcolm Gladwell, "Baby Boom's Urban Cradle Braces for Future Rocked by Crime," *The Washington Post,* 26 May 1994, p. A25.

34. Malcolm Gladwell, "In Today's Cities, There's No Room for Seclusion," *The Washington Post,* 11 February 1995, p. A1.

35. Jonathan Yardley, "We Have Met the Future and It Is Us," *Washington Post Book World* (11 June 1995): 3.

36. Sen. Daniel Patrick Moynihan, "A Cry for My City," *Reader's Digest* (January 1994): 77–79.

37. John O'Sullivan, "America's Identity Crisis," *National Review* (21 November 1994).

38. Will Lester, "Miami Anger at Protests Increases," *The Washington Times,* 12 May 1995.

39. Robert Reinhold, "L.A.'s Schools Chief Wants Power, and the Vote, for Immigrant Parents," *New York Times,* 29 November 1992.

40. Ton Bizjak, "Newcomer Voting Proposal Spreads," *Lompoc Record* (18 February 1992).

41. "What Hughes Said on the Air," *The Washington Post,* 22 February 1994, p. D10.

42. Richard H. Shultz and William J. Olson, *Ethnic and Religious Conflict: Emerging Threat to U.S. Security* (Washington, DC: National Strategy Information Center, 1994).

43. *Displaced in the New South,* Television Documentary produced by Georgia Public Television (1995).

44. Patrick J. McDonnell, "County Puts Some Limits on Laborers," *Los Angeles Times,* 16 March 1994.

45. Ken Cox, interview (20 May 1995).

46. Charles S. Lee and Lester Sloan, "It's Our Turn Now," *Newsweek* (21 November 1994): 57.

47. Pamela Constable, "Plan to Meld Cultures Divides D.C. School," *The Washington Post,* 26 October 1994, p. A1.

48. Richard Bernstein, *Dictatorship of Virtue: Multiculturalism and the Battle for America's Future* (New York: Alfred A. Knopf, 1994), p. 9.

49. Michael Lind, *The Next American Nation: The New Nationalism and the Fourth American Revolution* (New York: The Free Press, 1995), p. 14.

50. Roger K. Lewis, "Gated Areas: Start of New Middle Ages," *The Washington Post,* 9 September 1995, p. E1.

51. Edward J. Blakely and Mary Gail Snyder, "Fortress Communities: The Walling and Gating of American Suburbs," *Landlines* (newsletter of the Lincoln Institute of Land Policy), quoted in Roger K. Lewis, *The Washington Post,* 9 September 1995, p. E1.

52. Robert Bach, *Changing Relations: Newcomers and Established Residents in U.S. Communities* (New York: Ford Foundation, April 1993), p. 35.

53. Vicki Youne, interview (15 April 95)

54. Kathryn Wexler, "East L.A. Gangs' Uneasy Peace Hangs on a Wish and Prayer," *The Washington Post,* 29 March 1995, p. A3.

55. Ty Clevenger, "Youths 'Out of Control' in N. Virginia," *The Washington Times,* 1 September 1995.

56. "Global Mafia," *Newsweek* (13 December 1993); General Accounting Office, *Nontraditional Organized Crime* (Washington, DC: U.S. General Accounting Office, 1989).

57. Charles W. Hall, "Area's Ethnic Drug Rings Proving Tougher to Crack," *The Washington Post,* 2 October 1995, pp. A1, A12.

58. Michael Elliott, et al., "Global Mafia," *Newsweek* (13 December 1993).

59. Shultz and Olson, *Ethnic and Religious Conflict.*

60. Tom Horton and William M. Eichbaum, *Turning the Tide: Saving the Chesapeake Bay* (Washington, DC: Chesapeake Bay Foundation, 1991), p. 190.
61. Ibid., p. 188.
62. Ibid., pp. 3–4.
63. Lester R. Brown and Hal Kane, *Full House: Reassessing the Earth's Population Carrying Capacity* (New York: W.W. Norton & Co., 1994), p. 60.
64. Ibid.
65. Byron J. Bailey, M.D., "National Conference on Biological Diversity and Human Health," News Release of the National Association of Physicians for the Environment (13 February 1995).
66. "Interview: Thomas Lovejoy," *FOCUS,* vol. 4, no. 2 (Washington, DC: Carrying Capacity Network, 1994), pp. 63–67.
67. Bruce Finley, "Vanishing Wilderness: Recreation Surge Scars Landscapes," *Denver Post,* 3 September 1995.
68. Jerry Adler, "Bye-Bye Suburban Dream," *Newsweek* (15 May 1995): 41–52.
69. David Finkel, "Washington's Newest Frontier: Life on the Suburban Edge," *Washington Post Magazine,* 19 March 1995, pp. 18–33.
70. Joel Nilsson, "State Trust Lands Hold Key to Desert Preservation," *Arizona Republic,* 7 May 1995, p. F1.
71. "Texas Now Second Largest State, Nevada Fastest Growing, District of Columbia Fastest Loser, Census Bureau Says," *United States Department of Commerce News* (28 December 1994).
72. Nilsson, "State Trust Lands Hold Key," p. F1.
73. Thomas Heath, "Californians Crowding into Colorado," *The Washington Post,* 9 November 1994, p. A3.
74. Jim Lair, *Carroll County Families: These Were the First* (Berryville, AR: Carroll County Historical Society, 1991).

CONCLUSION

1. Jerry J. Jasinowski, "What U.S. Business Wants from Immigration," *New York Times,* 13 September 1995.
2. David S. North, *Soothing the Establishment* (Lanham, MD: University Press of America, 1995).
3. Joel Snyder, chairman, Institute of Electrical and Electronics Workers, statement at press conference, Washington, DC, 29 November 1995.
4. Edith Holleman, AFL-CIO, interview, Washington, DC, 29 November 1995.
5. Morton M. Kondracke, "Clinton Foreign Policy Improves, But Not on Cuba," *Roll Call* (15 May 1995): 8.
6. National Association of Manufacturers, *Talking Points on Business Issues in H.R. 2202* (Washington, DC: National Association of Manufacturers, September 1995).

Acknowledgments

A book like this relies on some fresh thinking and new reporting, but above all on mining the scholarship, reporting, and experiences of scores of others who previously have examined aspects of the book's topic. I gratefully acknowledge the contributions of all quoted within. The list of people who have personally taught me and helped me as I studied immigration-related topics in recent years is too long to include here, but I lift up for special recognition for their role in bringing this book to market: Louisa Parker (my research associate), James Placyk (the human "bookstore vacuum cleaner" and fax terrorist), the Winklers (providers of a writing hideaway and gourmet catering), the Yoders (frequent agents of miscellaneous assistance), the *Atlantic Monthly* (publisher of the article that led to this book), and Hilary Hinzmann (my tenacious Norton editor whose vision never wavered). I also thank all those associated with *The Social Contract* quarterly, John Tanton, Mount Olivet friends, and Sandy Maltby. It is trite and predictable that an author nearly always thanks a long-suffering family, but only a family in which a book has been created can understand the trauma, tension, and sense of separation a book brings to a household. My appreciation to Jeremy and Andrew for once again graciously doing without a father in their waning teen years and to Shirley, who has only herself to blame as she was the one who encouraged me to leave daily newspapering for more in-depth research five years ago and subsidized me when necessary. Finally, I acknowledge the parenting of Warren and Freda Beck. From them, and from many others in Marshfield, Missouri, I learned about the triumphs, frustrations, disappointments, solid dignity, and often extraordinary quality of just ordinary work—work that deserves governmental policymaking that does not stack the deck against those who perform it.

Index